# Conversations with Jerzy Kosinski

*Edited by*
*Tom Teicholz*

University Press of Mississippi
Jackson

Copyright © 1993 by the University Press of Mississippi
Manufactured in the United States of America

96  95  94  93    4  3  2  1

The paper in this book meets the guidelines for permanence and durability
of the Committee on Production Guidelines for Book Longevity of the Council
on Library Resources.


**Library of Congress Cataloging-in-Publication Data**

Kosinski, Jerzy N., 1933–1991
    Conversations with Jerzy Kosinski / edited by Tom Teicholz.
        p.   cm. — (Literary conversations series)
    Includes index.
    ISBN 0-87805-625-4 (alk. paper). — ISBN 0-87805-626-2 (paper :
 alk. paper)
    1. Kosinski, Jerzy N., 1933–1991—Interviews.   2. Novelists,
American—20th century—Interviews.   I. Teicholz, Tom.   II. Title.
III. Series.
PS3561.08Z464   1993
813'.54—dc20                                              92-44552
                                                            CIP


British Library Cataloging-in-Publication data available

# Conversations with Jerzy Kosinski

Literary Conversations Series

*Peggy Whitman Prenshaw*
*General Editor*

**Books by Jerzy Kosinski**

*The Future Is Ours, Comrade: Conversations with the Russians* (under the pseudonym
    of Joseph Novak). Garden City: Doubleday, 1960.
*No Third Path* (under the pseudonym of Joseph Novak). Garden City: Doubleday, 1962.
*The Painted Bird.* Boston: Houghton Mifflin, 1965.
*Notes of the Author on The Painted Bird.* New York: Scientia-Factum, 1965.
*Steps.* New York: Random House, 1968.
*The Art of the Self.* New York: Scientia-Factum, 1968.
*Being There.* New York: Harcourt Brace Jovanovich, 1971.
*The Devil Tree.* New York: Harcourt Brace Jovanovich, 1973.
*Cockpit.* Boston: Houghton Mifflin, 1975.
*Blind Date.* Boston: Houghton Mifflin, 1977.
*Passion Play.* New York: St. Martin's Press, 1979.
*Pinball.* New York: Bantam, 1982.
*The Hermit of 69th Street.* New York: Seaver Books, 1988.

# Contents

# Introduction

"There is a fleeting temptation, to suggest that there is no Jerzy Kosinski," Dick Schaap writes in one of the first interviews the author ever gave, "that he is a figment of his own vivid imagination." Reading the interviews collected in *Conversations with Jerzy Kosinski*, one would have to agree that Kosinski's public persona was one of his greatest creations.

There are few authors who were ever more adept at press interviews. For Kosinski, the interview was part performance, part public relations, part blind date. I interviewed him on two different occasions. Kosinski in person was different from the existential adventurer created by his novels. He was not so much engaged, as engaging; where his fiction was brutal, he was charming. Even his features, which in jacket photos appear harsh and angular were softer, and more handsome in person. The contrast between Kosinski and the intensity of his fiction created the background for the interviews.

Kosinski's interviewers, like his readers, were obsessed with the facts of his life. Over and over again, we watch as Kosinski toys with the question of the lines that separate fiction from autobiography in his work. "I never wrote my books as autobiographical," Kosinski tells Brandon Tartikoff. "I never claimed them to be anything but novels. Why I wrote them in a manner that suggests autobiographical elements stems from my basic notion of what a novelist is. I write because I feel that a novelist has a lot in common with others, not because he differs from them."

Yet Kosinski's life was markedly different from others. First, and foremost, as a young boy, he survived the Holocaust, when so many others did not. Then he escaped Communist Poland. Kosinski himself remarked to an interviewer that his life was the stuff of novels: he came to the United States with little money, no English, within a year he was a Ford Fellow at Columbia University, within a few more, he had married an American heiress and was living on Park Avenue. Nonetheless, Kosinski felt that his unique individual experiences, when transmuted to fiction, became a didactic lesson for others. "A human being is loaded with the greatest power, his imagination and the power to transcend his own conditions," he tells Jerome Klinkowitz.

The interviews gathered here are published, chronologically, in their entirety. Questions are repeated, and the answers vary. There are some discrepancies, and contradictions. "A good interview is," Kosinski once wrote me, "like truth itself, the temporary resolution of various contradictions." This makes the reading all the more compelling. For at the core, one continues to wonder about Jerzy Kosinski.

During the course of the interviews we learn a great deal about Kosinski: that as a youth, he raped and was raped; that he has a half-brother; that he has fathered three children. We learn the code names for a new novel, and then in the next interview, we see the impact of the completed work. We hear that he is thinking of moving to New Orleans. Should we believe him?

We also see his positions evolve over time. We read that Kosinski won't allow his novels to be made into movies. "Except perhaps, *Being There*." Later, we read several accounts of how Peter Sellers came to star in the film. Kosinski rails against TV and passive entertainment. We hear about his own experiences on the TV talk show circuit and of his own film acting experience in "Reds." We also watch as Kosinski grapples with his identification as a Jew, a Holocaust survivor, with the United States and with Poland.

The interviews give testament, as well, to the seriousness of Kosinski's purpose as a writer. Kosinski saw language, and his novels, as having a purpose. "A novel is nothing but . . . a larger aphorism," Kosinski tells one interviewer. For him books are weapons, and he strikes out against totalitarianism in any form. It is an intellectual dialetic in which Kosinski sees Lenin, Trotsky, and Mao, as writers. In other interviews, Kosinski lets us in on the way philosophical precepts informed the content of his novels.

Coursing through the interviews is the question of who is he. "I think we ought to define ourselves in terms of the language we use," he tells Daniel J. Cahill. Kosinski, who was mute for several years as a child, sees the protagonists of his novels as fighting muteness. His novels are devoid of traditional plot, he tells us, because he sees life as a series of heightened moments. This series of vignettes build meaning into the character and the situations he describes.

Finally, we realize that Kosinski is still at war. He hides himself, he wears disguises, he keeps survival kits in his car trunk. We are told these are games, and there are several descriptions of Kosinski's party tricks. Yet, the punch line is always that Kosinski escapes. In his private war, Kosinski remained the protagonist, using every arm in his arsenal. Sports, skiing, and polo are important for Kosinski, yet further extensions of his self. He is at play—and at war.

There is a gap in the interviews, with only one collected between 1982 and 1988. Kosinski did not publish any novels during those years, but the controversy that surrounded him during this period deserves mention.

Nineteen eighty-two was a tumultuous year for Kosinski. His eighth novel, *Pinball*, was published. There was a glowing front page profile in the Sunday *New York Times Magazine*. And then the backlash started. In June, the *Village Voice* printed "Jerzy Kosinski's Tainted Words," an article that accused Kosinski of not being the actual author of his works, of having used editors, and even writers to "improve" his work.

Kosinski denied the charges. Nonetheless, in November, the *New York Times* came to Kosinski's defense in a 6,000-word piece whose thesis was that Kosinski, as an anti-communist, had been under continuous attack by communists in Poland, and the leftists (including the *Voice*) in the U.S. since the publication of *The Painted Bird*.

Accusations about Kosinski's authorship had been circulating for years. In 1980, I had heard the same rumors and asked him about them. His answer (not included in my published interview) was that these accusations grew out of his idiosyncratic revising and editing process. He explained that he photocopied draft manuscripts (this was in the time before the ubiquity of the word processor), circulating them to readers and then incorporating those suggestions he agreed with. He then hired his own copyeditors, line editors, and proofreaders to bring the manuscript to a level he was satisfied with. This was all at his own personal expense. Much to his publisher's consternation, he continued to edit his books even when they were in galley form, where he was charged for each correction. In this way, he explained, he speeded up the editing process, allowing him to publish a novel every two years. Kosinski actually continued to revise his books after publication, and there are revised editions of *The Painted Bird, The Devil Tree* and *The Hermit of 69th Street*.

When at the time of the article, Kosinski made the same defense, the *Village Voice* journalists stood by their story, one of them, saying, "The point is that Kosinski has always insisted it was all him. Basically the story is that it isn't all him." The dispute ended on that semantic note. The irony was that on the one hand Kosinski had been "telling tales" for many years challenging people to determine whether they were true or not (it was clear he cared little); on the other, Kosinski's desire for control was so great, that it was impossible to believe that any book of his in print contained a word that he had not worried over himself.

No matter, the damage was done. Kosinski seemed to take it personally. "My political and moral credibility has been damaged," Kosinski told the *New York Times.* The charges continued to haunt Kosinski, and taint him. He took five years to write his last novel *The Hermit of 69th Street,* an unnaturally long period for him. Twice as long as most of his novels, it sought to "prove" all the sources by which an author created his work. In it Kosinski explored autobiography and personal issues more deeply and extensively than he ever had before. This exegesis, however, did not make for great reading. It was both a critical and popular failure. That too seemed to have its effect. It appeared to most as though the writer who once said his novel *Cockpit* was inspired by Melville's *The Confidence Man,* had lost confidence.

In the late 1980s, Kosinski visited Poland and Israel, and the interview conducted by Mike Leiderman attests to the way in which Kosinski had come to terms with Poland and both his Polish and Jewish roots. He became involved also in several business ventures concerning Poland. Then on 3 May 1991 he committed suicide.

As much as interviewers were obsessed with Kosinski's life, in reading the interviews he gave, I found myself obsessed by his death. In each I was drawn to those remarks that indicated Kosinski's attitudes towards life, death, and suicide. In my own first interview with Kosinski, he said, "My novels are largely concerned with characters pondering motives, inner decision makers faced with moral and ethical decisions." This resonates very differently for me now, than it did at the time. So too, Kosinski's comment to Gail Sheehy that, "I guess I simply worship feeling alive." Should we focus on the fact that Kosinski said "feeling alive" not "being alive"?

For as we know from the interviews, "feeling alive" had a specific meaning for Kosinski. It was the "heightened moment" that he brought to life in his novels. It was the tension that animated him. Over the course of the interviews, Kosinski struggles with aging. To Barbara Leaming in *Penthouse*, Kosinski said, "I see nothing wrong in using suicide as a safety device—one more guarantee of the decency of my life as it goes on."

Kosinski was a strong personality. His charm comes across in the interviews. We watch as he flatters his interlocutors: Dick Schapp reports Kosinski asking him if he would like to be one of his readers; Pearl Gefen says Kosinski asks her to "call him anytime." From Kosinski, there was often a follow-up, a thank you note, a drawing, an inscribed copy.

He had a deep connection with his readers. After reading about Kosinski's death, one reader Robert Preziose of Baldwin, N. Y., wrote to the *New York Post*: "Jerzy: Wherever you are now, there are no Painted Birds. Goodby Jerzy. Fly proudly with the rest of the birds. Sorry I never got to meet you down here."

This volume is a collection of people whose good fortune it was to meet and converse with Jerzy Kosinski. And I have edited this volume because I still feel engaged in a conversation with Kosinski. His death only poses more questions.

For me there is a central drama to the subject of a Holocaust survivor taking his life. Based on the interviews collected here, and my own conversations with him, I imagine Kosinski would probably have replied that he took his life, as any person has the power to take his own life, Jew or non-Jew, Holocaust survivor or not. He would insist, I believe, that he did not take his life as other survivor/authors Bruno Bettleheim or Primo Levi did, or for that matter as Goebbels did. No, I imagine the important thing for Kosinski was that it was he, himself, not the Nazis and not heart disease, who was the determinant.

When Kosinski took his own life on the night of 3 May 1991, he was once again reasserting himself as the protagonist in the story of his own life, taking away that which, in a sense, he had created. In the days that passed, I, who knew him slightly, like many others who knew him not at all—felt a loss. This collection of *Conversations with Jerzy Kosinski* is an attempt to recapture part of Jerzy Kosinski.

I would like to thank Seetha A-Srinivasan, Associate Director and Editor-in-Chief of the University Press of Mississippi, who suggested this volume, and was a constant help in each stage of its gestation. I am also indebted to Nancy Tritsch for her assistance, perseverance and detective work in helping to research the interviews and secure permissions. I must thank as well all the individual authors, editors and permission rights coordinators who helped in locating, and granting permission to the interviews herein collected. Special thanks to my two greatest fans: My mother, Eva Teicholz, who shared my interest in Kosinski; and my wife, Amy Rappeport Teicholz, whose love and support makes my work easier (and better!). Finally, thanks to all the interviewers. This volume is also the tangible record of their, and my, conversations with Jerzy Kosinski.

TT
September 1992

# Chronology

| | |
|---|---|
| 1933 | 14 June, born Lodz, Poland |
| 1957 | Arrives in New York |
| 1960 | Publication of *The Future is Ours, Comrade* |
| 1962 | Publication of *No Third Path*; marries Mary Weir (divorced 1966, deceased 1968) |
| 1965 | Publication of *The Painted Bird* |
| 1968 | Publication of *Steps* (1969 winner of National Book Award) |
| 1969–70 | Lecturer in English, Princeton University |
| 1970–73 | Visiting professor and resident fellow, Yale University |
| 1971 | Publication of *Being There* |
| 1973 | Publication of *The Devil Tree*; president of P. E. N. (served two one-year terms) |
| 1975 | Publication of *Cockpit* |
| 1976 | Publication of revised and expanded *The Painted Bird* |
| 1977 | Publication of *Blind Date* |
| 1979 | Publication of *Passion Play* |
| 1981 | Publication of revised and expanded *The Devil Tree* |

1982        Publication of *Pinball*

1987        Marries Katherina von Fraunhofer; publication in Poland of
            *The Painted Bird* in Polish language edition

1988        Publication of *The Hermit of 69th Street*; founds Jewish
            Presence Foundation

1989        Founds Polish American Resource Corporation (PARC)

1991        3 May, commits suicide, New York City; publication of
            revised paperback edition of *The Hermit of 69th Street*

# Conversations with Jerzy Kosinski

# Stepmother Tongue
## Dick Schapp/1965

*New York Herald Tribune Book Review* 14 November 1965:6. From
*New York Herald Tribune,* November 7, 1965; © 1965, New York
Herald Tribune Inc. All rights reserved. Reprinted by permission.

There is a fleeting temptation to suggest that there is no Jerzy Kosinski,
that he is a figment of his own vivid imagination, that, by all the rules
of logic, he could not possibly exist.

But he does.

He has black hair and dark, deep eyes, and he sits, at 32, with a drink
in his hand, and he talks, in English tinged with an Eastern European
accent, and explains, calmly, how he came to the United States late in
1957 without any knowledge of the English language and brought out
his first book in English less than three years later. His third book in
English, *The Painted Bird,* appeared last month—a haunting story of a
modern Mowgli, a six-year-old Polish boy raised among Eastern
European wolves in the jungle of World War II.

The book is Kosinski's own story, his life after he was separated from
his parents at the start of the war and drifted from village to village,
scorned as a Gypsy or a Jew (he is neither), beaten and abused and,
eventually, struck mute after being thrown into a manure pit, one of the
more chilling of the book's many chilling incidents. The story is told
without self-pity. "Frankly, I don't think I ever felt sorry for the boy,"
Kosinski says. "By East European standards, he had a very safe war. He
was free.

"The book is not literal," Kosinski says, "but it is almost all literal
incidents, shown in a way not literal, improved, cut up, fitted into a
pattern. I have used the stones of my life to build a new wall. I took the
literal and turned it into something symbolic. The book, I hope, is larger
than the literal and more concrete than the symbolic."

Just as the events in the book are reality heightened, Kosinski's own
progress since he came to the United States seems larger than life. He
had been an assistant professor in the Polish Academy of Sciences in

3

Warsaw and he had had a Ford Foundation fellowship offered to him for study at Columbia University. The Polish government, in a relaxed period, granted him a passport. Kosinski arrived in the United States with no grasp of the language and with no intention of returning to Poland. Between December, 1957, and July, 1958, when his Ford Foundation grant took effect, he held a variety of weird jobs—scraping ships with Greek and Puerto Rican crews (quitting suddenly when the Greeks ganged up on him because they thought he was a Greek who refused to admit his heritage), working as a truck driver without a license, while he covered for a moon-lighting driver who was too tired to handle his regular job and slept next to Kosinski in the cab.

Before he started school, Kosinski taught himself English, first by listening to the radio, then by translating English-language poets—Shakespeare and Poe, for instance—into Polish and Russian and memorizing the poems. "It is easier to memorize poems than individual words," Kosinski says. "The rhythm makes it easier." And, finally, he would get good translations of Polish and Russian works he knew and match them, word for word, against the original.

Quickly, as he entered the graduate school at Columbia and began work toward a Ph.D. in political sociology, Kosinski started writing in English and enjoying it. "I was acquiring a new tradition," he says. "I could never write fiction, for instance, in Polish or Russian because I would be suppressed by the linguistic tradition, suppressed by the grammar. And English is so much a richer language, ten times richer than Polish, eight times richer than Russian."

In 1960, Kosinski wrote *The Future Is Ours, Comrade,* and two years later, *No Third Path,* both non-fiction studies, based on his own experiences, of the mechanics of the collective society, and both strong arguments for the individual and against Soviet society. He wrote the two books under the name Joseph Novak. "I was a newcomer to the country," he explains, "and I was studying. I didn't want to enter into public disputes. And my spoken English then was very limited." Doubleday published both books. Between them, Kosinski met and married Mary Weir, the widow of Ernest T. Weir, the founder and onetime board chairman of the National Steel Corporation. Kosinski's new book, *The Painted Bird,* is dedicated "To my wife Mary without whom even the past would lose its meaning."

He started working on *The Painted Bird* two years ago and went

through nine full drafts of the book. He leaned heavily on the Rodale
Press dictionary and the large Webster's and the 26-volume set of the
Oxford Dictionary that his wife had given him as a present. "I keep
looking for the right word," Kosinski says. "There are so many
beautiful words that are not in usage any more."

As he wrote, he kept checking on himself for rhythm and clarity.
"English is easy to learn," he says, "but almost impossible to master."
He would recite three versions of a paragraph into a tape recorder, then
listen to the replay for the one that sounded best to his ear. When he
wondered whether he was getting his meaning across, he would call a
telephone operator, explain his predicament, read her a passage and ask
if she understood it.

"I was not in any way ashamed to expose my manuscript to friends
who would read it," Kosinski says. "I made 16, 17 copies of every draft
and showed it to people. I chose some people whose language was not
English and some who were Americans. I asked them to mark a little
cross next to anything that didn't sound right. If enough people marked
a sentence, I knew something was wrong with it."

Kosinski polished and repolished, completely redoing even the first
set of galleys, and the result is sentences as crisp and clear as: "She was
old and always bent over, as though she wanted to break herself in half
but could not. . . . She sometimes looked like an old green-gray puff-
ball, rotten through and waiting for a last gust of wind to blow out the
black dry dust from inside."

Now Kosinski is at work in New York on his next book. "It is the
first book in which I'll be able to be really free," he says, "free of
myself." He is still going to keep searching for the right words. "Want
to be on the list of people who read my manuscripts?" he asks.

# Trade Winds

Cleveland Amory/1971

Published in *Saturday Review* 17 April 1971:16–17. Reprinted by permission of Omni International Ltd.

We had brunch in the Manhattan apartment of Jerzy Kosinski, the multi-prizewinning author of *The Painted Bird* (Le Prix du Meilleur Livre Étranger), *Steps* (1969 National Book Award), and the forthcoming *Being There* (Harcourt Brace Jovanovich). Born in Poland and now teaching at the Yale Drama School, Mr. Kosinski is an intense, earnest, slow-spoken but quick-humored fellow who speaks with an intriguing accent but who, though his books have been translated into eighteen languages, writes only in English. Formerly married to Mary Weir, daughter of the late steel baron Ernest Weir, he dedicated his latest book to Katharine von Fraunhofer, who was also present and who is an attractive and able brunch-maker. "To Katharine v. F.," the dedication reads, "who taught me that love is more than the longing to be together."

"Nobody," Miss von Fraunhofer said, smiling, "reads dedications." Mr. Kosinski's apartment consists of a compact living room-bedroom, a kitchenette, a bathroom, and, for his photographic pursuits, a dressing room made into a darkroom. Small as it all is, however, Miss von Fraunhofer explained that it was still large enough for Mr. Kosinski to hide in. "And when Yurek *does* hide," she emphasized, "nobody can find him."

We queried the "Yurek." "It's the nickname for Jerzy," she said. "You also pronounce that with a 'Y.' Call him anything," she offered, "but Jerry. He hates that."

It was Mr. Kosinski's turn. "The only vanity I have is that 'Z,'" he said. "I even made the publisher make the 'Z' bigger than any of the other letters on the jacket."

We looked at the jacket. It was true—the "Z" was larger than any of the other letters. While we did so, Mr. Kosinski talked about jacket copy in general. "For a novel," he said, "there shouldn't have to be a description on the jacket. It's very upsetting. When I was working on the book, I could talk about it. Now, when it's complete, I can't."

"Chance," the jacket copy read, "is the quintessential antihero. His whole life has been spent in two solitary pursuits—tending a garden and watching television." Obviously, chance is retarded.

"That reminds me," Mr. Kosinski went on, "of a classic question I was asked the other day by one of the out-of-town reviewers. 'Would this book,' he asked me, 'like your other two books, be autobiographical?'"

Mr. Kosinski smiled. "The best I could do was tell him that to some degree we are all retarded. And one day, of course, we all will be retarded together." He paused. "In other words, it's not directly autobiographical in terms of my past, but it certainly is in terms of my future."

We asked him to explain. "Take my father," he said. "He was born in Russia. He saw the Revolution of 1905, then World War I, then he escaped from Russia during the Bolshevik Revolution, and then he lived through the Second World War. So if anyone had a reason to be fed up, he had. And he withdrew from the twentieth century altogether. He studied Ancient Greece, and the origin of the European languages. It was his escape device. He did have one narrow field of commercial excellence, though. He was an expert in the manufacture of felt. I have a similar way to survive," Mr. Kosinski went on. "Photographic chemistry. If I have twenty minutes' warning, I can go to work on it and support myself."

Mr. Kosinski was an only child. His mother was a pianist but was never allowed to perform in public. She is still alive, although very ill. "The war was when I was from six to twelve," he said. "I was alone in Warsaw, separated from my family. By the age of eight, in terms of character and what I wanted to do, I was already completely formed.

"When I was studying in Russia, at Moscow University, I would speak on the phone to my father in Latin. We were both quite fluent, and I would give him all the political gossip in the first ten minutes, because it took the Soviets that much time to provide a Latin censor. They were always sure we were speaking Rumanian. But finally the censor would come on and say, 'May I remind you, comrade, that you should use a language of a state recognized by the United Nations.' I could have asked them," he smiled, "'What about the Vatican?'" He stopped smiling. "The Soviet dictatorship," he said, "begins not in the Kremlin but in the kindergarten. I am basically very depressed about the twentieth century. It is a totalitarian century. This century, I am

convinced, will totally and totalitarianly get rid of the liberal mind, the
Renaissance man. This is the first time when there is a perfect match
between crude political ideas and the complex technology that makes
those ideas acceptable."

What, we asked him, could be done? "Nothing, really," he said,
"except to serve your own universe—of yourself—by not lending
yourself to this process. But even you may be too big a piece of real
estate. Too many things may have penetrated you already."

Mr. Kosinski, we learned, always wears a shirt and tie to his college
classes. "I like to feel locked in," he said, "against foreign influences."
Starting his undergraduate course, "Death and Modern Imagination," he
told his students, "I am not here to save you. I am not a missionary. I
am merely trying to save myself from what has happened to you.
There's a place in my boat for those of you who want to jump in."

Before saying good-by to Mr. Kosinski, we demanded a firsthand
look at his disappearance act. Miss von Fraunhofer ushered us down the
hall, while Mr. Kosinski hid. Then we came back. We looked everywhere very carefully—in the closets, under the sofa, behind every
cabinet, even in the darkroom. There was no question, the author of
*Being There* wasn't there. We gave up.

At that point, out came Mr. Kosinski. "Once," he told us, "I hid for a
whole weekend. I came out only for food and work. People were in and
out too, but they never found me."

# Jerzy Kosinski
## Brandon Tartikoff/1971

Published in *Metropolitan Review* 8 October 1971:104. Reprinted by permission of Brandon Tartikoff.

The mind that conceived the grotesque recollective of *The Painted Bird*, the fragmented, existential epic of *Steps*, and the recently acclaimed, debated, contested modern day parable of *Being There*, was concentrating its energies on the stack of "Modern Romance" and "True Confession" magazines piled conspicuously on the desk of the study. Jerzy Kosinski, 37 years old, winner of the 1969 National Book Award in Fiction, 1970 recipient of the National Institute of Arts and Letters Award for Creative Work in Literature, was taking it all in: "I Got High On Pot, And Gave My Baby Away", "I Gave Myself To My Father-in-law To Save The Family", "Midsummer Sex: The Orgy That Should Never Have Happened". "Reading these and other magazines allows me and my students to keep tabs on the changes in the language", he says, an intimation of a smile forming, perhaps.

After that the interview began abruptly, Kosinski speaking briskly, assuredly, point trammeling up point—photography, writing, the visual media, the cultural mapping of Western Man—until insight and sheer intellect rested their case.

The interview speaks for itself, because Koskinski doesn't subscribe to the notion that an author should be evasive and secretive about his writing.

The interview took place in New Haven where Jerzy Kosinski is currently Professor of English prose at the Yale University School of Drama.

**T:** I'd like to take a generic tact in discussing your writing, by initially focusing on that chapter of your artistic life when you were an internationally acclaimed and exhibited photographer. First off, what was your basic motivation in deciding to become a photographer?

**K:** I moved towards photography when I lived in Poland and in the Soviet Union, simply because I was opting for a medium that would allow me some degree of privacy, the sort of profession which incorporates removal from others as part of the vocational requirements. The second reason was aesthetical. I felt that even in photography I could use certain approaches to reality which would be judgmental and, to a degree, moralistic. By doing so, I couldn't be easily accused of political heresy, since photography, by its very nature, is highly objective. Thus, I opted for the only medium within my interests in which I could remain myself and yet express what I felt would be the very minimum an artist or a man preoccupied with human environment should express. As you can see, it was a choice not dictated by my drive towards visual arts— I don't have such a drive. If anything, I feel that the visual arts are separating us from one another because they claim such objectivity: they turn us into observers, and they take us away from ourselves by pointing out that as long as we observe, we remain detached.

**T:** What made you choose to approach the art of photography through a technical orientation (and eventual expertise) in photochemistry?

**K:** My learning photo-chemistry was part of my removal from the realm of Marxism-Stalinism (since my basic background was in political science and history); I moved to the medium that was least judgmental: chemistry, which was the only conceivable escape from the omnipresent dominance of Stalinist ideological oppression. The political spectrum available to me during 1950–56 I found absolutely unbearable: fraudulent, perverted, and blatantly anti-human. And I would do anything to remove myself and not to support it by my participation; and so I removed myself altogether by leaving the so-called "people's republics".

**T:** While there, did you ever attempt any writing?

**K:** I did not even consider it. Writing would imply my acceptance of the social context around me, the social order in which it took place: I hated that context. I still do. Writing, no matter how personal, is always social and political. It employs the language—the most social of all media—and no matter how egocentric and idiosyncratic a writer's vision, it is always a vision of the human self, of life, of forces which propel us in one direction or another. Thus, in a totalitarian state, the publisher publishes only books which are acceptable to the State. I would never commit myself to such cooperation; I would not write.

**T:** What about keeping a personal diary, or perhaps writing some poetry just for yourself?

**K:** It would be cheating: In the final instance, I believe, one writes a diary or poetry for others; one does not write it for oneself.

Photography was more personal. I could come up with only one photograph. I would develop it myself. I was in charge of the whole process. And, at the worst, I felt that if my life was to be spent within the totalitarian state, I would become a photographer. I would photograph children and the old and incurably sick people, both the most innocent citizens of such a State, and I would remain within what I considered surface expression. Therefore, once I left Eastern Europe behind and settled here, in America, I had to look at my past life with an entirely different perspective. I had to part with many motives which were no longer valid, one of which was photography.

**T:** And yet I detect much of the photographer's eye evident in your writing . . .

**K:** Or you can do the opposite. I like to believe that there was a lot of the writer's eye in my photographs. Many of them almost "told stories". There was some humor in them, (unlike in my writing!). But you are right in a sense that the guiding principle of my fiction is one of reducing human reality to what I consider its most immediate dimensions. My photographs also were stripped of all "secondary" details. I used a lot of black and white with almost no gray tone in between. I would often set objects in the very center of the photogram, and in doing so defied the prevalent trend of setting them off-center. I felt that this would confront the observer with the incident portrayed, rather than distracting him by the composition of the picture. In my writing I note the same tendency to develop more and more the contrast, and to remove the tones in between. Perhaps my removing the gray in the photographs could be compared to my sustained pruning of adjectives and adverbs, and my great belief in the verb, as the most involving, the propellant prose-element of writing.

**T:** I imagine that you are constantly called upon to attest whether or not all the gothic happenings, bizarre sexual encounters, and horrific incidents described in your novels, are derived from your personal experience. How do you reconcile the autobiographical element in your writing with your personal definition of a novelist?

**K:** I never wrote my books as autobiographical; I never claimed them to be anything but novels. Why I wrote them in a manner that perhaps suggests autobiographical elements stems from my basic notion of who a novelist is. I write because I feel that a novelist has a lot in common with others, not because he differs from them. Because he's very much like others he feels that whatever he depicts also has to make an impression on others. If I describe my emotions, I do it believing that I'm describing your emotions as well, because both of us, being human, have so much in common. This goes for the French, Chinese, for the Eskimos, for the Latin Americans, for the East Europeans, and for the natives of this land of ours whose language I adopted to write in. In terms of human situations, in terms of our imagination, we all differ very little. We do differ only in the rudimentary aspects and ways of our upbringing, of certain environmental, marginal properties relating to our emotional make up.

In my view, the 20th century man reflects the major Western cultural thrusts; hence the novelist is a topographer of the emotional, moral and socio-political paths which are equally evocative for people in Europe as they are for people here. This view precludes writing fiction as an autobiographical exercise since even the writer who feels he is writing from a strictly autobiographical perspective conveys nothing but human experience—an experience which knows no private property, no monopoly and no copyright. It knows, however, aberrations—some writers see themselves as missionaries of their own private gospel; their novels are so "way out" that they indeed have little to do with the human condition. And the form, the language they employ, often attracts attention only to itself, to its own "composition," thus failing as conveyor of a human incident and of a human emotion. Such novels are to me nothing but old telephone books; the names and numbers are all there but if you should dial by a mistake, there will be no answer.

**T:** You've been known to answer the question of whether you have actually experienced all that you write about with the mystical response—"If I haven't already experienced them, I could and I might." What did you actually mean by that?

**K:** What I mean is that if they didn't "happen" to the reader when he read them then they didn't happen. For it is the reader who must make them real. If a novel succeeded, then the reader should have imagined these events as happening to him—and so be purged, be enriched, be moved. If a reader doesn't believe, for instance, that *The Painted Bird* evokes the reality of his immediate existence here, in New Haven, or in New York, Long Island, or in any other place, then clearly it doesn't matter whether "it" happened to me or to someone else or not happened at all. And I'm not going to give my reader, whoever he might be, excuses from the violence of his own environment, by telling him that "painted birds" live only in the cages of rural Europe, because I believe that he also is living in a cage that is full of them, that he himself is one of them; he paints them, but he's also painted. The violence of *The Painted Bird*, of peasant villages, is comparatively minor to the trauma of living in a major industrial city. A small peasant community offers many escapes which the human birds trapped in New Haven, New York, or Los Angeles, Paris or London, Moscow or Berlin do not have anymore. And so I repeat: it is the reader who makes the book happen. Hence, explaining the book with fragments of the author's life is an attempt to torpedo the evocative thrust of fiction. By doing so the human experience the novel portrays becomes grounded like dead lightening. It does not confront the reader as potentially his anymore. It does not threaten him—he is "safe": he has nothing to fear. It "happened" to somebody else (the Author!).

**T:** If you were to write *The Painted Bird* over again would you write it in the form of *Steps*?

**K:** I wanted to write *Steps* first. I had the detailed design for *Steps* before I decided to write *The Painted Bird*. But at the time I felt that *Steps* had to be far more exact, in terms of the language I needed, to express some of its ambiguity. I knew I would need additional control over the language, so I postponed writing *Steps* and embarked on writing a novel in which the elements of nature, of folklore, and of definite history were present. As if stripping a novel of all such "specific" elements, wouldn't make it equally true, or even more accessible. Now, I think *Steps* is more accessible precisely because it is not fixed in any specific place. Unlike *The Painted Bird*, *Steps* doesn't offer its reader any easy way out.

**T:** Did you conceive *Steps* in its present fragmented, timeless sequence, or did you write it in chronological action-blocks and then put it together in the fashion of a New Wave film director editing his work?

**K:** Since there is a clear progression which I had in mind *Steps* was written in exactly the same order as it was published.There is, I believe, a progression in *Steps*, a staircase of sorts, from the formed mind of the protagonist (in the beginning of the novel) when he sees himself as a unique manipulator of others, to the stage (at the novel's end) when he realizes that he is nothing but a composite of various steps of culture. In the beginning of his voyage he still sees himself as a highly individual being even though already holding a credit card. He still tends to think that he doesn't buy the culture at large, but just a specific sexual encounter. Throughout the incidents of the book he becomes more and more aware that he is the credit card of Western civilization. He's sold in mass, and he's bought in mass. Once realizing this, his ultimate goal is to acknowledge this, to surrender, to vanish.

**T:** While both *The Painted Bird* and *Being There* depict the trials and subsequent survival of an innocent protagonist making his way through the societal mire, they seem to end on a note of ominous inconclusiveness. How would you compare the fates suffered by the Boy and Chauncey Gardiner? And do you see them making a finite statement about the human condition?

**K:** At the end of *The Painted Bird* the Boy is at the most destructive part of his journey; from now on he will speak the voice of revenge: he knows no other voice. He's a potential Eichmann, standing on the balcony, full of contempt for mankind—and for himself as a former victim. After all, even the great men, the great killers in history, spoke of revenge from some sort of balcony. And that's where the Boy is standing when the novel ends. So his regained voice might tell those who will listen to do what others have done to him. If he's wiser, he's wiser simply by acquiring an experience of hate, of suffering and terror, of power which he may want to pass onto others. Perhaps mankind would be better off had he been killed.

The end of *Being There* is, at least for me, equally foreboding. In terms of our individual fate, we can no longer influence Chauncey Gardiner's, while he is unwillingly—influencing ours—a process we are unable to stop, indeed, are not quite aware of its taking place day after day. Thus, nothing prevents social forces, which appear anonymous to us, from retrieving Chauncey Gardiner from his anonymity and from putting him back onto the national screen to face the nation on television. Chauncey Gardiner may be no more than a composite of all of us—and this includes our politicians, our actors, and our instant culture heroes.

**T:** Why did you choose to portray Chauncey Gardiner as being a bit retarded? What did this add towards his interaction with society?

**K:** I don't think he is that defective. To a degree, so are people around him. In his context Gardiner is the only man who truly reflects the contemporary life. He's at peace with the environment, which is already so broken, that he, as a little fragment of it could not survive in it on his own. Some of those around him, but not all of them (or all of us) are "split"; they still belong to some "private" gardens of individual idiosyncratic experience which demands moral judgments since it includes notions of justice and morality; but at the same time they have been excluded by modern life from any meaningful action which could alter their lives; their condition precludes even communicating their judgments to others or to one another. The television becomes the guiding force for all of us. In spite of our remaining differences we're all united within the most insidious frame of reference—the visual medium, the television. In this new era Chauncey Gardiner is ahead of us, since he is already the complete product of what is in store for us in the imminent future. He has no other awareness (not even a sexual one) while we still claim to have one. He's the first in the Videot's Paradise. He doesn't need to communicate with anyone,—he has nothing to tell others that they don't already know—(visual culture being the source of knowledge and experience) and therefore he is adaptable. People around him, all of us, who should be able to decipher him, who should be able to disengage ourselves from his vacuum (since we are still armed with another sensibility), are already unable to do so. We have been disarmed by the medium which daily feeds all of us.

That's why, I think, among all of us Gardiner is a man to watch. He is the voice of the TV set, he is the image on the TV set. He functions smoothly; but we don't. We are defective. We can no longer find out who we are—whose standards of reference are we to employ?—or what the emotions are that guide us—are they the emotions of our real life, or imitations. We have lost the way to find out who the others who surround us are, since the only way to find them out—intimate contact—has been replaced by the multi-channeled TV set. And so it is only natural that we vote for people and are led by people and behave like people who come to us through these channels only.

**T:** Critics like Anatole Broyard of the *Times* and John Updike in *New Yorker* have reacted violently towards *Being There* and what they claim to be your criticism of America and its Establishment. Turning positively for a moment, how could you, if given the power, correct the evils and inadequacies you ascribe to television.

**K:** Television is the total medium; it almost becomes a substitute for tangible reality. Its accessibility, its digestability is far greater than that of any other medium. Because it is visual, and because of our preoccupation with visual culture (witness our belief that seeing implies active participation) television fulfills what we want our life to be. For many hundreds of years Western man longed to be at peace with himself even though threatened by his physical and emotional existence, yet, simultaneously, he was afraid to be separated from it. Television offers such illusory compromise. Hence, its nature cannot be altered, and it is too late to alter ours. The medium prevents any other identity than the one it develops. Give it to a totalitarian system, and you will see how manipulative it can also be politically. At present, American television still reflects the pluralistic aspect of American society, and as such I don't think it is consciously manipulative. I may see certain tendencies among the officialdom to force it towards another chapter of its influential history but if it happens I hope I won't be here to witness it. But if I am, I have no doubt that some of my critics who defend this officialdom today will tomorrow hand me the warrant of arrest.

**T:** According to an article about you in *Look,* you have received dozens of film offers for *Steps*, and for *The Painted Bird*. Do you think you will ever consider having these works adapted to film? They both seem to lend themselves extremely well to a cinematic interpretation.

**K:** I don't want *The Painted Bird* or *Steps* to be illustrated by an actor, to become permanently set via the visual medium in one concrete dramatic situation. As I stressed before, I don't want to prevent my readers from having to "stage" my novels in the life of their imagination.

**T:** Even if you yourself were personally involved and responsible for the adaptation?

**K:** Perhaps in the case of *Being There*, which would lend itself more to a cinematic interpretation simply because of its story. A film could show how feasible and believable Chauncey Gardiner is. But to portray Gardiner I would insist on an actor who has not been known. Only through the visual medium could you see how acceptable he would become. Perhaps the film audience could then understand more of the nature of the visual media and be made suddenly aware of all the Chauncey Gardiners there are around.

**T:** I noticed recently that you appeared on the Johnny Carson

"Tonight Show". I wondered if there wasn't an element of black humor lurking behind your appearance, knowing how you portrayed the talk show in *Being There*. What is your view of this type of program?

**K:** Anyone who has watched talk shows can imitate the behavior expected by them; since the medium allows for the most elementary mode of expression. A one-liner, a joke, a three-minute story, and of course anything gestural is its ideal format. That is why every statement Chauncey Gardiner makes seems to be tailored to fit this format—and the format of our life as well. In my first appearance on the talk show, I made this very point. Here I was, a foreigner, speaking with a heavy foreign accent, with an entirely different idea of humor and conversation, but because that format required so little it could accommodate me; what's more I find it quite acceptable too. After all, Talk Shows managed to turn a conversation into a visual act—one more relief for a tired man! I am no exception to the rule—the medium proved it to me and I proved it to the medium. Remember: I am the actual father of Chauncey Gardiner. . . .

**T:** How do you react to the prevalent snobbism of many noted writers, towards appearing on television and talking about their works.

**K:** Personally, I see no reason to dismiss a medium to which 6.5 hours a day are devoted to an average American. For one, it is still politically free and, a quite liberal medium—and think how many people it reaches—even if so slightly. When on television I have attempted, for instance, to alert the parents—since I teach their sons and daughters—to the emotional and intellectual dangers the medium has created for those children who watch it indiscriminately. I did not talk about my novels or the craft of writing them but about the experience of teaching videots, the television generation.

**T:** Outside of the last 25 pages of *Steps*, *Being There* constitutes your first work grounded in American culture, your first "American" novel. It's interesting that you chose to express yourself as Antonioni did in his first "American" film, *Zabriskie Point*—in the form of a myth or fable. Did you find this form conducive to your vision of the medium's arresting takeover of American society?

**K:** I don't think *Being There* is a fable. To dismiss it as some critics suggest, as a sort of contemporary *Candide*, reflects a simplified vision of reality. It's a novel about a social and emotional process which is by now so common that we don't even perceive it anymore in three dimensions. When you have people competing on national television for the image and nothing else (e.g. the Kennedy-Nixon debates), when people devote so much time to it that it patterns their lives, then this process is not a fable anymore. After all, television registers primarily the visual and not the verbal—whatever is said on its screen is clearly secondary to what is shown. Television establishes this priority, and its "message" isn't absorbed by the viewer because he has dismissed the language while focusing on the onrushing images. This is the substance *Being There* is made of. Is it a fable? A science-fiction? Utopia? I wish it were. The very issue of *Time* magazine which reviewed *Being There*, noted that McCloskey polled those who voted for him in the 1967 election; 84 percent admitted not knowing his background or ideas, but voted for him because he looked sincere and honest on television. Even Chauncey Gardiner could not have hoped for better results! That's why I am convinced that Chauncey Gardiner is not only someone we know very well, but that we know him for what we think we know him, not for what he really is. Our tradition of Enlightenment tells us he must have "something" if he becomes that prominent, instead of assuming that he is prominent because he might know nothing and that's why he's the least objectionable to everyone of us.

**T:** But you cannot deny the predominantly mythical format of *Being There*: the Garden, the plot transpiring in seven days, a protagonist named Chance, a seductress named EE (Eve). How would you explain this cultural role myth seems to be playing in the development of *Being There* and your other novels?

**K:** All novels rely on myths and mine are no exception. However, Chance is a common American name. So is Elizabeth-Eve (EE). *The Painted Bird* can be seen as the myth of the travelling child. Every single incident in *Steps* is built along a very obvious myth, what's more a myth already incorporated in the tangible aspects of our lives. For instance, the philosopher's grail becomes the omnipotent credit card. These myths are the "steps" of our culture, and of our daily existence; and of our drama, film and fiction. We walk this veritable staircase of myths and fables unaware of their origins, or of the "stories" they once were. A businessman lifted by helicopter over the East River heliport is not aware of the Icarus myth, or of the Jules Verne novels which quite likely stimulated the invention of this flying bird.

The Staircase of myths, of culture is the only one available to us. We can walk it slower or faster, we can walk it backwards, we can walk it comfortably or uncomfortably, but it's the only one we know, and there is no escape. The staircase—with us walking it—is sealed. Today, when the pains of living are greater than ever, and when life demands of society, the mechanics of which we no longer understand or perceive, the television comes to "rescue" us from the discomfort of the unknown. Television, the finest embodiment of our old predilection towards visual culture is the latest best-selling chapter in Western Man's history—long escape from facing his own predatory condition. He has always suffered when he confronted it from within—this after all, included realizing one's mortality. So out of the hopeless despair, he, the spoiled child of the universe, created a truly magic window, a silverish screen, which he believes will allow him to look perpetually outside—into the show of life, somebody else's life. He himself feels outside—peaceful, at ease, a mere observer, always busy watching, too busy to reflect and ponder. It is for him—for us— that we have invented television rather than, let's say, an equally clever contraption which would enable us to come to terms with our being here, to accept our temporal, physical existence, our emotions, our fears, our joys, our pains, and our Death.

**T:** What is your personal relationship to television, meaning: do you watch it, and if so, with what intentions?

**K:** Of course I do watch it, I watch if often—I think I know all the programs quite well. And as you reminded me, I am from time to time even on it. Since I teach contemporary English prose, I observe television very carefully. As a visual medium I consider it to be the ultimate enemy of language, of imagination, and insight. And therefore I have to know it very well. Just as anyone preoccupied with nature has to fear the industrial pollution, anyone preoccupied with literature, writing, and drama has to watch television. Watch it in double meaning. And so, on one side I am astonished by this medium's so easily acquired power over us, but on the other I think its influence is the punishment for our committing the ultimate sin: for losing the awareness of the Self. In television we found the device which buries us without any possibility of our ever getting out. It immobilizes us, and we are dying mute in front of a live talk show.

# The Art of Fiction XLVI—Jerzy Kosinski

George A. Plimpton and Rocco Landesman/1972

Jerzy Kosinski, born in Poland in 1933, does not like to talk about his past, although the events of his life correspond almost exactly to those described in his novels. While still a young boy, he was separated from his parents and wandered from village to village in war-torn Eastern Europe. His life in postwar Poland was collective, structured and ordered—the very antithesis of the traumatic experience of his youth. From 1955 to 1957 he was an Associate Professor at the Polish Academy of Sciences in Warsaw. In 1957, he left Poland and arrived in the United States as a "private individual" with no knowledge of English and no established means of support. "I did not like myself in Poland," he says, explaining that it was the country of a past from which he was trying to separate himself. Why did he choose the United States? "Argentina and Brazil would not let me in. And so, I started at the other end of the alphabet."

In 1962 he married Mary Hayward Weir, "a wealthy, white Anglo-Saxon Protestant who grounded me very definitely in purely American experience." After her tragic death in 1968, he continued teaching as a professor of English—first at Wesleyan, then Princeton, and now at Yale, where he is Resident Fellow at Davenport College.

Kosinski has had twenty-five Manhattan addresses, and travels frequently in Western Europe. He has never had children, explaining that "my orbit does not make provision for the giving of life." He will not accept the responsibility of bringing others into the world and feels that if he did, his children would be burdened with his past and the vision that developed from it. He has no desire to project himself beyond his books, over which he can exercise complete control. Children would be "yet another fragmentation, another split in the self. If that self is to be free," he adds, "I must depend on no one and no one must depend on me."

After two volumes of nonfiction under the pen name of Joseph Novak, in 1965 he published his first novel, *The Painted Bird,* using his own name. It has been translated into thirty-four languages, and was awarded *Le Prix du Meilleur Livre Étranger* in France. For *Steps,* published in 1968, he received the National Book Award. *Being There* was published in 1971. He has also written two collections of essays, *Notes of the Author* (1965) and *The Art of the Self* (1968).

**Interviewer:** If you had continued to live in Poland and written in Polish, do you think your books would have been published? And if so, would they have been popular?

**Kosinski:** It's not even a matter for speculation. I would never have written in Polish. I never saw myself as a man expressing opinions in a totalitarian State. Make no mistake about it: all my generation was perfectly aware of the dimensions of our existence. To be a spokesman in a field which used language would require one to be a spokesman for a particular political situation. My generation considered this a trap; we would not speak for it; nor could we speak against it. So what happened was that I slowly moved toward visual expression, and became a photographer. Of course, there were some other reasons. I was bilingual— my parents spoke Russian at home while I was studying Polish in school. But there was a touch of disdain for Polish literature, which in their opinion was inferior to Russian literature. I was split, like a child who grows up in two different families; studying in Polish at the University, but at home, really, all that mattered was 19th century Russian literature.

**Interviewer:** Could you express in photographs, given the dimensions of the trap, anything you felt?

**Kosinski:** Within the limits of photography, I could point out certain aspects of human behavior as contrasted with collective behavior. I could show old age which knows no politics; I could show the solitude of a man lost in a large field; I could point out that there is, after all, an independent, naked, human being. This in itself was a sort of political statement. I even produced some nudes of rather attractive, non-socialist female forms. It ended on a very unpleasant political note: I was accused of being a cosmopolitan who sees the flesh, but not the social being.

**Interviewer:** Who accused you?

**Kosinski:** The members of the Photographic Society. The same thing as the Writers Union, you know. These groups are geared to this sort of policing; that is what they're there for.

**Interviewer:** Can one defend oneself?

**Kosinski:** Within the limits of the totalitarian doctrine—hence there is no defense. When I was growing up in a Stalinist society my guide-lines were: Am I going to survive physically? Am I going to survive as a sane being? Since I was in conflict with the society, my real plight had to remain hidden. I avoided having close friends, who would know too much about me, and could be used against me. Until I left for America I lived the life of an "inner émigré," as I called myself.

**Interviewer:** An inner émigré?

**Kosinski:** Yes. The photographic darkroom emerged as a perfect metaphor for my life. It was the one place I could lock myself in (rather than being locked in) and legally not admit anyone else. For me it be-came a kind of temple. There is an episode in *Steps* in which a young philosophy student at the State University selects the laboratories as the temples. Well, think how much more of a temple a darkroom is in a police state. Inside, I would develop my own private images; instead of writing fiction I imagined myself as a fictional character. I identified very strongly with characters of both Eastern and Western literature. I saw myself as Petchorin, in Lermontov's novel, *A Hero of Our Time,* as Romashov, the hero of Kuprin's *The Duel,* as Julien Sorel, and once in a while as Rastignac, facing the society and being at war with it. I wrote my fiction emotionally; I would never commit it to paper.

**Interviewer:** Paddy Chayefsky said recently that he felt these sort of oppressive strictures were really quite important in producing fine litera-ture. He felt that a strait jacket was essential to a writer.

**Kosinski:** Easily said. One could argue the opposite as well and make a point for the Byronesque kind of expression with its abandonment, its freedom to collide with others, to express outrage; for Nabokov's kind of vitality. Or we can make a point for a man who chooses a visionary strait jacket which is self imposed, perhaps the best form there is. Look at Balzac, Proust, Mann, Camus, Faulkner.

For every Solzhenitsyn who manages to have his first novel published officially *(One Day in the Life of Ivan Denisovitch),* there are probably hundreds of gifted writers in the Soviet Union who create emotionally in their "darkrooms," and who will never write anything on paper. Or those very desperate ones who do commit their vision to paper but hide their manuscripts somewhere under the floor.

**Interviewer:** What was the reaction of the Polish press to your achievements in English prose—to *The Painted Bird, Steps,* and *Being There?*

**Kosinski:** The reaction of the Polish press in Poland towards *The Painted Bird* was pure propaganda. They reinvented the content of the novel. Their major effort was to prove that any Pole who settled abroad, writes in English and is published by various western publishers had to do it either by selling himself to the CIA, Radio Free Europe, or to the Library of Congress. According to the official Party journal, the most damaging proof of my collaboration with the White House was that the novel carried the Library of Congress number . . . which, of course, is automatically assigned to every book published in the U.S. There were a few things, however, which they couldn't quite cope with: *The Painted Bird* was warmly received by, among others, Sartre's *Les Temps Modernes,* the Communist *L'Humanité* in France, *The Daily Worker* in London, and the progressive leftist press in the rest of Western Europe. To counteract it, the Polish bureaucrats said that being a Jew, I sold myself to Zionists and *had* to write an anti-Polish book to achieve "success" in the West. They stressed my anti-Polishness. *The Painted Bird,* of course, was not set in Poland, it was set "somewhere in Eastern Europe." After this, they dropped me altogether. When I got the National Book Award, there was not a single mention of *Steps,* nor later, of *Being There,* as if I ceased to exist. Anyone who leaves Poland and doesn't come back, sells out his Polishness: if he left for political reasons, that would be applauded by the Poles; they would say, "Well, we all have our relatives in America, how nice that he is there now." But if he simply leaves for personal reasons, he has turned against his very element," *his nationality.* The Polish population didn't know *The Painted Bird;* they *assumed* that I had whitewashed the Germans, that the book glorified the SS, and they were authentically enraged. I received mail not only from Poland but from Poles in the United States, who hadn't read the book either. I received thousands of angry letters and at one point I had to register some of them with the police because they were threatening in a very specific form. But, of course, I remained a free man: I was here. Can you imagine the predicament of someone who writes in the Soviet Union, feeling that this is the best thing that he can do for his country, delivers his manuscript to the Soviet publisher, and is persecuted promptly from the next day on—his case discussed in the Writers Union because, apparently, according to the accusations, in his manuscript *he reveals himself as an anti-Soviet character.* This was the case of Pasternak. When he wrote *Dr. Zhivago,* he thought that he was writing a book of great human import, showing the predicament of a man caught in the changing patterns of socialist history. Well, the Party didn't see it that way. Look at Solzhenitsyn; apparently, he feels the same way. He doesn't write anti-Soviet books. It seems that he is writing books which are Russian *and* Soviet in the ultimately positive way. Again, this has not been the view of the Writers Union.

**Interviewer:** Who are the people in the Writers Union in Poland?

**Kosinski:** They are journalists, novelists, literary critics, poets.They have to live, and to live they have to be published from time to time by the State. I think many of them are primarily concerned with survival in their profession. It's easy to attach labels. You have to remember, they have to function within a most threatening and un-predictable reality governed by the Party bureaucracy and the total State. Hence, many of them are extremely cautious, many tend to be dogmatic, many are just desperate and some are servile agents of the State organs. The creative man in a police state has always been trapped in a cage where he can fly as long as he does not touch the wires. The predicament is: how to spread your wings in the cage. I think the majority of them fight for their own sanity and when suddenly one of them says I don't like this cage, I want out, and does something about it, the others descend upon him because he is threatening the safety of all of them.

**Interviewer:** Given the unusual circumstances of your life, many people think of your work—the first two novels, anyway—as non-fiction.

**Kosinski:** Well, to say that *The Painted Bird,* for example is non-fiction, or even autobiographical, may be convenient for classification, but it's not easily justified. What we remember lacks the hard edge of fact. To help us along we create little fictions, highly subtle and individual scenarios which clarify and shape our experience. The remembered event becomes a fiction, a structure made to accommodate certain feelings. This is obvious to me. If it weren't for these structures, art would be too personal for the artist to create, much less for the audience to grasp. Even film, the most literal of all the arts, is edited.

**Interviewer:** You once said that *The Painted Bird* is the result of a "slow unfreezing of a mind long gripped by fear." I assume this fear refers to the horrors of World War II.

**Kosinski:** I see no essential difference between World War II and any other traumatic reality. For example, I know many people whose childhood in the United States was in its own way just as traumatic as that of millions of Central Europeans.

**Interviewer:** Yes, but in this case a whole generation was affected by the same event. A noted American critic spoke of a "brutalization of the imagination" produced in many writers by this one catastrophe.

**Kosinski:** World War II is something which I think might have affected some American critics more than it affected some of the European writers. I don't believe that human experience, as reflected in fiction, can be graded, from less brutal (presumably North American) to extremely brutal (Russian, Central European, Chinese, Bengali, and so forth). It depends on how it affects the creative mind. Among the East Europeans I know, I think I was no more, no less affected by the war than millions of others.

**Interviewer:** You sound like Polanski, who says that violence is horrible and traumatic only when you look at it from a particular point of view.

**Kosinski:** If you—or anyone else—had been surrounded by it for years, you'd perceive it also as human, natural—and expected. You get used to it. A needle or the sight of blood may be as terrifying to a North Dakotan as a bomb is to a Vietnamese.

**Interviewer:** So in your view, experience is arbitrary; X pretty much equals Y, or Z?

**Kosinski:** Pretty much.

**Interviewer:** But the experiences that you deal with in *Steps*, for instance, are certainly not what we might call "ordinary" experiences. One episode takes place in an asylum, another in a rest home, another in a lavatory, another in the New York underworld. And you continually choose incidents that to other people, at least, seem unusual.

**Kosinski:** I don't know who those "other people" are. The asylum in itself is not a very unusual institution; many of us are well on the way to it. Take the number of mentally disturbed people in any industrial society, or the number of psychiatrists practicing in New York.

**Interviewer:** If all our institutions and experiences have equal value, that is, if anything goes, isn't there a corresponding reduction in the immediacy or intensity of your response?

**Kosinski:** It depends, I think, primarily on your outlook. If you look upon the incidents in *The Painted Bird* and *Steps* and *Being There* as peripheral and insane and not too common, then you are bound to have a shock almost every day; but if you will see yourself as part of the larger community, if you will not keep yourself in a locked compartment marked "for sane only," then you won't be very surprised when confronted by murder, persecution, or old age. Perhaps such an attitude would make you "less sensitive"—but, conversely, that would mean that the least aware, the most provincial among us, is also the most sensitive.

**Interviewer:** It would seem then that no one thing would faze you more than anything else.

**Kosinski:** Well, on one level, that's true: humanity does not surprise me. I accept the reality the way I have perceived it in my life.

**Interviewer:** Why did you choose the United States when you left Poland?

**Kosinski:** When I left Poland, I was not leaving for any specific place. I had three priorities on my list, in alphabetical order: Argentina, Brazil, and the United States, all large multiethnic societies where I could find anonymity. I remember that first I carefully began collecting Spanish and Portuguese dictionaries. Only later, English and American ones. I knew a bit of French and Latin and Esperanto in addition to Russian. I assumed it would have been easier for me to pick up Spanish or Portuguese. But I was turned down by both Argentina and Brazil. They wouldn't accept me because I had a "Marxist" background. Having studied in the Soviet Union, from their point of view I was potentially a threatening element. On December 20, 1957, I was admitted to the United States, and had to decide what to do next. I was twenty-four. I did not believe in cumulative riches, as I do not believe now, because I know that the world disintegrates from time to time and even the best furniture is destroyed. Hence my faith in "portable skills," originally photography, now writing—which leave me mobile, free to *exit—to exit* is a very important verb. When I reached the United States, I said to myself that since photography, unfortunately, requires such expensive equipment, my exit would have to be language itself, writing prose.

**Interviewer:** How long did it take you to learn English?

**Kosinski:** I am still learning. I think I will always be learning. My attitude towards the language is like my attitude towards a woman I love; she might leave me at any time. In other words, I shouldn't leave her alone for too long. When I travel abroad for a long period of time I get very insecure because I feel that I am forgetting English. Do remember, I was already twenty-four when I began learning English and it has to be constantly pressed deeper and deeper. Otherwise it might evaporate.

**Interviewer:** When did Joseph Conrad leave Poland?

**Kosinski:** He left for England when he was twenty-one. He wrote his first novel, *Almayer's Folly,* when he was thirty-eight, and he collaborated for a while with Ford Madox Ford. What is of interest is that he had difficulty expressing himself vocally; apparently his accent was unbearable. He probably considered speaking a nuisance—a writer is not supposed to speak, he's supposed to write. Similarly, when I wrote my first book in 1959, *The Future is Ours, Comrade,* about a year after I arrived in America, I found that I could *write* the book, but I had great difficulty discussing its chapters with friends of mine at the University. Conversing in English, though, did not interest me. I was aiming at an expression which was articulate but abstract, a language without sound. I didn't want to meet my audience, or know it in any way; I just wanted to manipulate a part of myself.

**Interviewer:** What are the advantages of a writer working in a language which is not his own?

**Kosinski:** English helped me sever myself from my childhood, from my adolescence. In English I don't make involuntary associations with my childhood. I think it is childhood that is often traumatic, not this or that war.

**Interviewer:** Could you see yourself starting all over again—new country, new language?

**Kosinski:** It's a nightmare, but I do think about it. Yes, I could. French perhaps, though I speak and read it very poorly. Whenever I am in France, I notice that in French I am a different being than I am in English. French connects me somehow with my Polishness; its culture is similar, the culture of rigidity, of bureaucracy, of fear of others, all the standard European props. But then French allows you to refer to human situations in a highly abstract way. I notice that when I'm in France my "English" vision gives way to a "French" vision which is less idiosyncratic, more Cartesian, less personal, really.

**Interviewer:** Do you ever think about abandoning writing altogether, be it in English, French or whatever?

**Kosinski:** I do. What if I found myself again in a police state? Or, to be more exact, what if a police state found me? I find it very telling that during the fourteen years of my existence in the U.S., I have always kept a photographic darkroom in my apartment. The darkroom remains even today my device for escape from the ideologies of political terror.

**Interviewer:** Have you ever used it?

**Kosinski:** Occasionally I develop photographs for friends of mine who don't want to use the neighborhood's photo shop. I haven't done any creative photography. But as it turns out, the darkroom has another use. Recently I learnt that my eyesight was in danger. I took another look at my darkroom, and I thought, "Oh my God, maybe it will become a metaphor for my American existence as well." I used the darkroom to practice dictating to a tape recorder just in case I would become blind. While dictating in darkness I noticed I developed a new kind of freedom—the tape recorder prose seems to be looser, less controlled than the typewriter prose of *Steps,* for instance, or *Being There.* Afraid that I would lose my sight any minute, I prevented myself from editing: all I wanted to do was to develop the ability to be articulate while dictating. The rest I would somehow learn later. All I wanted to do was to permit my "vision," born in a darkroom, this inner vision, to reach the tape recorder.

**Interviewer:** Did you have it read back to you?

**Kosinski:** No, I didn't want to be stopped: I just wanted to pour it out.

**Interviewer:** What do you do with the drafts?

**Kosinski:** I put them away in a bank vault. I am secretive. I close things. I lock them. I have fifteen different places where my things are hidden. Some of the bank vaults where I send the drafts are almost bigger than my apartment. I am always afraid that some societal force will go after me, and will try to penetrate not only my apartment—let them do it!—but my inner life, which is reflected in my writing and in my letters.

**Interviewer:** What I meant is, do you rework the "darkroom" pages?

**Kosinski:** I am looking at them now, but I don't want to start depressing my text too much, de-escalating it, as I always did with my previous manuscripts. I used to count words the way Western Union does; my prose was like a night letter. Every word was there for a reason, and if not, I would cross it out.

**Interviewer:** You said once that you wrote dozens of drafts of your manuscripts. Did you want to be sure that each word had exactly the power and meaning you intended, or was it a more general stylistic thing you were looking for?

**Kosinski:** In addition to the advantages I mentioned before, there are, of course, disadvantages to writing in an adopted language. The main one for me is that I am never certain whether my English prose is sufficiently clear. Also, I rarely allow myself to use English in a truly spontaneous way and therefore, I always have a sense of trembling— but so does a compass, after all.

**Interviewer:** So you are simply checking and rechecking your use of the language?

**Kosinski:** I wanted to make the language of my fiction as unobtrusive as possible, almost transparent, so that the reader would be drawn right away into each dramatic incident. I suppress in my prose any language which calls attention to itself. What I've just said carries no value judgment. It is the opposite, for instance, of what Nabokov does. His language is made visible . . . like a veil or a transparent curtain with a beautiful design. You cannot help seeing the curtain as you peek into the intimate room behind. My aim, though, is to remove the veil . . . altogether if possible. I think in *Steps* I came closest to what I really wanted to do with English. The vision demanded a clear language, a language as detached as the persona of the novel. For me a novelist is not a displayer of stylistic bonfires; he is primarily conveying a vision. Of course, whether the vision will "ignite" the reader's mind is something the writer will never know.

**Interviewer:** But can't the relationship you wish to exist between you and the reader be established just as well with embellished language? Too many authors who really have such fun with the fireworks would have to be stricken off your list.

**Kosinski:** Certainly some writers feel that by exploding language they can bring the reader's awareness to several layers of existence at

the same time. But I aim at narrower situations, not at the totality of
human life, as so many Anglo-Saxon writers seem to do. Maybe from
their point of view the society hasn't disintegrated. They believe that
there is a totality of experience, and that a human being can encompass
in his perception many layers of his existence. I simply am not of this
generation. At best, I think that if I can retrieve *one* fragment of reality
I am lucky—not a house at large, but just a chair, a sofa, at most one
small room, that's all. A writer's ultimate vision demands the language
he uses; my vision demands the language I use.

**Interviewer:** What about your working habits? Are you Protestant
and disciplined, or European and dissolute?

**Kosinski:** Being a part of the Protestant ethos for less than one third
of my life, I acquired only some Protestant habits, while maintaining
some of my former ones. Among the ones I acquired is the belief that I
ought to answer my mail—a belief not shared by many happy intellectuals in Rome. And, of course, I am employed by others. I teach English
prose and criticism at Yale. I am a member of the community. Occasionally I give public lectures, and I tend to talk as a social-scientist, not
as a novelist. Some of my collective responsibility is clearly inherited
from my Marxist training, some has been borrowed from Protestant
America. However, in terms of my actual writing habits, I remain an
East European. I write only when I feel like it and wherever I feel like
it. I do it in a restaurant, on a plane, on a train, in a car. I wake up in
the middle of the night to make notes to myself and never know when
I'll sit down at the typewriter—or the tape recorder. The new book
stays with me all the time, so I don't feel the urge to impose any
strictures about "writing output."

**Interviewer:** How long is the time of actually putting words to
paper?

**Kosinski:** It varies. I think the longest uninterrupted stretch I ever
had was twenty-seven hours. I produced nineteen pages of *The Painted
Bird,* which in the drafts that followed shrank to one page. On an
average I probably produce about a page, maybe a page and a half, in a
sitting. I write very much the way some of my poet friends do. I begin
with the sentence, a fragment of a scene I like, and then go either
"above it" or "below it." Since I start with an image, let's say, of a man
being driven in his car through the West Virginia countryside—a scene
from my new book—I might write about the rain, and the end of the

drive, and then go back to the scene's beginning. I still haven't written the scene's middle, so you can see that it's very much written in fragments. I always start a novel by writing its first page and its last page, which seem to survive almost intact through all the following drafts and changes.

**Interviewer:** Do you have a title for the new book yet?

**Kosinski:** Only a code word: *Greenback.* Its protagonist is my ultimate polarity. He is young, he is American, he is an heir—I envy him and, therefore, I have to be very careful not to take revenge on him; I must not cripple him with European afflictions. I think the tape recorder–darkroom experience I mentioned before helped me retain his fluidity. I notice I cross out less when I consider him in the drafts. I look at a sentence and immediately reach for a pencil to cross it out, but the lead is soft—so that the line it makes can be easily erased, and I promptly erase it. I don't want to cross out too much.

**Interviewer:** Have all your books had code words?

**Kosinski:** Yes: every book had a code name before I had a title for it.

**Interviewer:** What was *The Painted Bird*'s?

**Kosinski:** It's code name was *The Jungle Book. Steps* was *The Two.* And *Being There* was *Blank Page,* and sometimes *Dasein,* a philosophical term, difficult to translate, which could mean the state in which one *is* and *is not* at the same time. One has to be careful with titles. If I had kept to that initial code name it would have connected the book, possibly, with the philosophy of Heidegger. As a matter of fact, one of the American critics learned from my publisher that *Dasein* was the code name, and months later wrote a very negative review of *Being There* as a Heideggerian novel—a terribly unfair thing to do. Had the code name been *Kapital,* he probably would have considered the book a Marxist novel.

**Interviewer:** Unlike many writers, who are forever denying that they read their reviews, you seem to be rather interested in criticism.

**Kosinski:** I am attracted to literary criticism. In fact, to test my interest I wrote two critical essays on my own novels. I see no essential difference between various acts of creation. I think that literary criticism is just as creative as writing novels or poetry. It is unfortunate that in this country it has often been assumed, perhaps by the wives of the writers, or maybe the wives of the critics, that it is more glamorous to be a novelist than a critic, because as a novelist you are assumed to have lived your novels. Some of the Hollywood movies have contributed to this notion, I think. Also, a novelist can more easily claim that writing is hard work since you have to live all the awful things you are writing about. Conversely, being a literary critic is often considered "intellectual" and parasitic. You are living off the "hard gut" experiences of the novelist.

**Interviewer:** Are you upset by adverse criticism of your work?

**Kosinski:** I am, but only when it is also bad art: poorly written, unimaginative, *ad hominem*, propagandistic, commercial. Among my favorite critics are some who claimed all my work to be inferior, overrated, crude, amoral; but they wrote all this creatively.

**Interviewer:** To what do you attribute the success of your books?

**Kosinski:** I can only speculate, and judge by the echoes from reviews, letters, and some direct contact with the audience. I suspect my books are read for other reasons than the ones I would attribute to them. The younger Americans, the college generation, seem to see *The Painted Bird* as a symbolic novel about their lives: they are "the painted birds" in the hostile environment of industrial America. *Steps,* on the other hand, typifies to many of them the deadness of a man who is a product of an indifferent, atomized society, a society in which he is not only manipulated by others, but cannot help manipulating others. He becomes the walking credit card, removed from whatever vital forces he might have had. As for *Being There,* the reaction from younger audiences concerns their relationship to Chauncey Gardiner: they're afraid they're being turned into Chauncey Gardiners, that their parents have already elected him—a Reagan, the impact of the Nixon-Kennedy debate, the value of image making. They're upset by the findings of one candidate whose private poll showed that only 5% of those who voted for him knew his views, while the remaining voters claimed they liked him because he came across well on television. There's more and more preoccupation with the visual aspects of American political life. Think of the priorities given to the looks of our candidates. They all come across well on TV. Do we have a hunchback? A man with a missing jaw? A man with a nervous tic? No, he simply wouldn't make it. Can you imagine an American politician, however bright, with a damaged face, or with one eye? Moyshe Dayan, all right, he's up there; he's theirs, not ours.

**Interviewer:** What was the reaction to your books in England?

**Kosinski:** The British tended to be upset by *The Painted Bird,* abhorred *Steps,* and accorded *Being There* a higher status than anywhere else. So the reception seems to vary from book to book, and from period to period. One has to assume that at different times different people will be reading the book for different reasons.

**Interviewer:** Doesn't it bother you that there are so many different reactions and interpretations?

**Kosinski:** No. How do we know what Camus wanted to say in his novels? We only know what we perceive, and we read Camus for whatever we get from him now. A writer prompts a certain vision; he does not delineate it. His purpose is to awake, to trigger; the rest cannot be guessed. After all, if the writer's imagination is free enough to arrive at this triggering moment, why shouldn't the reader's imagination be equally good? A writer is not superior to anyone; he merely reflects a human ability to evoke.

**Interviewer:** After the success of your early nonfiction, did you find it difficult to get your first novel, *The Painted Bird,* published?

**Kosinski:** Yes, I did. When I had the manuscript in its finished form, the first step was to show the book to four friends of mine, who were all editors in very large, respectable publishing houses in New York. All four had an interest in my work because of the nonfiction, and all four told me in very plain language that in their view the novel was not publishable in America.

**Interviewer:** What were their reasons?

**Kosinski:** That it was a book dealing with a reality which is alien to Americans, set in an environment that Americans cannot comprehend, and dealing with situations, particularly the cruelty to animals, that Americans cannot bear. No fiction could possibly alter all this, they said, and certainly not *The Painted Bird.* Their verdict was: Go back to writing nonfiction. I asked them who, in their view, would be the *least* likely publisher for this book. They said short of Vatican City, I should try Houghton Mifflin in Boston. I sent the manuscript to Houghton Mifflin, and a few weeks later they cabled that they wanted to publish it. It appeared in the fall of 1965.

**Interviewer:** Since you do teach English prose, what is your feeling about the future of the written word?

**Kosinski:** I think it will survive where it has always really been—at the edge of contemporary sensibility. I think that's the proper place for

it anyhow. Reading novels has always been an experience limited to a
very small percentage of the so-called public. Increasingly, it's going to
be a pursuit for those who seek unusual experiences, fetishists perhaps,
people of abnormal imagination.

**Interviewer:** Why such a limited audience?

**Kosinski:** Today, people are absorbed in the most common denomi-
nator, the *visual*. It requires no education to watch TV. It knows no age
limit. Your infant child can watch the same program you do. Witness its
role in the homes of the old and incurably sick. Television is everywhere. It has the immediacy which the evocative medium of language
doesn't. Language requires some inner triggering; television doesn't.
The image is ultimately accessible, i.e., extremely attractive. And, I
think, ultimately deadly, because it turns the viewer into a bystander. Of
course, that's a situation we have always dreamt of . . . the ultimate
hope of religion was that it would release us from trauma. Television
actually does so. It "proves" that you can always be an observer of the
tragedies of others. The fact that one day you will die in front of the live
show is irrelevant—you are reminded about it no more than you are
reminded about real weather existing outside the TV weather program.
You're not told to open your window and take a look; television will
never say that. It says, instead, "The weather today is . . ." and so
forth. The weatherman never says, "If you don't believe me, go find
out."

From way back, our major development as a race of frightened beings
has been towards how to avoid facing the discomfort of our existence,
primarily the possibility of an accident, immediate death, ugliness, and
the ultimate departure. In terms of all this, television is a very pleasing
medium: one is always the observer. The life of discomfort is always
accorded to others and even *this* is disqualified since one program
immediately disqualifies the preceding one. Literature does not have this
ability to soothe. You have to evoke and by evoking, you yourself have
to provide your own inner setting. When you read about a man who
dies, part of you dies with him because you have to recreate his dying
inside your head.

**Interviewer:** That doesn't happen with the visual?

**Kosinski:** No, because he dies on the screen in front of you and at
any time you can turn it off or select another program. The evocative
power is torpedoed by the fact that this is another man; your eye some-

how perceives him as a visual object. Thus, of course, television is my ultimate enemy and it will push reading matter—including *The Paris Review*—to the extreme margin of human experience. Ultimately, it's going to be a pursuit for those who seek the unusual, masochists probably, who *want* sensations. They will all read *The Painted Bird*, I hope.

**Interviewer:** But couldn't the masochists get enormous pleasure out of watching *The Painted Bird* as a film?

**Kosinski:** No. At best they would become voyeurs, which is a low level of experience. No. The very fact that it is happening on the screen tells the viewer two things: one, it is *not* about him; and two, it is not real. It is already *there,* it is artificial, it is about someone else.

**Interviewer:** Doesn't one identify with Gary Cooper or John Wayne?

**Kosinski:** Very fleetingly. It's merely recognizing the symbol, saying, "This is John Wayne playing so and so." The optimum that the visual medium can aim at is the moment when the observer decodes what he sees on the screen. In a curious way, the better the film the more it reminds the observer that he is only observing; in the moment of ultimate terror on the screen the man in the audience says to himself, "Come on, hang on, it's only a film." With the novel, you cannot escape the evoking which is done within you since the screen is inside—and that is a very real and often painful process. But I never considered literature to be as important as the public highway system, for instance. Reading fiction is an esoteric pursuit; it aims at the blind and at those who can evoke, and the majority today don't have to. They are all provided with TV sets. I don't think literature ought to compete with cinema or television, though indeed it performs the essential function of the highest art . . . to bring man closer to what he is. The old Aristotelian idea: to *purge* him from his emotion—not merely to *show* him the emotion.

**Interviewer:** You say that literature demands more involvement and more effort from the reader than the visual media. Is this why your last two novels have been so spare?

**Kosinski:** Yes. I do trust the reader. I think he is perfectly capable of filling in the blank spaces, of supplying what I purposefully withdrew. *Steps* attempts to involve the reader through nonuse of the clear and discernible plot. From the first sentence of the book, "I was traveling further south," when the reader starts traveling down the page, he is promised nothing, since there is no obvious plot to seduce him. He has to make the same decisions my protagonist is making: Will he continue? Is he interested in the next incident?

**Interviewer:** Your intent, then, is subversive. You want to involve, to implicate the reader via his own imagination.

**Kosinski:** I guess I do. Once he is implicated he is an accomplice, he is provoked, he is involved, he is purged. That's why I won't give him moral guidelines. The reader must ask himself questions. Was it his curiosity that dragged him into the midst of my story, or was it recognition, his complicity? For me this is the ultimate purpose of writing.

**Interviewer:** Do you want to be remembered as . . .

**Kosinski:** I don't want to be remembered. These are dehumanizing times—it's best to be forgotten. Continuous membership in the Atomic Age does not interest me.

**Interviewer:** Yet you make copies of everything, file things away; you're very meticulous about preserving your work.

**Kosinski:** I merely facilitate the work of the executors of my Last Will. They will follow its text; meanwhile, I take care of its prefaces, footnotes, postscripts, etc.

**Interviewer:** You always expect the worst?

**Kosinski:** No: the expected.

**Interviewer:** But all the preparations against the future . . .

**Kosinski:** The future? All my plans have always turned out to be for yesterday.

# Jerzy Kosinski: An Interview

Jerome Klinkowitz/1973

Published originally in *Fiction International* 1(1973):31–48. Reprinted in *The New Fiction: Interviews with Innovative American Writers*, ed. Joe David Bellamy. Urbana: University of Illinois. 1974:142–68. Permission granted by University of Illinois Press.

"His art has dealt with the fangs and colors of dream and of daily life among the violations of the spirit and body of human beings." So read the statement of the National Institute of Arts and Letters when it granted Jerzy Kosinski an award "for creative work in literature," just before the publication of his third novel, *Being There,* in 1970. Kosinski is among the more widely honored American novelists writing today, winning the Prix du Meilleur Livre Etranger for his first fictional work, *The Painted Bird* (1965), and the National Book Award for *Steps* (1968).

We cannot know how close Kosinski was to the wartime horrors of *The Painted Bird* or the transitional agonies of *Steps,* although the themes of those novels, of *Being There,* and of the book he was completing when our interview took place (*The Devil Tree,* 1973) center philosophically on "the self." Reviewers sense the problem and make the most of it, as when John Updike, careful as always about a book's design, noted that the typography of *Being There* "suggests that Kosinski's biography is the last chapter." His life does present a high profile: the professorships, awards, and degrees, but also the exposure as a talk show personality, as world traveler while the husband of a steel heiress (now deceased), and even as a late-comer to a party he could not have regretted missing, at the home of his close friends Roman Polanski and Sharon Tate on August 8, 1969. But besides the public record of his own self, Kosinski has studied the role of selves in modern life, not simply as a novelist but originally as a professor of sociology. It was to have been his career in Poland, where after a chaotic and catastrophic childhood (which left him mute and illiterate into his teens) he quickly approached the top of academia, earning graduate degrees in history and political science and undertaking as his special interest the self in

collectivized society. Two of his scholarly works were published in
Poland, and after his dramatic emigration to America in 1957 at the age
of twenty-four he drew on notes for a third to produce *The Future Is
Ours, Comrade* (1960) and *No Third Path* (1962), written under the
pseudonym of "Joseph Novak."

Jerzy Kosinski invited me to meet him at Yale University in November of 1971—a few weeks earlier than originally planned; the night
before (Halloween) I'd seen his friend Roman Polanski's *Repulsion* for
the first time and was still reeling in nightmares when Kosinski's
morning phone call summoned me from Chicago to New Haven. With
books and notecards and personal emotions all in great disarray, I
arrived at Kosinski's residence in Davenport College late Sunday
evening and was met with a graciousness and candor which made a
solid eight hours' conversation (four that night, four the next morning)
possible. Kosinski's presence is commanding: physically tall, thin, and
of intense personal bearing, he impresses one with his great range of
knowledge and personal experience. Yet my own comfort seemed
foremost in his mind, and the contagion of this attitude (plus a healthy
supply of Heineken's Light) moved us into a good talk about his literary
achievement.

Our most substantial discussions centered on his theory of writing and
how he followed the involved course of moving from sociological study
(in Polish) through award-winning international photography to his
current success as a novelist writing exclusively in his adopted language, English. Since *The Devil Tree* was then in progress, I have
omitted the few references he made to it in favor of Daniel J. Cahill's
interview with Kosinski (*North American Review*, Spring, 1973), which
is devoted exclusively to this latest work.

**Jerome Klinkowitz:** Many people would like to ask you, I suppose,
whether all those incidents in *The Painted Bird* "really happened to
you." I won't ask that, but you did tell Cleveland Amory [*Saturday
Review*, April 17, 1971, p. 16] that during World War II you were
separated from your family.

**Jerzy Kosinski:** Yes.

**Klinkowitz:** Was it really for a period as long as in the book, six
years, that you were on your own?

**Kosinski:** Yes. From 1939 until 1945. But I was mute for a longer
time than was the Boy in *The Painted Bird*. He's mute for about three

years, from 1942, let's say, to the end of 1945, when he regains his speech. I was mute from 1942 until 1948, more than six years.

**Klinkowitz:** At what stage did you begin your formal education, such as learning to read?

**Kosinski:** Formal education? Kindergarten before the war. Then, at the age of twelve, as a mute in the special school (1945–1947); and then two years later I was transferred, still mute, to be taught to write and to read by my father and privately hired tutors. When I got my speech back (1948) I went directly to the Gymnasium and Lyceum of Humanities.

**Klinkowitz:** The first edition of *The Painted Bird* closes with an italicized postscript I don't find in subsequent editions.

**Kosinski:** The postscript resulted from a mistake. Initially in my correspondence with the publisher I often defended the idea of the book. In one letter I speculated about the "future" of the novel's protagonist, about the fate of the Boy "after the War." I wrote this letter from Europe where I was traveling. The editor at Houghton Mifflin thought that this was a "very telling letter," and she also thought that it could—indeed, should—become a postscript to *The Painted Bird*, and apparently she cabled me about it; since the final galleys were just about to be sent to the printers, she rushed and used the negative option: if I would not reply she would assume that I agreed. Well, I was in France, staying in a large, disorganized hotel, and I never received that cable. Sometime later the book was published with that italicized ending. Unlike this unintended "epilogue" there were, however, many well-intended passages, paragraphs, and phrases of the original manuscript which did not make their way to Houghton's edition of *The Painted Bird*; even though they appeared in the final corrected galley proofs they were dropped "in the last minute"; we had an argument about it. All omitted parts were reintroduced in the Pocket Book edition [1966], to the revised Modern Library edition [1970], and to the forthcoming Bantam Book 1972 edition.

**Klinkowitz:** That very postscript suggests, of course, more of your own experience, particularly the Stalinization of Poland and the introduction of collectivized society, which you subsequently studied and wrote about in *The Future Is Ours, Comrade* and *No Third Path*. I am intrigued by how your career developed from these roots—how you moved from sociology to photography and finally to fictional art.

**Kosinski:** First, when I saw myself as a sociologist, as a social scientist, I assumed that I was already operating on a high level of abstraction. Indeed, equal to that of fiction; after all, a sociologist abstracts certain social forces into meaningful formulas which could be perceived by others in an act of self-recognition. During the Stalinist period I became aware that this was not possible, that being a sociologist I was not only writing fiction, but that "the plot" of my "fiction" was given to me by the very forces which I resented and abhorred and was terrified by—the Communist party and its totalitarian system. Of course, I realized that as a social scientist I was not at all a writer of "sociological fiction," so to speak, but that I was writing a script for Stalinist policemen, who might use my abstract script to arrest living people. My sociological dissertation would be used as a program for a pogrom, as any other piece of social writing would be used. Or, if I refused to make it politically "valid," it would be used as a program for a pogrom of me, of my family, and of my friends. Hence, I began moving towards chemistry.

To make this sudden new interest legitimate I enrolled as an auditor in the courses in photographic chemistry; otherwise, abandoning Marxism and Leninism for the sake of black-and-white photography would be considered a political act of antisocialist character. Later, as if by accident, I began taking pictures as well as developing them—my first black-and-white photographs had a very good reception by the official photographers of the Soviet Union and—later, in Poland also— and I became a member of the photographers' union; I was officially allowed to practice photography; I received access to the university's darkroom. Then I received an official permission to read Western photographic books, magazines, and catalogs which were kept in a restricted part of the university library. Several of my better photographs I submitted to various national and then international exhibitions of photography; some of them won prizes. By 1957 my photographs were exhibited at more international exhibitions than anybody else's in Eastern Europe. And so I moved even futher away from language.

The photographic darkroom became a symbol of my life. Only in the darkroom I could function without being watched. While safely locked inside there, I would turn the lights on; then I could read from time to time some of the forbidden literary works, but not that many—I was too careful, and after all, the darkroom was used by many people, and since anyone could be accused of having brought these books inside, I would bring them with me carefully packed inside photographic paper ("sensitive to light—open only in the darkroom"—how appropriate!). That was frightening, frankly. I didn't read much. I managed to get some volumes of Nietzsche in Polish prewar translation. I read some of Dostoyevsky, which was not readily available, but I could always claim that, after all, Dostoyevsky was published by the Soviet publishers, so my crime was not that great. Nevertheless, photography became my ultimate interest at the time, and I felt that becoming a professional photographer was the best thing I could do as long as I was in Poland or in the U.S.S.R.

But I wanted to escape, and I embarked on a very long and complex process of preparing my escape, a process which took me almost two years. In my scheme I had to literally invent people who would sponsor me in my actual departure from Poland. Since I would be leaving my parents, my adopted brother, and some of my friends behind, I wouldn't want anyone to be responsible for my escaping. Hence I *had to* invent people of authority. Only they could help me; I could trust them. They couldn't be blamed; their families couldn't be arrested. Within the totalitarian bureaucratic jungle it was not that difficult to invent a few additional bureaucratic animals; the jungle would absorb them readily. And I invented four eminent scholars, all highly placed in the academic hierarchy, who sponsored my departure. Three of them were in favor of my departure; one was against my leaving Poland. Even though this was for the sake of plausibility, I didn't like him, I remember, and I had some difficulty writing critical letters which "he" had to write about me, so to speak, since in these letters I had to produce some authentic negative aspects of my personality. I remember resentment I felt towards *his* correspondence, and great apprehension towards the answers he was receiving from other, real, bureaucrats about me, particularly from those who had agreed with him and who volunteered negative opinions of their own. The other three kept writing basically in my favor—three to one in my favor! Not bad in a police state.

Only after I arrived in the United States I realized that my interest was not photography; even though I had my cameras with me and could have accepted various jobs as a photographer, I refused to do so. I felt that I had to concentrate on language; I had to acquire language as quickly as possible. Not only for the purpose of speaking (this even today is not my prime interest), but for expressing myself in writing.

Now a darkroom became a writing desk, and paper remained sensitive to light, but in a different way. I, not the manufacturer, would make it sensitive and I would make it sensitive by the inking I would place on its surface. As a photographer I knew that the basic purpose of the photographic process was to reproduce the reality and that photography would actually accomplish it. If there was a tree in the field and I photographed and developed it in my darkroom, I actually could do this so it would match exactly the imaginary photograph in my mind. Well, I found this profoundly distressing. If my imagination was able to conceive of the images which could be so easily reproduced in the Soviet darkroom—in any darkroom—then clearly there was not much to my imagination. I found it very humiliating.

With writing I can only approximate the vision I have. I can only encode it, and by encoding I'm sending a cable through an abstract messenger to an unknown receptor. I don't know whether it will be read or who will read it and what it will mean to him. And this *not knowing*—it's exactly what I cherish in writing novels, since I'm basically concerned with *my* imagination and with *my* encoding; not with anything else, not with anyone else. I assume that my using the language connects me and my readers—whoever they are—in the most profound of ways, but I'm not giving my reader every detail of black and white, or of Kodacolor, with all the shadows in between. I am merely pointing out the tree in the field. Whether my reader will "see" the field or a tree or my intent to show them in a certain manner is something I will never know. How he will see it and what it will mean to him will remain, for me, a mystery. This is why I think I would never be able to go back to visual arts of any kind; even if I would write nothing but telephone books and list names and phone numbers, they would still have for me greater evocative power than the best of my photographs.

**Klinkowitz:** At times in the books on collective behavior you do present images almost as a novelist would. In *The Future Is Ours, Comrade* there's one incident in which you had a shop window where there were all sorts of goods, radios, appliances, and there were the pictures of the party leaders among them.

**Kosinski:** In *No Third Path* you might have noticed the metaphor of the painted bird. That is when the embryo of my idea of the book was born.

**Klinkowitz:** And in *No Third Path* there are dramatic scenes, where the interviewer talks to an old man in the park, a little child comes rushing up and is scared away; this seemed to me more literary art than detached sociology.

**Kosinski:** I don't think that there is a detached sociology. It is merely another form of encoding; perhaps a different form of literary fiction.

**Klinkowitz:** So many incidents from these two books appear later in your fiction: the "painted bird," as you mentioned, the Soviet officer Gavrila (whom you visit as an old friend in *No Third Path* and who appears in *The Painted Bird* as the officer who adopts the Boy), the wrestler in the concentration camp, and even the character who, in the collective state, can find privacy in lavatories. Would you contrast the different uses made of similar incidents in the fiction books with the nonfiction?

**Kosinski:** The difference is that my nonfiction grounds it in a specific place—the U.S.S.R.—and by doing so torpedoes its immediacy, its proximity to the reader. On the other hand, the fiction invokes the reader directly. He cannot discard it by saying, "It already happened to someone else, hence it won't happen to me. I'm excluded; I'm a bystander." Perhaps the "nonfiction as literature" aims at nonevoking; it aims at reassuring the reader that the event had taken place or that it's a large historical process, hence that there's no direct threat to the reader. Fiction assaults the reader directly as if saying: It is about you. You are actually creating this situation when you are reading about it; in a way you are staging it as an event of your own life.

**Klinkowitz:** You mentioned once on *The Tonight Show* that as a friendless young immigrant in the United States you would sometimes call telephone operators to help you with matters of stylistics for your first book in English (*The Future Is Ours, Comrade*).

**Kosinski:** Well, not quite. I did not expect telephone operators to help me in matter of style. It was a problem of simple communication. Knowing no one who could "play back" the idea which I tried to express in written English, it occurred to me that in the middle of the night in New York there was, after all, a person who was available, a voice which would answer, and who would have to perceive my images only through the words.

In other words, the level of abstraction was maintained; *I* would not be seen; my gestures would not "be read"; *I* would use only the sound of the language. Thus, I would call a New York telephone operator and I would describe my predicament. I would tell her that I was a foreigner, that I was writing a scholarly work in a recently adopted tongue, and that since some of the passages of this work described situations not commonly known in the United States, I wanted to make certain that they would be understood and that she understood them. Then I would read a passage describing, let's say, a multifamily apartment in the Soviet Union, in which people would use one common bathroom and kitchen, and so forth, and I would ask her: Did she understand the paragraph? How would she see these people? Could she now tell what it all meant to her? This was a simple case of finding a potential reader, so to speak. . . . Very often a telephone operator would say "I'm not sure I understand it. What do you mean that everyone would use the same kitchen? Would this mean that they all had their own utensils? Or would they share the same towels?" Good questions. I was asked, "When they use the same bathroom do they bring their own things with them each time they go to the bathroom? . . ."

In *The Future Is Ours* when I would say that the Russians find their privacy on the street this came as a great shock to the telephone operators, who couldn't see how any privacy could be found in the street. Hence, in the book, I had to illustrate a bit more, by making a point that unlike Americans who are pleased with changes in their immediate surroundings, in things they own—a better car, newer furniture, a bigger house—Russians often find pleasing change in the way the street is "furnished"—a new building, a new monument, a new traffic system—all the embroidery which the government creates for the street, which of course to the citizens typifies the progress. This was the initial stage of my writing of the book: I looked for an ideal reader. I dialed "O."

**Klinkowitz:** But it had nothing to do with language itself.

**Kosinski:** Nothing to do with language as structure, as style. Of course not. I had access to all the grammars I wanted and to all the dictionaries I needed, and I had maintained a very elaborate correspondence with my father which runs into almost 2,000 sheets, three letters a week, dealing only with the English usage. My father was a philologist—he knew English quite well. With his help I was well equipped to use the dictionaries, the synonym finders, the word finders, the grammar manuals. I couldn't speak, of course. I had great difficulty explaining to the telephone operator what I wanted from her; I would have to write it first for myself—a little screenplay, almost—and read it to her so she would know what I expected of her. Very often my foreign accent interfered, and some telephone operators were not quite certain what was actually the word I used. There was no one else I could really do these tests with, since during the day I worked as a truck driver.

**Klinkowitz:** You wrote *The Future* in 1959–1960—it was published in 1960. This is a bare three years after you'd arrived. . . .

**Kosinski:** Actually I arrived in December, 1957; the book was published in May, 1960.

**Klinkowitz:** So two and a half years. I'm just wondering at what point do you feel you really gained a facility with English?

**Kosinski:** In terms of writing? Or in terms of speaking?

**Klinkowitz:** In terms of writing.

**Kosinski:** In terms of writing, I would think about nine months after I arrived, but this has been a never-ending process. In terms of speaking, about a year and a half later, but I am still working at it. No prison is as impregnable as that of language.

**Klinkowitz:** In the Dutch edition of your collected essays you add a statement that writing in an adopted language offers you "one more curtain that separates [you] from spontaneous [and hence uncontrolled] expression." Does this mean that raw experience cannot spill over into your work—that it must be refined by some artistic process?

**Kosinski:** Well, yes. I think language is both a maze and a veil. I think all men perceive themselves and their environment in a verbalized form; by comparison with a man who speaks the stepmother's tongue, a native perceives his reality in a perhaps less organized way. His consciousness of the "form" of his language seems to be of a slightly diluted character. Perhaps he remains more emotional, more spontaneous, and less aware of the censorious processes which language imposes on him. He might not fully realize that his emotions have been fitted already into the molds of the language. Hence, in my view, a "lower-class" experience is different from the "upper-class" not only in terms of the content of the actual experience but in terms of its organization, its ordering by language at the time when it had occurred. For instance, a peasant does not perceive his reality as brutal. However, his language transcribed and read by the middle class indicates brutalizing experience, since it is perceived in a different fashion.

Now, conversely, if this is the case, then something else also is taking place. Language connects us not only with our primary reality, with the reality of the self, with the reality of the emotion; it also connects us with a certain social reality outside us. Language becomes the connective link. One is traumatized by the language when one is growing up. In our society the adults use the language as a reprimanding device. A child often cannot help feeling that certain words hurt just as much as certain gestures do. A native, because of this, is at the same time more idiosyncratic to certain aspects of his language, of his self, than a foreign-born writer who adopted a new language long after his formative years. One can ask which are the formative years. I think had I come to the United States at the age of nine I would have become affected by this traumatizing power of language. At the age of seventeen it would have been too late. When I came to the United States I was twenty-four.

Hence, I am not traumatized by my English—no part of my English affects me more or less than any other one. For instance, a writer who writes in his native tongue may feel emotionally uneasy about using vernacular even when he knows why he is uneasy about using vernacular. When manipulating the language a native writer faces many conflicts. Even though he remains spontaneous he avoids certain language, exposes another, and his creative choices are determined to a great degree by his adolescence and by his childhood—by the period of his initial entry into the language, into the very language which orders experience.

Now, a man who at the age of twenty-four, for example, arrives in a new country with an entirely different set of encoding—emotional encoding stemming from another language—in the beginning finds himself in a vacuum. His language makes no sense in the new environment, and the language of the new environment evokes nothing in him. However, once the newcomer masters the new language he discovers two sets of responses within him. One to his native tongue, which he might classify as an adolescent response. It is the immediate response which evokes almost uncontrollable reflexes, particularly towards the vernacular, the language of reprimand, the language of abuse, etc. Another response is almost nonemotional, and it is caused by his acquired stepmother's tongue, which doesn't have the ability to traumatize. No matter how well you know this tongue (providing you did not grow "in it") and how well you manipulate it, it lacks the edge of spontaneous reflex. Hence, a foreigner, one could claim, has certain emotional advantage in the new language he has chosen to use. It won't traumatize him easily. For instance, in the U.S.A. my fear of bureaucratic language, my fear of the language of the law, is "intellectual"; there is no emotion which similar Polish or Russian language evokes in me.

**Klinkowitz:** Are you saying that the foreigner is in control of his stepmother language, while in his mother language he is more determined?

**Kosinski:** Perhaps one could claim the paradoxical: that a native is less in control of the language. The language controls him.

**Klinkowitz:** Is it the foreigner's practice, then, that makes great art? Or even art per se, as opposed to a native speaker working purely out of experience, which, when we trace back, we see he's really not in control of?

**Kosinski:** I think this differs from writer to writer. What is the function of literature? What makes literature? I think those who write and who think about what and how they write have their own answers. I thought about it simply because I wanted to find out exactly what is the actual prompting which makes me do what I do, particularly what are the promptings which *prevent* me from doing what I want to do very often. I know there are certain areas of the Polish or Russian or English language which touch me emotionally more than others. And maybe because of my awareness of the English language imposed on me by circumstances since I was twenty-four, I have adopted an outlook which I might never have acquired had I decided to write in my own language. And maybe that's why I have never written anything creative in my own language. Maybe that's why I would never have considered to write anything in Polish or Russian (I was bilingual). I think that a foreign-born writer who manipulates the adopted language (as opposed to the native who is more manipulated by the language) more consciously selects from "the verbal environment" its pivotal aspects.

For a foreigner writing in an adopted tongue, the act of perception is edited already; it means that if I am aware of the new language and if I am also aware of the process of editing which had already taken place, I might as well carry it to a very definite conclusion.

A man who returns home and tells about an accident cannot possibly convey *all* of the accident—allness is simply not conveyable. He has to select what he considers the crucial ingredients, the most pregnant symbols. He doesn't bring slides, after all, or photographs. He must select certain basic ingredients out of "the vocabulary of an accident," assuming that those he will tell it to will supply their imagination and their knowledge of accidents as well; that he will thus tap *existing* knowledge about accidents—their imaginary knowledge—the cultural knowledge—which will make his experience conveyable to them. You could certainly use all of the large Oxford dictionary, all 450,000 words, to describe one accident. You still could have run out of words. Then you'd perhaps use some French. And some German.

It follows, then, that a novelist cannot aim at conveying the most. He fits his language into the preexisting body of imagination in such a way that his language prompts those who are "on the receiving end" to provide the rest since they clearly *can* provide the rest. They embody the collective experience of "an accident." (Unless, of course, one would want to communicate with people from an entirely different realm of cultural experience.)

You asked me before how a writer selects "the bare minimum." I think there's no predictable way to do it. He simply has to trust his own judgment and decide what is the most concise "code" for a given situation, since clearly "the situation" is much larger than "the code." However, being in the business of encoding, he ought to behave as an encoder. He should make certain that the code he selects is the best he can come up with. Hence, his contact with the language should be maintained on a very technical level. He should be aware of the existing usage; he should be aware of the language which had died. In other words, he should "feel" the language around him. He may feel an urge to use a work simply because it's pleasing, but at the same time the social connotations of this particular word might have changed. Conversely, he might like to use the work which had just emerged as a fad, not realizing that as a fad it may die very soon.

**Klinkowitz:** I was just going to ask you if you think ideally, you can be sure that the reader will *have* the response that you calculate. How far do you think a writer can control his reader's response?

**Kosinski:** Clearly he cannot gauge the response of the readers; a novelist will never know what the response to his work is. He can poll all his friends and what he might receive might not be typical at all.

The only way is to assume that the code he provides will trigger *some* response.

Hence, I believe, the more pertinent the code, the more of a response it will produce. One piercing can be felt more than fifteen taps on the shoulder. If you pierce someone with a small needle the response might be greater than, let's say, twenty-five moderate blows. The man can dismiss them: "Well, he hit me *several* times." That's all. For me to evoke more means to describe as little as possible. Trust the power of words. Trust the collective imagination. A writer does not create the reader's imagination; he merely evokes it. That's why a novelist must assume that if he writes it is not because his perception is different from others, but that his perception is similar to the perception of others and that the only difference between him and others is that he decided to sit down and to encode in language what others encode in metal, in clay, in concrete, and so forth.

If the purpose of fiction is to tap, so to speak, the imagination of the reader, then the novelist should always consider—indeed, like Western Union—the price of the words. I tend to believe that "the more" of the language, the less evocative its power. The danger begins when a novelist calls attention not to the entity he attempts to create through the language, but to the language, to the code itself. Language is also reality; words have specific independent existence. But if the language on the page attracts attention to itself, to the form, the way an actor once in a while attracts attention to himself rather than to himself as an actor, then the language fails as a conveyor. In the essay on *The Painted Bird* I speak of an actor as Hamlet. In the play, are we supposed to meet an actor, or are we supposed to meet Hamlet? We expect to meet Hamlet—not the actor.

**Klinkowitz:** How do you avoid that danger?

**Kosinski:** I discipline myself to write with a very clear notion of an incident I want to describe. First, I pick up words rather indiscriminately and I type them on the page almost as if it were a poem. And then I begin to remove as many of them as possible. This is the initial stage. I realize that during this process of de-escalating I am quite likely altering not only the language but to a degree the vision. There is a price I pay; perhaps language which I thus employ strips the incident of certain aspects, but, on the other hand, perhaps other aspects are made more perceivable. I feel that for a native novelist who is doing the same thing this process is very often unconscious. His promptings are the forces of his life, of his growing up, of his adolescence. I can't help remaining aware of every stage of my writing even though often I would like to forget. But I can't.

You asked me before about the relationship between the sociological awareness, and, let's say, the literary one; and I said that political writing is for me a sort of literature which aims at different properties— instead of projecting toward an individual situation, sociological imagination, for instance, aims at abstracting situations, larger social forces— which does not aim at a "finished form." My attraction towards sociology and political science was caused by their attempt at abstracting the totality of human experience.

The fact that some of the political writers would later become personally engaged in politics was to me an act of ultimate betrayal on their part as writers. A writer called Lenin later became a bureaucrat; a writer Mao turned into a bureaucrat; a writer (and art critic) Trotsky turned commissar of war. In terms of their creative ability, I found this tragic, since their language and their encoding had enormous appeal to a great number of people. Hence it once was literature. We might question its moral message (many critics question the morality of the protagonist of *Steps* or the morality of the Boy in *The Painted Bird*). However, one cannot deny that their encoding was properly chosen— Lenin, Trotsky, Mao did communicate with the masses of people they did not know; they did evoke certain emotional states, even purgatory ones, the reactions they could not foresee and predict.

The attempt to dismiss all of this sort of writing as a mere propaganda is, I think, something which future generations, if they will be here, would have to ponder. I think Hitler—in terms of the popularity of *Mein Kampf*—must be paid attention no less than popular novelists of the time. And Lenin and Stalin and Trotsky and Mao in terms of my life would certainly deserve attention as great fiction writers of the twentieth century.

**Klinkowitz:** How exactly do you see them as literary artists?

**Kosinski:** I see them as men who at the onset of their creative effort instead of opening a factory or starting a shop would use language, inking, a symbol, through which they attempted to abstract the major forces operating in a society, the major instincts, the minor vices—they wanted to evoke certain images, passions in their readers, and they achieved this; from a purely novelistic point of view, therefore, they aroused emotions. Some of their writing first purged men of their dangerous emotions, since anyone who read Lenin authentically hated the imaginary enemies of the proletariat, and in an Aristotelian fashion, during the act of reading, he was purged of dangerous emotion. The tragedy was that the writer who first managed to purge the emotions would feel that he had to purge people rather than their emotions.

I think the misfortune of Western culture is that often it calls on the writer to prove that he can physically do what he had imagined so well. And this temptation leaves none of us free. We all give in to it one way or another. I mean my talking to you right now is in a way my mistrust of my art and my believing that perhaps my fiction does need explanation. I think that this trend of Western culture makes us move towards a lower level of perception, towards the visual. The preoccupation with the image conveniently frees us from the predicament of being involved with the reality; now we can simply observe it.

**Klinkowitz:** I wonder; do you agree then that when the writer takes life and transforms it (by controlled selection) into what we call art there's this great danger that it might turn into life again and become truly potent?

**Kosinski:** Why is it a danger? I see the writer primarily as evoker. He merely taps what's there. He doesn't create any new worlds. He doesn't exist outside of the existent. He is not creator of new reality. He is merely a refocuser; not a transformer.

**Klinkowitz:** I like the metaphor, as you mentioned, of "tapping," because it seems that he taps the source of power and makes it available.

**Kosinski:** The power is there, yes. A human being is loaded with the greatest power—his imagination, the ability to transcend his own condition. No other creature, as far as we know, has the ability to transcend itself, to bypass the "real" condition. A dog cannot imagine itself as anything but a dog. Hence he cannot modify his existence in any way. He's at the mercy of the ultimate gravity—reality. But nothing prevents us from lifting ourselves above it. The greatest ability we have is the ability to transcend our own condition. The crudest man, the most crippled mind, the most retarded child, has an ability which no atomic bomb, no hydrogen weapon, could possibly create.

**Klinkowitz:** I was wondering if you feel art or fiction can be more real than reality. I'll read you a sentence from your *Notes of the Author:* "*The Painted Bird*, then, could be the author's vision of himself as a child; a *vision* not an examination, or a revisitation of childhood."

**Kosinski:** Yes, such a vision is total. It encompasses any aspect of our temporality, of our empirical presence. Hence, our tangible confinement in time and space is inferior to the play of our imagination. In the moment of this interview you can see yourself conducting the interview with me, but nothing prevents you from "departing" (while you are still bodily here) to another presence. In other words, the vision is always greater and truer, since a vision encompasses both the actual, "horizontal" condition and the transcendence into a new "vertical" mode, self-generating within its own confinement.

**Klinkowitz:** And art becomes the unique vehicle.

**Kosinski:** Art becomes the only vehicle which directly leads to this unique awareness and to this singularly human ability. What's more, art exists only because of it.

**Klinkowitz:** In *Notes of the Author* you talk about the function of memory as an artistic device. How memory *edits* is the word you use. I might say memory selects, memory filters.

**Kosinski:** I think memory discloses, since selecting, editing, and filtering would mean a conscious effort, or at least a consciousness of the fact of selecting; I think that memory discloses involuntarily in the process which we have no control of. We tend to perceive ourselves either in a very general way or in a minutely idiosyncratic one. And what fiction can do and what fiction has done, I think, was to bring certain functional elements into the awareness of our "reality." I don't think there's a possibility of truly knowing "the edges"; the reality fuses with our vision of it. The edges are like photographs developed on an aged paper—they are blurred, not clear.

**Klinkowitz:** Are remembered events fictions?

**Kosinski:** Yes, they are fictions; even though they accommodate "autobiographic elements" they are edited out. I think our notion of ourselves is a fiction which is composed of what we have memorized, edited, created, imagined. Our recollection contains, for instance, fleeting moments of the childhood, highly telescoped, a few events from the boyhood and adolescence. What else is there? There's no continuity. Is there a plot? A plot, a sense of destiny, is provided for us by family tradition, by society, by a political party, or by our own indoctrinated imagination. The plot is given by outsiders—parents, for example—who insist on destiny of some sort. Psychoanalysts would insist on a destiny we can't quite control; Marxism insists on a societal destiny, on realized necessity; an existentialist points out our constant split and our tragic plight. What is our individual consciousness, or our individual awareness? It is composed of very short incidents. Our memory is the great short story writer. Maybe that is why we believe that everyone has one novel in him: his own empirical existence—if he can extract his self from it. I think it's quite appropriate: our memory is our supreme writer and editor. It is the aesthetic dimension of our life.

**Klinkowitz:** So these fictions are an accommodation to the past, then? Or they can be?

**Kosinski:** Your memory accommodates according to "the general style" of your mental fiction-writing process. In terms of your memory you as a fiction writer, encode events of your life either by rejecting this "novel" of your life, or you encode them as highly acceptable and pleasing. In both instances you free yourself from the oppressive presence of everyday existence by substituting your own little fictions. The idea of the happy end, the notion of the tragic end, are all devices originated in our memory. By observing our memory we have arrived at a notion of writing fiction. Writing fiction is, after all, a recent enterprise; claiming that there is a clear pattern to individual life was reinforced when so many of the nineteenth-century philosophers supported the notion of destiny. We were surrounded by things which we were told had beginning and end and a purpose; we were surrounded by animals which would always behave in the same way; we were surrounded by social institutions which would start wars and make peace, but somehow our own life seemed to be composed of tiny little events selected at random. Why we would remember our father more than our mother, why we would remember a minor quarrel more than a serious one, why we would not recall a fight in which we had lost our teeth—all this bothered us, and the collective psyche came up with the notion of individual destiny. I think Freud—a great novelist of his time—supplied the notion that there is a plot to our life. Proust named the plot: remembrance of things past.

**Klinkowitz:** So you can't really control this part.

**Kosinski:** No, these are the blurred edges. These are the margins which we have not been able to manipulate at all.

**Klinkowitz:** You have described *The Painted Bird* as being the result of a slow unfreezing of a mind; are these the edges coming into focus?

**Kosinski:** Maybe not the edges, but only the central darkness. We often are polarized between the edges only, losing the sight of this central darkness. We give plot to our lives—pleasure, vice, fetish, family—"I am a businessman," "I am an engineer," "I enjoy my work," "I love my work," this sort of bland vision—without ever coming to terms with the essence of one's existence. The edges are easily lit, but the area between very often remains completely obscured. I think the unfreezing of the mind only fiction can accomplish . . . but it's only an unfreezing, it's all there.

There seems to be hidden in both the Protestant ethos and the Judaic ethos an excessive fear of this central darkness; the fear of the discovery of the real, not merely acceptable, reasons for our harassed existence; a certain mistrust of creativity, of imagination, as a force which illuminates the meaning of our lives.

This fear of imagination as a probing force is probably the reason why a work of fiction is so often ascribed to a specific experience of someone else who has experienced it and written about it and "it is autobiographical"; that is, the reader is excused from assuming that it might happen to him.

If literature has been a conveyor in this country, it was often a conveyor "moving backwards" to an act which had already taken place in the work of fiction—back to the author. This manifested itself often in those American writers who volunteered an imaginary act of ontological reduction in their novels, who would then attempt to prove that even though they hadn't done it before they wrote about it, they, as creators, had "to return" to the world of "lived experience," of empirical temporality. What a tragic reversal: imagination needing a stamp of approval from reality. I think such an attitude reflects fear of a work of fiction which abandons the personal self to address itself to a different reality which lies beyond the novelist's volition, and in which the reader might discover ("hear in retrospect") what without the novel he would have never suspected in himself.

**Klinkowitz:** Can we discuss more specifically the literary form of your works? All three of your fictional works are written in different forms. I wonder if you have any general idea about literary form that perhaps unifies this development.

**Kosinski:** I think the form of each novel stems very directly from what I wanted to say. I think the form reflects the specific content, and I couldn't think of any other form which would do it better.

For instance, everything I think about language was reflected in *Steps* by ascribing to the dialogue an independent function; *dialogue became an independent incident.* Each of the incidents in *Steps* is independent; they are connected by the picaresque, but they are also connected by the cumulative awareness of the protagonist—his awareness of the self and of the society. The destiny-oriented Western culture insists—even in a novel—on a guiding principle, and hence on a plot. Maybe that is why so many people found *Steps* extremely difficult to follow—some critics saw in *Steps* several different male protagonists—as if afraid to recognize that our lives are not based on a single plot; nor, for that matter, is our fiction.

Confronting oneself developed in *The Painted Bird* through the series of exposures with the natural world, with the supernatural world, with the societal world of the Boy. And in *Being There* the language avoids highly complex metaphors; it reverts primarily to a garden and to television, and that's all. In *Being There* the same double metaphorical system is operating for those who are not "on Chance's side": Benjamin Rand, his wife Elizabeth Eve, and people around them.

**Klinkowitz:** In our own day, in our own culture, do you think such a popular medium as television does anything to our concepts of time and space which in turn might be reflected in a literary work written from our times?

**Kosinski:** I think its impact is already visible. I think the American novelist will have great difficulty in fencing off the influence of television and of film, the media which have very short attention spans, which bombard quickly, which are gimmicky in their attitudes; but, conversely, some novelists will quite consciously try to do the very opposite.

*Love Story*, for instance, comes very close to a screenplay—it reads very much like a screenplay. Some of the novels of Jacqueline Susann, of Harold Robbins, of Wallace have that obvious cinematic dimension. And they were immediately translated into the medium which they resemble anyhow—into cinema. But on the other hand there may emerge a novelist who might not necessarily follow the easily perceivable pattern of TV and film.

**Klinkowitz:** I would also like to talk about the ideas in your books. John W. Aldridge has called you a philosophical novelist, a man concerned with the nature and meaning of the human condition. Along this line I see in all five of your books, including the two on collective behavior, a basic concern with the individual in relation to other selves and to groups.

**Kosinski:** I guess I'm preoccupied in my nonfiction and in my novels with—what interests me most—the relationship between the individual and the group. During the war, as a child I lived in small villages, and as an unwelcome outsider I couldn't help noticing how each peasant personified the whole village, with all its system of beliefs, with all its systems of property. Perhaps then I realized that each of us is a microcosm of societal forces which operate outside and inside of us. I became aware of it again during the Stalinization of Poland, when for various political and ethnic reasons I was cast aside. By then, to a degree, I probably provoked some of it; I really didn't mind it. When I look at the pattern of my life I note that I often invite the penetrating force of society to approach me—and to reproach me—for not giving in, to remind me, as it were, where I stand as an individual. I considered ideology to be basically a form of fiction.

I once remarked, and this almost removed me from the Soviet University for the third time, that in my view Stalin was "an ideal novelist," a kind of writer every writer secretly would like to be—to have your books published in millions of copies by the state (all the volumes beautifully bound) and to have all your potential critics arrested and exiled on the day of publication. What a dream! (By the way, no one in the history of literature could ever match Stalin, since he would not only arrest the critics who actually were critical of his work but even those who were potentially critical.)

I saw myself imprisoned in a large "house of political fiction," persecuted by a mad best-selling novelist, Stalin, and a band of his vicious editors from the Kremlin, and quite logically I saw myself as a protagonist of his fiction. What kind of a protagonist? I could have selected many examples from the Soviet literature which would somehow make me the cheerful inhabitant of a labor camp or a prison. But in my darkroom I also read *The House of the Dead*, and I really saw

myself living inside of a "novel" called "the Soviet Union" created by
the crude imagination of bad artists, and then I realized that my ultimate
goal was to escape (if necessary, to die by committing suicide).

**Klinkowitz:** I would like to ask you about possible affinities which
might exist between your work and the films of Roman Polanski. Did
you know him in Poland? He was in Lodz. . . .

**Kosinski:** Yes. We have known each other since 1950. I was taking
the history of film in the Lodz State Film School, where Polanski
studied, since the University of Lodz, where I was studying, did not
offer the history and theory of film, and as this was one of my minor
subjects I was allowed to take the history and theory of film for two
years at the Lodz Film School.

**Klinkowitz:** For two native Americans, if they had both come from,
let's say San Francisco at the same time, you would study these people
for affinities that they might have. Do you think the same affinities
spring from Lodz? Was there an essential experience?

**Kosinski:** I think there was an experience far more important than
Lodz; it is commonly referred to as the Second World War. It is a film
made with a lot of extras, some of whom were not destined to live
through the film. We were both six years old when the war began, and
our perceptions were quite likely similar. Then during the Stalinist
period its totalitarian measures equally hit our idiosyncracies which we
had developed to survive the war.

**Klinkowitz:** We've mentioned before how a liberated self can be
a very terrifying thing, particularly because of the conditions which
society sets up, which one has to work against to become liberated. Just
last week I saw for the first time Polanski's movie from 1965, *Repulsion*
(which is the same year the *The Painted Bird* was published) in which
he presents the young girl in her apartment, excluded from society,
totally within herself. Do you see tonal similarities between this film
and *The Painted Bird*? The horror of the liberated self impressed me in
both works.

**Kosinski:** A point well worth making. Perhaps war does accentuate
both the "liberated" individual and the enforced collectivity. In 1939 in
Central Europe a Jew who had considered himself a peaceful member of
a community in which he was accepted became the ultimate threat to the
safety of this community on the day of Nazi invasion. These rapid up-
heavals in the relationship between the individual and society were very

clear already at the age of six to Polanski and to me. Suddenly, each of us became the enemy of our environment, and the environment turned into our supreme enemy. Maybe this accounts for some of our vision.

**Klinkowitz:** In *The Painted Bird*, the Boy, of course, does survive, he does maintain a self of sorts, but it seems a very terrible survival. I think in a battle between the self and society most people would probably favor the self and condemn the society as a terrible, repressive power. But I'm wondering if you would agree that maybe the self can have a terror all its own in its survival. I'm thinking of the Boy in *The Painted Bird*—all these images of death, power, control, and revenge; they become almost lyrical, as when the narrator recounts the bombing of the apartment building, with the walls tumbling down, the grand pianos spilling out, and so forth. . . .

**Kosinski:** Yes, the props of traditional individuality are being suddenly shattered.

**Klinkowitz:** Those are lovely lyrical images, one of the most beautiful passages in the book, and yet it is all death and destruction. There's also the scene where the peasant carpenter is tossed into the cistern, which is literally boiling with rats . . . that's a lovely lyrical image— how he is so almost beautifully devoured alive.

**Kosinski:** In our society destruction and death often have the embellishments of a beautiful ritual. Those who go to war march very lyrically. Wives are kissing husbands goodbye, and there are flags and music and usually blue sky. The war is ugly only for those who lost— for the pianos blown into pieces that cannot produce a tone anymore. Maybe this is the merciful part of our existence: when we die our destruction is given an acceptable form by those who survive us. The terrors of the self, once they are realized, are greater than the terrors of society because they lack the embellishments.

**Klinkowitz:** How?

**Kosinski:** Society penetrates the individual claiming that he cannot survive the terrors of the self without the protective blanket of societal rituals and institutions. Our religions, our myths, our taboos, our mores, all reflect it.

**Klinkowitz:** One last question: After fourteen years, do you imagine that you will remain in America?

**Kosinski:** I don't know.

**Klinkowitz:** You don't know?

**Kosinski:** I don't know. I don't want to live in a non-English-
speaking country. I would like to retain direct access to the language.

**Klinkowitz:** Are there any particular reasons why you would like to
remain within the English language, since you know at least four or
five, as I'm told?

**Kosinski:** I don't know them well. I couldn't possibly write in any of
them. That's the reason. It's a simple but main reason. I can only write
in English.

**Klinkowitz:** Oh, I see.

**Kosinski:** And I love English. I really do. I find it fitting my de-
escalating process; it allows constant pruning more than French, more
than the Slavic languages I know. Its verb is powerful: the language
lends itself to the vision I have chosen for my art.

# Jerzy Kosinski Reaches Down into Life and Writes

Wayne Warga/1973

Published in the *Los Angeles Times*. 22 April 1973:1ff. Reprinted by permission of the Los Angeles Times Syndicate.

That "writers must write about what they know" is an adage so frequently heard in the community of writers it must by now be a cliche. Yet it is nevertheless worthy, particularly so for writing fiction. Fiction somehow needs more resource, a resource used primarily to evoke powerfully a time, a place, a deed or whatever else is needed to tell the story. Thus it follows that if one is to write fiction, it would really help to have led a fascinating and different life.

Such is the case with Jerzy Kosinski whose fourth novel, *The Devil Tree* was just published. Kosinski's life is a passenger train rattling its way across continents full of torturous curves and long, desolate open spaces. Kosinski the novelist has an uncanny knack of stepping out of the train and up to some special perspective so as to look at his life and write. He seems to do so by reaching down and quietly lifting the roofs off of the passenger cars while the occupants look up in horror and confusion. The passengers might or might not be his readers, but whoever they are he demands a great deal of them.

In 1917 his Russian parents fled communism and settled in Poland where their only child was born June 14, 1933. Two months after the German invasion of Poland in 1939 he was separated from his parents who assumed him dead. The next six years the young boy wandered throughout the villages in Eastern Poland believing he was either a Gypsy or a Jew, knowing the German penalties for harboring either.

In 1942, at the age of 9, he lost his speech. In 1945, he was found by his parents in an orphanage, a half-mad, terrified, speechless child suddenly reunited with his family and civilization. For the next two years he remained speechless and slept in his clothes, refusing to leave the house during the day while at night he prowled the streets as he had done in Eastern Poland.

Slowly, he began to recover and reenter civilization. By the time he was 14 he had become an avid skier, but he still could not talk. And, at 14, he had a serious skiing accident which hospitalized him for months. While he was recuperating he regained his speech. With his father as tutor, he worked his way through high school in one year.

Years later he chronicled all of this in *The Painted Bird*, his first novel. *Painted Bird* not only established him as a potent literary force, it created a global cult as interested in Kosinski the writer as it was curious about Kosinski the man.

He continued his education at the University of Lodz, carefully avoiding encounters with communism. His academic excellence nevertheless brought him to the attention of the Party. He resisted them and his rights as a student were suspended twice and he was threatened with "resettlement," the euphemism for being sent off to a labor camp.

He became a scholar, prize-winning photographer and skier, completed his first and second master's degrees and was finally dispatched to the Soviet Union for his doctoral studies. There he became convinced that if he remained in a Communist country his fate would be sealed: He was philosophically and morally opposed to communism and, as such, was faced with a lifetime in labor camps or prison. He decided to escape.

In 1957 he took advantage of his position as a scholar, using the bureaucracy and confusion of the aftermath of the Hungarian revolution and Khrushchev's bent for liberalism, to obtain a passport. He intended to go to either Argentina or Brazil ("large, multiethnic giants where I could be altogether left alone," he says), but both countries denied him entry because of his Marxist upbringing. The United States quickly issued him a visa as "a highly skilled alien."

On Dec. 20, 1957, he arrived in New York with what was left of the $5 he had when he got to Copenhagen, where he tasted his first Coca-Cola (hated it) and his first ginger ale (still addicted). He entered the United States with $3.80 and no knowledge of English.

He relied on his ability to be mute to communicate and began still another incredible odyssey. Through the good graces of the manager of the YMCA he settled in beside the building boiler and began memorizing Russian-English dictionaries, accepting any odd job offered him. He was paid 35 cents an hour to scrape ship bottoms and his employer deducted 10 cents every hour for "transportation" to and from the shipyard. He was hired to clean bars after hours because he did not drink. He parked cars at Kinney. He became a film projectionist and perfected his idiomatic English by watching *The Barefoot Contessa* 35 times in a row. By March, less than four months after arriving in America, he spoke fluent English. He then joined the Teamsters Union and drove trucks and trailers throughout New York and New Jersey, fascinated all the while by the political undercurrents in the union. He moonlighted as the chauffeur for a black harlem entrepreneur ("A far cry from my vision of *Uncle Tom's Cabin*) where he learned about drug traffic and car racing between city blocks. He also learned a terrifying game in which innocent bystanders were murdered.

All of this he chronicled in *Steps,* which was published in 1968 and won the National Book Award for fiction. Kosinski was the first foreign-born and foreign-educated writer of English fiction ever to win the award.

His first summer in the United States he applied for a Ford Foundation fellowship, received it, and enrolled at Columbia's New School for Social Research. One of his class presentations inspired a classmate, who was an editor at Doubleday, to suggest he write a book. It was published in 1960 under the pen name of Joseph Novak and was called *The Future Is Ours, Comrade.*

The book was immediately serialized by *Saturday Evening Post* and condensed by *Reader's Digest.* A delighted Kosinski found himself $150,000 removed from poverty and suddenly in vogue among the political-literary crowd. Bertrand Russell wrote to congratulate him and Konrad Adenauer was reported in the press as "disturbed" by the book's implications. Among the thousands of letters he received was one from a woman named Mary Weir, who wrote from Europe that her late husband would have praised his book highly and she, too, wanted to congratulate him.

"I wrote back to thank her," Kosinski says, "just as I wrote all the people who wrote me. But I remembered the name from somewhere and finally I found it. He was Ernest Weir, founder and chairman of the National Steel Corp., this nation's fifth largest producer of steel. At the time he died at 83, he was an anachronism and a political visionary. He was the last American tycoon as history has known them."

In her letter, Weir's widow suggested that when she was next in New York perhaps she and Kosinski could have dinner.

"We corresponded infrequently for the next four or five months and then one day I had a telephone message from her suggesting dinner. I felt somewhat curious but mostly dutiful. After all, she must be an old woman—I imagined her in a wheelchair—so I chose a restaurant near her address."

The night of the dinner Kosinski dutifully arrived on time and was greeted by a young woman whom he assumed to be Mrs. Weir's companion. They chatted a moment or two and finally Kosinski said:

"Is Mrs. Weir feeling well?"

"Oh yes, very well."

"Shall we collect her, then?"

"I'm right here."

"I was astounded. She was more than 40 years younger than her husband and she looked like Susan Hayward, which in fact was her maiden name. She lived in an incredible environment. She was shy and withdrawn, the widow of a man who gave all his time to his business. She was rooted; I had been totally uprooted. She was astonished to learn there was no subway under Madison Avenue and I was astonished to find myself riding in a chauffeured car—in the back seat."

They became, at first, friends: "It was a case of mutual discovery. I showed Mary the world I had known—the shipyards, bars, Harlem, and she showed me hers. In order to see hers, I gallantly spent all of the money I earned from *The Future Is Ours, Comrade*, on her."

"There was a missionary zeal in Mary's attitude to me," he says. "She felt it her responsibility to make up for my experiences in life."

They married on Jan. 11, 1964, and Kosinski took up residence at 740 Park Ave. along with the Rockefellers, Mellons and others living at the prestigious address.

"It was a time of mutual discovery. I had lived the American nightmare and now I was living the American dream. As Weir's fourth wife and his widow, Mary had access to his homes in Europe, his yacht in Greece and always traveled by chartered airplane, and four years before I had been scraping the bottoms of ships. Mary came out of her long, lonely seclusion and together we rediscovered how to live. Her special joy was in showing me Europe and America."

Shortly after the marriage, his second book—nonfiction and under his Novak pen name—*No Third Path* was published. He decided to turn to

fiction and began to work on *The Painted Bird*, which he dedicated to
her.

"It was an attempt to somehow balance the reality of my past with the
reality of my present. She, in turn, learned of my past through my
writing. Our style of life was such that the money from *Painted Bird*—
no small amount, either—paid for my suits, luggage and tips. I'm
probably the first man in the free enterprise system who spent all of his
income on tips. It was the only financial responsibility I could assume."

Mary Weir Kosinski died of brain cancer before *Steps* was published,
causing Kosinski's already heavily contrasting life to take still another
sharp turn. They had been incredibly rich, but not really rich at all.
Upon her death, the money allotted her by Weir's estate reverted to the
estate, and Kosinski's inheritance was the memory of six years of
marriage.

"I had lived at the roots of the Protestant ethic and now I wanted to
see the branches, to know the whole tree. I wanted to see where the
sons and daughters of the Protestant ethic went to school and what
became of them."

He taught first at Wesleyan and, for the last three years, at Yale. His
third novel, *Being There* was published in 1971 and promptly landed on
the best seller list.Critics liked it, but said that his two earlier books
which they felt were more autobiographical had been better. Much the
same response has been given to *The Devil Tree*, though somewhat
more negative.

"Critics say I wrote about capitalism and money in the last two books
because of my sadistic imagination. I laugh. They were willing to accept *Painted Bird* and *Steps* as a reality of my life, but not money and
industry. If anything, *Being There* and *Devil Tree* are more autobiographical than my other books. I consider *Devil Tree* my private joke on
American critics."

Perhaps it is because Kosinski sees quickly and acutely the dark side
of the American dream. He writes in lean sharp compositions which cut
through to the core of thought and feeling. *Being There* is about a man
with no past suddenly and fatefully thrust into prominence, a prominence enhanced by the media. Kosinski himself talks little of his past
and has never publicly spoken of his marriage until now.

*The Devil Tree* is his second incursion into the nature of American
life and mores and it aims—and hits—at the rattling hollow core of

the American dream by looking at the son of a business tycoon from Pittsburgh, scratching heavily into the external as well as unconscious aspects of his life and mind. It is hardly what one might call a hopeful novel, but in a way it is hopeful because it asks us to examine the reality of our lives for in examination lies knowledge and knowledge is the way to change and improvement.

# The Devil Tree: An Interview with Jerzy Kosinski

Daniel J. Cahill/1973

Published in the *North American Review*, Spring 1973:55–66. Reprinted by permission of the *North American Review*.

Born in Poland in 1933, Jerzy Kosinski is an American novelist who writes exclusively in English. Since his arrival in the United States in 1957, he has published two books on collective behavior, *The Future Is Ours, Comrade* and *No Third Path,* both under the pen name Joseph Novak. His first novel, *The Painted Bird* (1965), was awarded France's Prix du Meilleur Livre Étranger. For *Steps* (1968) he received the National Book Award. His third novel, *Being There* (1971) was a fable version of Kosinski's continuing meditation on the theme of violence, a "conceit" concerned with the phenomena of masses of men dead from an assailant so far removed as to be entirely invisible.

In the new grammar of violence, *The Devil Tree* (1973) moves the "danger" signs closer to the edge of the well-traveled road. This fourth novel is a recreation of the schizoid ethos of the American dream rapidly disintegrating into the American nightmare. Kosinski's new protagonist, Jonathan Whalen, comes to discover that "the escape route has no exit: for some in America, coming of age is coming apart." In a rare interview, Mr. Kosinski expands upon the idea of what it means to become a personal "event" in a modern society falling into ethical turmoil.

**Cahill:** Your previous novels presented an enormously different atmosphere and dramatic situation. Do you see *The Devil Tree* as thematically related to your earlier fiction?

**Kosinski:** I think there's a greater similarity between *The Painted Bird* and *The Devil Tree,* at least in terms of my attitude, than between, let's say, *The Devil Tree* and *Being There,* or *The Devil Tree* and *Steps.* I think that if I'm to judge somehow, *Steps* and *Being There* were responses to and comments upon a certain very specific character and a very specific situation, while *The Devil Tree* is more of a meditation without an attempt to respond to and to comment upon the fictive reality it creates. In my own attitude toward my novel, I felt a substantial difference throughout the writing of the book; I policed myself not to respond to Whalen, whom I would not like, and not to really comment upon him, since my practicality and my own background would clearly either get rid of certain predicaments of his life or would modify them for him. I had no right to do that. In both *Steps* and *Being There* I was in a position of responding to and commenting upon; they were, so to speak, at my disposal. Here the events and the protagonist were not. I think this is one difference. I also think that *The Devil Tree* is very much like *The Painted Bird*, yet more than *The Painted Bird*. It is the most societal of all the novels because an attempt has been made to condense and to crystallize certain situations which are common to all of us, at least in my view, and known to all of us—unlike the other three novels in which one could claim that they were not necessarily the episodes or experiences of everyday quality. *The Painted Bird* relies on the Second World War, the event which is gone. *Steps* focuses on the events which could be dismissed as indigenous, simply because they could feasibly take place, or could have taken place, in another land. But *The Devil Tree* is a composite and condensation of something which is over-familiar, as opposed to the other novels, which were not. Also, if you take some of the basic components: the plight of the young man, which again typifies countless similar situations among my students at Princeton and Wesleyan and at Yale. The family trust, a very common middle class institution by now in the United States; the history of drug use and abuse, perhaps—the young people going to Europe or to the Middle East or to Africa to use it as a playground for an exposure to drugs which they cannot that easily pursue here. The group therapy proliferating over the nation.

And I think the major issue is the inability of the young to fulfill the trust imposed on them by their parents while living off the financial trust their fathers or mothers established for them. The ambiguity even of the very idea of trust—"I trust you, and yet you will live off that trust, financially, so to speak." So, those are my very random comments I make to myself ordinarily. But I did notice that in the notes written for *The Painted Bird*, and that's what?—seven years ago, the initial paragraph reads: "The transfer of fragments of objective reality to this new dimension in which the literary work arises has a logic of its own and requires the selection and condensation of a large number of phenomena which the writer believes to best 'document' his imagination." I think this statement is much more true in *The Devil Tree* than *The Painted Bird*, about which I wrote these notes.

**Cahill:** This "document" of the imagination is therefore a reflection of a contemporary reality. . . .

**Kosinski:** Yes. This is a part of reality which I feel is contemporary to all of us in the United States. There'll be a large part of the book, unfortunately, which will require some rather elaborate footnotes in the European editions. The very notion of a trust is really unknown—of this sort of a trust. And then of course the word *trust*—there's a trust in someone and a trust by which you live. But I think the climate of the book is something which is quite prevalent in the large body of the society in which, and perhaps vaguely *for* which *The Devil Tree* was written.

**Cahill:** *The Devil Tree* is structurally close to the same frame or tableaux method of *Steps*, but a progression of story is more defined. Are your narrative methods the same in both novels?

**Kosinski:** I think that . . . this book incorporates the various patterns of all the other ones. The fact that I use a set of incidents, separated by spaces may superficially resemble the technique of *Steps* but the function here is quite different. While in *Steps* it was an obvious break between the incidents, in which the reader, so to speak, could abandon it without any damage to himself personally—other than just escaping from an experience—or to the narrative, since he was promised nothing. The white spaces here simply indicate the space . . . they are Jonathan's—they are not the reader's and they are not the author's. This is the place where the experience first occurs. There's a specific story progression in *The Devil Tree*. We do move from the roots to the branches—and there's a resolution of sorts: Jonathan in Geneva looking back at the origin of all the trip, as it were. If there is a point to the book, maybe that's the point: that somehow we all should find out what is the source of what oppresses us, or what is the source of what gives us joy, and confront it directly. If we want, we would be brought to confront it, either on a stretcher or in another way. I think his going to Geneva may mean feasibly he's coming to terms with the ideological roots of his being. Is he going to accept the ethic which brought him up,

the tree which somehow erupted from the soil of West Virginia? Even
though the climate was transplanted, it's really from there, it's in
Geneva. That may be. There is a cumulative story—we know more and
more and more about Jonathan and Karen.

In *Steps* we knew really less and less and less, since the protagonist
was purposefully rejecting large chunks of his own staircase, so to
speak; he was abandoning various aspects, he was reductive. Here I
think the story is cumulative. Presumably between the moments of
crystallized feeling or crystallized reflection, Jonathan—not the reader,
but Jonathan—is vacillating, because this is the life which goes on
unnoticed, this is the vacuity of the existence. This is opposite to what it
was in *Steps*. I also thought it would be unfair and untrue and ultimately
artificial to have the book organized in chapters, since they are not
chapters to Jonathan Whalen; they are fragments which foretell an
imminent reality perhaps, but they are not chapters in his life. The fact
that part of the narrative of *The Devil Tree* is written in the third person
and part in the first person doesn't even imply that he survived altogether. These may be the remnants of Jonathan Whalen. The last parts
are in the third person; he may be dead by now. I think the writing of
the whole narrative in the first person would somehow have implied that
he's alive.

**Cahill:** Jonathan Whalen lives quite handsomely from a financial
trust but he seems to have rejected the values which made this great
fund of wealth available to him. But there are many people in many
places who are engaged in fulfilling or failing to fulfill the aspirations of
those people or generations just ahead of them . . .

**Kosinski:** Of course. They have to. And this is another predicament
of the societal devil tree. How does a child fulfill the trust of the parents
if the periods are separated by profound changes in society in which the
very notion of the trust is changed? I mean trust morally speaking, even.
And in a protestant society particularly, how does a child match the
vested energy of the parents who went very often into the empty countryside and populated the countryside with chimneys and skyscrapers
and businesses, when the child is already born into this jungle? The very
idea that the child is supposed to do better than the parent can be
metaphysically and sociologically a tragic idea. It implies somehow a
cumulative power which grows with generations, while one could argue
that it is the very opposite. Such power diminishes, it gets diluted in a

large collective process in which the individual matters less and less and less. Frick, Carnegie, and a few other ones, a few other originators, today would go to college. Their efforts at the age of 19 or 21 or 22 would be diluted in a vast pursuit of intellectual subjects. There would be no time for going to the factory every day.

**Cahill:** In almost all of your novels you've appended certain aphoristic statements, too. Do you find a special need for those aphorisms in the book? For instance, the epigraph for *Steps* from *The Bhagavadgita*.

**Kosinski:** The epigraph gives a miniature argument. But to me the whole principle of fiction is that of a reality condensed and crystallized, not only by having selected certain incidents, but by the very principle of language which does not in itself reproduce anything but the inking on paper. The language in its making is "aphoristic," so to speak. The word written in itself means very little. It is the implication, the decoding process, which takes place in our mind which makes the principle of literature and the principle of language meaningful. Hence a novel is nothing but slightly larger—spatially, a larger aphorism. It is what we make of it. What about the Ten Commandments? What are they? What about the Bible, both the New and the Old Testaments? What about the Koran? What about the Talmud? I think the whole principle of the language is aphoristic, and therefore it would be only appropriate for me, I thought, in the beginning of the book, to indicate that this is not a computer, 1001, model 40 which can retrieve any aspect of objective reality—tell you the size of the streets, the number of vehicles, the registration numbers—it cannot. It can do only what a small aphorism in the beginning, perhaps, could do as well, that's all.

**Cahill:** I would like to ask you, as you view your own work now in the novel as a form, do you have a sense of a strong deliberation, or a line of progression, that you're trying to pursue in the novel?

**Kosinski:** In which terms? In terms of the control of the language, in terms of proposing a certain social philosophy . . .?

**Cahill:** Yes, that would be the kind of thing I have in mind.

**Kosinski:** I think in terms of proposing a certain way of evoking . . . You must remember that from the very beginning I insist for myself, or to myself, on one major aspect, that a novel is nothing without its reader. In other words, had I to write a novel knowing that it would never be read, I wouldn't have written it. Now this may sound as a sort of highly egocentric statement, as it probably is. It presupposes the act of reading in the act of writing. It assumes that the act of writing has to lead, must lead, to the act of reading. And when I used the word *decoding,* what I meant is that my encoding is of no use, since in itself the work of fiction has no meaning. It acquires meaning only in the process of being decoded by another psyche. Not by the psyche I can approximate but by the psyche I *cannot* approximate. How do I know anything about you? Is there any way to know anything about you? There isn't. There is a solipsistic quality to it—that it has to be decoded. If there's an element of having benefited by my previous works, I do not feel that I have learned anything, I do not feel that I am at a different stage than I was when I was writing the first one, since the guiding principle is basically the same: language aimed at the psyche I do not know. I have no way of knowing how it will be decoded. All I can assume is that there isn't much of a difference between my psyche and the collective psyche which surrounds me, and therefore quite likely what I encode, the other will be able to decode within a vaguely similar frame of reference. And the *frame of reference* is a crucial phrase. Frame of reference meaning the societal components which are rather readily accessible. The fact that I make such a judgment, "readily accessible," means both that I consider myself egocentric enough to make such a judgment but at the same time totally collective in my outlook, assuming that others will be able to perceive them as common events.

**Cahill:** I was thinking of a sense of beliefs that may be developing and unfolding in your work.

**Kosinski:** No other sense of belief than the sense of belief that there is a possibility that the other, collectively speaking, the reader, will be able to decode it and that he might, through the very act of decoding, feasibly bring some order into the otherwise unstated reality, psychic and collective. The act of reading can therefore make him, just as it made me in the act of writing, more idiosyncratic and more aware. It does not mean to make him better or worse, more or less moral, human or less human. In other words, if there is an optimum I would aim at, it is exactly what I aim at in myself. The act of writing makes me by its very nature more aware of my own relationship to my own self, to my own environment. Ideally this should also happen to the reader. If awareness is the purpose—*what* awareness? This is something beyond even my speculation.

**Cahill:** And you're offering no directives for that channelizing . . .

**Kosinski:** The directions are implicit. The directions are implicit in the fact that from my point of view, and I do believe it, a man more aware of himself is less of an animal. A lion or a mouse are not aware of who they are. A man who is more aware of himself and of his environment is by the very nature of the awareness more human. The more human he is, the better for all of us. The more human I am, the better for me. The more I understand myself, I think, the more at peace I am with myself, with my ultimate plight, the unfortunate death which somehow no author can escape, nor for that matter a reader. And I think this is the ultimate belief, that the act of awareness, the act of experiencing oneself in a process in which one can state certain things about oneself and one's connection with reality is a profoundly human process. I remarked somewhere in the past that the animals react even to music but they do not react to the printed word. The principle of literature is a sublimely human principle. It activates the brain, and of course it utilizes the brain, and only the brain. And because of this, of course there is this moral; this partly answers your question: there is definitely an implicit moral statement.

**Cahill:** I want to pick that up if I may, go to Whalen for a moment and then perhaps back to Karen by way of a slightly different idea, too. Early in the novel Whalen sees many people, and they appear to him as distant, as alien, and he dismisses them, and in the next sentence the novel reads, "He was his own event."

**Kosinski:** Yes.

**Cahill:** Which seems to suggest his egoism, the way he's locked into himself. Whalen characterizes himself as a vagrant, an outcast, and he recognizes the duality of his personality. He says that his very real self is violently antisocial. There are two important motives that seem to operate in his character: one is to confront his own contradictions, and the other is to admit the impact of his childhood. Again the issue of the past is sounded—he is born under the sign of Saturn, which gives him the feelings of separation and estrangement.

**Kosinski:** And he mobilizes whatever he can, however mythical, to reinforce whatever he thinks is to be reinforced; I mean, he mobilizes astrology on one hand and the background of his father on another. That is the ambiguity.

**Cahill:** The point I was thinking of, and relating backwards to

Karen—that there's a great play made in the book of manipulating people, for example the early scene with Barbara in Rangoon, and how Whalen manipulates Barbara by leading her to believe that he has murdered Mrs. Llewellen. I was interested in the way in which every-one is manipulating everyone. Karen is manipulating Whalen; Whalen is surely manipulating Barbara—this seems to be one of Whalen's games. Is this manipulation of people one of the special targets of the book?

**Kosinski:** I can only speculate, but in the absence of meaningful definitions of the self and in the absence of meaningful relationships, what surfaces is the most elementary aspect—that is, not who I am, and not who the others are, but who I am in relation to others. In other words, to what degree I can push them around, or to what degree they can push me around. So, I think, because of the absence of knowing exactly who he is, because of the inability to know who the others are, because of being incapable of creating a lasting and meaningful relationship of any kind, either with his own past even, or with his future, so to speak, which dwells in him . . . what remains again is the most elementary sort of game playing. And what is the encounter group? Isn't the encounter group the ultimate game playing? It is of interest that we finally object, and your voicing the problem is a reflection of it, that we feel that manipulating Barbara in Rangoon is manipulating, but playing one's line in front of a psychoanalyst, or playing one's past in front of an encounter group, somehow is not.

**Cahill:** But the point I was thinking of here is again the problem of defining self, and Jonathan speaks of the aspects of his personality that are very deep within; there are special references to "the struggle within me" and the talk of this kind of dualism; "They did not understand that I was pushing myself to extremes in order to discover my many selves." And I think of the multiple experiences of Whalen here, and notably his ambiguous relationships with Karen.

**Kosinski:** I think one ought to define oneself in terms of the language which one uses. The passage which you mention, when Whalen says "There's a place beyond words where experience first occurs to which I always want to return," is important. The point now is, *is there such a place*? By its essential nature, language pronounces judgments. There is no place beyond words where experience first occurs. This is, of course, wishful thinking. Jonathan here wants to return to a non-existent place, to the place beyond judgment. He says, "I suspect that whenever I articulate my thoughts or translate my impulses into words, I am betraying the real thoughts and impulses which remain hidden." To me this is the source of what I consider to be the modern—Protestant, perhaps— suspicion of the language altogether. There is a feeling of not trusting the language. And I think it is implicit in the acts of many people who feel somehow that the language, because it has the power to confine meanings, reduces and cripples us. Whalen also says, "Instead of expressing myself, I produce a neatly ordered document about someone else's state of mind." This may be the source of some of his pre- dicament. You may recall that in *Steps* I was also concerned with the role of the language. The protagonist of *Steps* at one time feels that he could free himself by abandoning language, that the state of muteness is something which is superior to the state of being talked about or of talking oneself. There is also a passage in *Being There* about the very suppression of articulating one's thoughts as an ultimate goal to which we may willingly or unwillingly be moving. And then, of course, the boy in *The Painted Bird* becomes mute. I think that modern society is a derivative of the Protestant ethos, the most universal of ethical forces in terms of the history of culture. It is the most universal ethos, since it not only incorporates all the other ones, but leaves them permanently present by not suppressing, by not counteracting them ideologically. Max Weber knew what he was pointing out: the element of "calling" is extremely important to create the skyscrapers which you can see from this window, and everything we have talked about. Within the Prot- estant ethos, because of the constant stress on action and on societal aspects, the element of individual expression is always questionable. To what degree is an individual experience a valid experience? Hence our constant stress on autobiography, our attempt to dismiss the imagination and to ground the experience as narrated, as having actually taken place in a specific environment, to ground it in an acceptable mode of events. Therefore, Whalen's conflict begins when he begins to see himself as an event. His father would never say that; his father would say "I consider an event what affects thousands of people. When it affects me it is of no importance; therefore, my own son is not an event to me. The events are the children of my workers, of people who are not even *my* workers." He would say "the company's employees." This is the tragedy of Jonathan, that he's born into the society which in some way is promis- cuous enough within its Protestant tolerance to allow him to consider himself an event, without any mercy given to the pursuit of one's self as a meaningful event. The final sentence, "I regret having made myself so accessible," is part of his tragedy of self-perception, since he cannot accept the self words reveal. He abandons language because he is no longer an event.

**Cahill:** I'm interested in what you say about this muteness, this preverbal state that seems to carry with it some aura of mystery, some aura of superiority—that people define themselves, but refuse to place that definition into verbal forms. There is a wonderful phrase by T. S. Eliot in which he says, "If you haven't got the word, you haven't got the idea." One does not have a grasp of a concept until he can give it shape in words. In the last sentence that you read in regard to Whalen, "I regret having made myself so accessible," he is putting himself into words and now would rather retract because that admission is a show of his banal naiveté . . .

**Kosinski:** Jonathan realizes that he must make himself as accessible as possible; this is the only way to a meaningful contact with oneself and with the others. By not making himself accessible he withdraws to the place where the experience first occurs, which means to a place from which he cannot communicate with anyone. This is the ultimate tragedy of Whalens, that they refuse to make themselves accessible through imagination, that they perceive themselves neither as an event nor as a collective entity, that they are in that awful limbo in which one is willing to talk about one's background to a psychoanalyst, but one cannot really accept oneself fully, for whatever reasons one exists. In other words, is it a hedonistic pursuit or is it a meaningful pursuit of business? Because of his ambiguous relationship to the language, which is the only way to make himself accessible to himself as well, he is pronouncing a verdict, a tragic verdict, upon himself. And so is Karen; she's no better in that respect.

**Cahill:** But your own idea of the tragic verdict—I suppose it's even wrong to say they pronounce it on themselves; they simply don't allow it ever to come to the fore, and they refuse to formalize a whole hazy body of feelings that are underneath, because to formalize them is to define them and be the thing they say.

**Kosinski:** Yes. Exactly. So the mistrust of the language here becomes the boomerang, and of course that's what happens, that unless you can dissolve yourself in a pursuit as grand as that of Horace Sumner

Whalen—in which the corporation becomes the language, the corporate venture takes care of the expression—unless you can do that, what is left to you?

**Cahill:** Silence.

**Kosinski:** Macaulay, the corporate man in the new conglomerate which old Whalen left behind, hides behind his desk, and the desk speaks 50 different languages—visual language, video language, and so forth. He is in no way concerned with what he himself is; he is really what his action is. He claims that his images can be transferred straight across the corridor or across the ocean. He is very much like Whalen's father, beyond the self. But Whalen is not. What you said in the beginning of our conversation, that many young people are in the position today of Henry James' characters, is very telling—they really are. They could pursue a meaningful search of who they are precisely because others, senior Whalens, Macaulays, take care of them but many refuse to engage in the pursuit of who they are, because they are offspring of a very tragic tree in which the imagination has never been allowed to emerge as a meaningful way of communicating. The only avenue left to the definition of the self, and the only avenue left to self expression has been really blocked.

**Cahill:** Yes. Their engagement in multiple and erratic experiences, always entering down dark corridors . . .

**Kosinski:** Eventually, and listening to music, which is not verbal, watching images which are not directly communicative. I think part of the preoccupation of the very young ones with the rock groups is linked to the feeling created that these popular stars manage to define themselves through their medium, through the intensity of music, and therefore they became freak-like, free, and ungrounded. And all the kids who watch them, of course, are very much like Whalen, they are very much grounded, but they are grounded in the environment which they refuse to accept as meaningful. Jonathan says somewhere in the book that he envied the great leaders because there was never any mention of their fathers. Of course, younger Whalens, Whalens who are 14, 15, look at the rock stars with exactly the same feeling. They are liberated from the family ethos, producing their own sound, which is a nonlanguage.

**Cahill:** And the music is therefore, I suppose, the extension of their essence.

**Kosinski:** Yes. Exactly.

**Cahill:** Do you feel that Whalen is the complete exemplar of the failure of values?

**Kosinski:** That is not a judgment I would make, you must remember. That is the judgment you have to make as a reader. I don't know what it evokes in you. To me Whalen is no more, no less, than a man, so frankly lost, like the majority of us, between his roots and his branches. The particular predicament of Whalen is that he is confronted with a highly perplexing and complex reality, which by now, particularly in the United States, has managed to mix the technological with the psychic, managed to submerge the encounter group in the computer print-out. It is no surprise that so many places now mate people by computer, an unthinkable arrangement to a generation of 25 years ago where even a dance floor was not sufficient grounds for knowing someone. One had to "go out" several times. Various "dates" had to somehow precede even a superficial knowing of each other. Now it is the computer. I think what is fascinating in contemporary America is this very mixture of artifacts which are of physical and of metaphysical nature all in one, including the family situation. Within our technological and legalistic society, there is a strange ambiguity in which ethical and moral values can be completely dismissed.

**Cahill:** As I think of your recent essay, "The Lone Wolf," I also think of this image as representing a concept, a certain mode of encountering life. The image of the lone wolf is woven throughout all of your work. It seems to have an immediate relationship to the image of the painted bird, the individual standing alone, removed from the crowd by conscious choice. In *The Devil Tree* the following statement appears: "To say yes is to follow the mass, to do what is commonly expected. To say no is to deny the crowd, to be set apart, to reaffirm yourself." It seems that between the concept of *The Painted Bird*, or the image of the painted bird, and "The Lone Wolf," there is a significant relationship.

**Kosinski:** We die alone. The pack doesn't die with us. The statement which you just read is a mere indication that, no matter how strong the collectivity, it will allow us to die alone. This is the truth which Whalen could have achieved, and he could have developed a sense of serenity almost; he could certainly come to terms with both himself as a branch and himself as a root. But he abandons it altogether from the mid-story on. The motive of the lone wolf is the motive of all the novels, with the one exception of Chauncey Gardiner who is really unable to even realize that there is such a possibility. He's externalized beyond the collectivity, indeed. Beyond the garden, but also beyond the collectivity.

**Cahill:** Yet to the pack he seems like an ideal leader.

**Kosinski:** Of course. But it's because the pack lost the very sense of its individual components as well.—*The Painted Bird*, *Steps*, and *The Devil Tree* share this ultimate quest for identity. Jonathan Whalen is the spiritual descendant of the other protagonists. But ultimately I think we all are.

**Cahill:** Is Whalen lost in the end? Is he lost to any kind of meaningful engagement of life with others?

**Kosinski:** I think no more than the rest of us. How can he combine the sense of heritage with a society which is changing so rapidly from year to year that it discredits any sense of history? Both the notion of heritage and imminent history are lost. How can he possibly find a meaningful life, a search he is forced to abandon altogether, the way many of us are forced to abandon the central effort of purpose? What is the need for the encounter group, if not the search for a meaningful other? How, in the crowds of people who work with us, who walk the streets and take the subways with us, how do we find a meaningful relationship? We are now at the stage of finding the meaningful moment. How does one explain the prevalent depression in our society? How do we explain the fact of the industrial society caught in psychic turmoil by a drug problem unprecedented in history? Jonathan Whalen functions in a highly schizoid environment, an increasing pressure we all feel. Life loses meaning. It neither terrifies us nor pleases us. We are in a strange limbo of growing indifference not because of ideological reasons—because simply it would take too much energy to understand the chaos of our times. And that is the schizoid ethos.

**Cahill:** I want to go back for a moment to some of the things you were saying in regard to psychiatric deformities. The themes of insanity and incipient madness play a prominent role in *The Devil Tree*. What we do to those people who are deformities of the standard or norm is to lock them up in order that the rest of us can lead our lives without the visible presence of those who cannot be mentally and physically absorbed into the contemporary moment. Jonathan Whalen comments at one point in the novel that no corporation will hire a hunchback. We tend to eliminate differences that we cannot understand.

**Kosinski:** Yes, but we also do it to ourselves as well. The fact that we reject so many aspects of our lives which could make them more meaningful is an illustration that part of us is chained in the attic. And we will never let it out. This is what I meant by the ultimate tragedy— what we do to others we really do to ourselves. The fact that the national insurance would not make provision for the mentally ill is of course the most damaging aspect, not to the mentally ill, but to any of us who are going to require that sort of help. So there is a strange blindness, a refusal to recognize tragic aspects of life. In *The Devil Tree*, there is an ironic reference to Samuel Tewk, an English reformer, who in 1813–1814 created the first asylum for the mentally ill based on a different principle. Until the first decade of the nineteenth century, the guiding principle was that lunacy could be cured through punishment; it was not the mentally ill who were being punished but the evil forces within them. And therefore when they were chained to the walls and beaten, they would eventually emerge cured. But what we need to do, Tewk believed, is to make the afflicted people function socially in an acceptable way so that they will not upset those who are not mentally ill. And therefore he was hailed as a very humane philosopher, since he did away with the cruelty. Now the mentally afflicted were to be trained how to behave at tea parties; and they were taken to church, and then dressed the way everyone else was dressed, so no one would recognize them as being mentally ill. Of course the pain they suffered, and the anguish of the mentally ill remained their private property, so to speak. We, presumably the healthy ones, were not supposed to be disturbed by the presence of those whose universe was so different from ours. Of course I don't think there is a school which could possibly be named after Samuel Tewk, even though he's, again, highly regarded. But I think all our schools and universities ought to be.

I think many of our educational institutions reflect some of the symptoms that we have talked about, especially in their isolation of the young from the genuine difficulties and responsibilities encountered in the larger social experience. During the educational process, the child or adolescent remains cut off from the society outside, the very society on which his life will depend. The young person is growing into society, yet he is kept really outside of the society into which he is growing. So, metaphorically, his roots are kept away from his branches. The sooner his roots become the branches, the better for the tree. He is kept within a peculiar dimension in which his roots are not really brought into practice. The schools are not emphasizing tradition, history, heritage or family origins. As if they are not important and may be safely discarded. At the same time schools are not moving into another dimension of values. So there's a strange and a very curious way in which young people are emotionally retarded. They may be intellectually trained, but they are ill equipped emotionally to confront the turbulence of modern society. They are removed from the source of emotional turmoil which is functioning within the industrial society, and functioning among others who are lone wolves. During the college and university years, the feeling is somehow created that the dining room typifies sort of a United Nations of human nature. We all sit at one table here, and there are no differences, and we are all united by the same pursuit. But what happens to us outside is ultimately tragic. To me, this is one of the reasons why so many young people turned to drugs, to reinforce themselves, to create some sort of stimulus from within in order to make up for their inability to function from without. They felt that they were not equipped emotionally, and therefore they needed an injection of strength; and some of them took to drugs to provide this misleadingly reinforcing element.

**Cahill:** Which can only indicate a refusal or a complete failure to engage with complex issues.

**Kosinski:** Or what's far more important to me, to confront one's own self. And therefore they would be left at the mercy, not only of the unknown society, of the society unknown to them, which would traumatize them all the time, but they would also be faced with something far more unknown, their very ownselves.

**Cahill:** Which is the obliteration of history, of course, too.

**Kosinski:** In purely practical, individual terms, they would be left with the unacceptable self, and that is a heavy burden to live with and to die with.

**Cahill:** In the epigraph from Marcel Proust's *Remembrance of Things Past,* you give an oblique reference to history, notably the history of an individual. There's the phrase, "our future dwells within us." Whalen is a man in a time and in a place, a wealthy American who rejects the history imposed on him—that is, the life of responsible action in the whole corporate web of social reality. What was the future dwelling within Whalen that foreshadows the adult Whalen we see in the book?

Is his plight a situation in which there is an internal future destroyed before it can be realized?

**Kosinski:** He begins with emptiness. He will have to. This is something which he has no choice but to begin with. He cannot possibly embrace his roots as the context of his psyche. One cannot embrace heavy industry as the spiritual origin of one's development. I think this is true of all Whalens everywhere. In other words, one's father should never be a source of one's own development, because then one discards history; one assumes that the father and son have a lot in common, and they have probably less in common than anyone else. They are two different people growing up in two different climates. The very fact that this is the son of a father means that some awful, terrible change has taken place outside—one is old, one is young. What therefore I think Whalen could pursue would be a pursuit of the new self which could make use of history, but very often by a conscious discarding of it. I think this could lead to a true progress in which a new sort of awareness would be developed, one which would allow Whalen and his contemporaries to come to terms with who they are. Indeed, the attempt would be made at a self-definition. If there is a value to having a well defined father, collectively defined, financially defined, politically defined, it is that it could force the child to seek a new definition. This is the future which theoretically dwells in Whalen, the search for a new self. If he is to abandon it, and I think he does abandon it, then of course he reverts into a father in miniature, which means he becomes Horace Whalen 50 years later, and that is of course an anachronistic animal which is going to be destroyed by the jungle. But the jungle makes no provision for the species which don't exist anymore. A dinosaur would die in today's jungle; the jungle is not high enough to hide him. And this is I think the ultimate tragedy, that young Whalens are condemned to extinction. Their attempt to kill Howmets is a desperate attempt to kill those who know about their roots. But of course it is doomed to failure. The society outside will always be composed of many generations superimposed on each other. It's a child-like attempt to remove the roots, so to speak, because he has nothing else. So the drive becomes ultimately destructive. With the drugs, the drive was to suppress the psyche. With the murder towards the end of the book the drive is to suppress the collectivity. Both are doomed to failure. Whose failure? Whalen's failure. And so this is, I think, the imminent reality which is foretold, at least for me.

**Cahill:** I associate this kind of emphasis on a controlling past with the title of the novel, and I think the immediate past out of which Whalen emerges seems one that's invested with a kind of moral stupor. Is Whalen then one of the young ones being destroyed by the devil?

**Kosinski:** If the devil is the contemporary society, then yes. Because the tree will grow, and only the big ones will survive, and there will be a shortage of young ones. But ultimately it is the tree itself which is punished. It is the society on which a terrible punishment is being inflicted, because the society needs—we all do—we need Whalens. And of course we need more Baobabs. If the society is going to destroy the young ones, and only the full-grown Baobabs will be left, then we are in trouble, because then we, very much like Whalen, are at the mercy of forces which are not of "today." Then we would be strangled by the roots of the past which have nothing to do with our branching out into the contemporary society. We may therefore have to put up with the reactionary philosophy, we may have to put up with reactionary legislation, we may have to put up with the politicians who will be reflecting the ethos of 50 years ago, rather than the requirements of the contemporary life, and eventually we may end up in a madhouse in which no one will make provisions for the mentally ill.

**Cahill:** Is Whalen being obliterated from the landscape . . .

**Kosinski:** Yes. As a species, of course.

**Cahill:** . . . and there is the continuance of the old trees, but they're not food for the present times.

**Kosinski:** The parents of our students are not falling apart; the young ones are. Of course in the past it was the opposite. The old ones were out of touch with society. The general complaint of the 19th Century parents was that Julien Sorels were born, Fabrizio Del Dangos, Rastignacs—they were the ones who were taking over. And of course the parents were then pushed back to their futile or semi-futile retirements and totally out of touch. But now it's the opposite. This is what I meant—a madhouse in which no provision is made for mental illness. The old Baobabs, somehow, remain in power because the young don't vote.

**Cahill:** Which is one of the great ironies of our time, because the forces of change seem to come from the young people, but they're doomed to failure. They're doomed to failure because of sheer practical and political inaction.

**Kosinski:** Like Whalen, somewhere in the middle of their development they say, "I am a son of . . ." And at the police station the ultimate test of who are you, your identity, that's where they give up. And they say "I am a son of . . ." Well, from then on we don't deal with the son anymore, we have to deal with the father—alive or dead, metaphorically present or spiritually present, if you prefer, or present as a corporate body—and that's what happens.

**Cahill:** Many critics have noted a persistent strain of violence which informs your fiction. Do you find the same landscape of violence in *The Devil Tree*?

**Kosinski:** Yes. Far deeper, I think, and more penetrating, since unlike the violence of *The Painted Bird*, external to a large degree, unlike the violence of *Steps*, brushed off by the protagonist who is capable of protecting himself. The violence of *The Devil Tree* is far closer to the violence of *Being There*. I think of all the four novels *Being There* is the most violent book, since there the whole notion of violence has been already discarded, but the protagonist is an ultimate victim of the ultimate violence, and therefore the violence is not something which he can define as violence. Hence he cannot defend himself against it; he is really the ultimate result of it, the ultimate victim really. I like to believe that *The Devil Tree* incorporates all the other novels in a sort of dialectic fashion, Hegelian fashion; but then perhaps because of also denying the other three, it creates a new entity and therefore, for me at least, it's far more difficult to deal with. My ambiguity towards *The Devil Tree* is far greater than towards any other of my works because I think the work is far larger than I am. I sympathize and empathize with the boy in *The Painted Bird*; I understand very well the man in *Steps*; I have pity and no connection, really, with Chauncey Gardiner, he doesn't concern me, he's too predictable for me, and too obvious. However, I'm very ambiguous towards Jonathan Whalen. On one hand I understand him and some of me is in him, but on the other hand I find him naive and I find him also rudimentary in terms of life; he is someone I can analyze rather easily. Yet he has many components which I know nothing about. What do I know about growing up with roots which are not severed? What does any Central European know about growing in a progressive, cumulative fashion? All

of us had our childhood chopped by various events, and the childhood
of our times was chopped as well by wars, by revolutions, by sudden
uprooting. And so in many ways I feel that *The Devil Tree*, in terms of
my old relation to my work, did something which puzzled me; I'm far
more perplexed by *The Devil Tree* and by Jonathan and his environment, than by anything I have ever done in the past.

**Cahill:** If the violence is revealed in its most acute and painful forms,
there are elements or scenes of sexual violence—ones far outside of that
popular realm of affronted sexual mores. Generally, these are situations
in which people abuse each other for devious self-serving ends.

**Kosinski:** That's right, the sexual violence is accepted by them, and
therefore they may not necessarily classify something they would consider done to them. This is the way things are, they say. That's what
I meant by being penetrated by the violence which loses the definition
almost. So I think this is a different violence, since to the protagonist of
this violence it becomes a way of life in which they don't feel that it
could be otherwise. Indeed, they don't think it *should* be otherwise.
What's more, I think the basic difference between the violence of *The
Devil Tree* and all the other books, except of *Being There*, is that the
violence is insidious, and it comes camouflaged as something else. We
all know that some of the protagonists of *The Devil Tree* would say that
there are certain business requirements; if you want to play the game
you have to play with the small tricks. If you want to live in a fun city,
this is the price you pay for fun. There is a sort of jungle philosophy
in which the protagonists don't call the shots by their proper names.
Language again becomes a traveler's check, really; it is plastic money in
the form of a credit card. I think a traveler's check may be a good code
for this book. In other words, it is not the real thing anymore; it has the
various curtains. Language performs the camouflage function, the
veiling of the events. What's more, all of these protagonists, unlike
Chance in *Being There*, who is imprisoned in his garden, and perhaps
is retarded and therefore cannot get out of it, these people in *The Devil
Tree* have all the options—you said it yourself, they have almost the
Jamesian option of getting out of their own predicament, providing they
know what their predicament is. They don't know it anymore, but they
refuse to realize this. Why is Jonathan coming back from Africa to New
York? What for? Is the meaningful search for the self to be conducted
only in the fun city? Couldn't it possibly be conducted in another cul-

ture? So, we are back to the same aspect of the self from which they all, I think, progressively depart, further and further, until society becomes the "great" encounter group; the self becomes a conversation with a psychiatrist. I think the individual lends himself as a victim by an open inability to counteract even the most elementary pressures. Part of this is, of course, the inability of the men and women to see themselves as victims. That is, I think, the tragic predicament . . . this is the ultimate defeat of the imagination, and the defeat of the language. A man as a protagonist of his own life, ceases to see his own life as eventful enough to be tragic.

**Cahill:** A number of the people in the novel seem to be infected with a diseased will, a complete suspension of power to know and power to act. Does this seem a fair statement to you?

**Kosinski:** Yes. Actually *The Devil Tree* may be in some remote way an attempt to state it. How does it happen? What are the ingredients of this paralysis—are they individual? Or are they perhaps derivative of the situation which is nonhistorical, precisely because it is not historical? What are the collectives between the generations of fathers and the generations of sons and daughters? Are there any? Is there any heritage—meaningful heritage—left to us, and if so, what is it, other than the meaningless trust administered by people whose contact has been neither with the roots nor with the branches?

**Cahill:** Does the novel offer any kind of relief or repair or restoration from the unholy state of disease?

**Kosinski:** I think the novel does it, any novel does, in the process of being read—this is what we said in the beginning, that the act of connecting the imagination of the reader with the imagination implicit in the language is already an attempt at the self, in this case the self which is reading. Hence any act of reading—indeed the act of reading anything—is an act of activating the projecting ability of the self. From this point of view, if one insists on a moral judgment, and very often one does, I think perceiving any art, the very act of perception is already humanizing, since it activates the profoundly human ability to project oneself into another situation. If I were to define the goal of the literary experience, this would be the ultimate goal—to make the man more aware of who he is, and of how eventful he is, since he is event to himself. He ought to be. Otherwise what is he? Is he a number in the telephone book? Is he a social security number? All the jokes which we

make about a man being nothing but computerized phenomena ironically may be true, unless the man is an event which begins and ends,
and which has to be accepted with full recognition of its eventfulness.
Unless this takes place, the man then is not only a victim, he can also be
an oppressor; he can be used one way or another. He becomes an agent
of forces he doesn't know, he doesn't understand. Even violence
inflicted on him, in which he's a subject, a very definite subject of
cruelty, passes unnoticed. He's lost the ability to perceive himself, and
this is ultimately a threatened and threatening individual, an individual
who doesn't know who he is. He's pitiful because the life beautifully
vested in him is a loss, but he also is, I think, dangerous to other men,
since indeed he becomes an agent of other forces.

**Cahill:** How should one in the turbulent times of today begin to seek
out viable, meaningful, self-definitions when seemingly trapped now in
a moral morass?

**Kosinski:** I could almost say that it's much easier for someone who's
trapped to define himself than for someone who has a feeling of relative
freedom. Hence I think that if, there ever was a time in which the act
of self definition was needed, if it's precisely what you have said, it is
now, because of the sense of entrapment at least we should know . . .
we may not know who traps us . . . but we should know who is
trapped. So the *trapee* . . .

**Cahill:** You may have invented a new word.

**Kosinski:** . . . the immediate *trapee* should know who he is if he
lacks the ability to find out who trapped him. And I think this is
understandable; I think it's very difficult to find out by whom one is
really trapped, in a world as complex as this. However, the means to
find out who is trapped are still open to us, I think more than ever
before. Before, outside of our taped reality, you and I talked of the
sudden emergence of pornography and the sudden, what I call the
masturbatory culture, which really aims at the solitary man, the solitary
social animal prevented from establishing meaningful sexual, or any
other contacts with other people of the same kind. I think the symptoms
are clear; we can see that there are more and more people who have
been abandoned to their own fate, somehow, who are unable to "cope,"
as they call it, with the external social reality; they are also quite unable
to express in any meaningful way, in any functional way, some of the
most basic elements of, or aspects of, their nature; they cannot function
sexually, they cannot function emotionally. So we don't like the indica-

tions that we are trapped, that man becomes more and more imprisoned, so to speak. Ironically at the same time there seems to be greater urgency than ever to escape from the situation of entrapment into some sort of vicarious experience.

**Cahill:** Isn't this explosion of pornography functional in that it allows people to escape, too; that it makes for them a world in which they can see themselves as the aggressor, the conqueror, through all kinds of fantasies . . .

**Kosinski:** Or, openly admit that they are victims. But the spectrum is so crude, the actions of anonymous bodies so elementary, that one can only speculate and perhaps regret that with all the options left to the trapee, from all the available means of escaping imaginarily, he would select the crudest, the most elementary form. And that is of course very bad. It's a sad comment on the final inability to perceive one's self as trapped.

**Cahill:** One final question about Jonathan at Geneva. The closing scene reads: "The smell of moss spread through the air. He sniffed the dew, listening to the lapping of the water against the stones and felt the skin on the back of his neck prickle. The fog began to lift. He stared across the lake and saw the lights blinking of the villas and hotels of Geneva." Is Jonathan here caught in "the drift towards death," or is the phrase "The fog began to lift" an affirmation of new life?

**Kosinski:** I think I leave it to interpretation. Can we take it for what it is? He's in Geneva, probably in a clinic; he may have gone through a nervous breakdown as a result of breaking all the relationships, and of course the murder, and trying to get rid of his roots, and unable to keep up with the branches. And it may be that from now on he will live a life of an expatriate, a playboy perhaps, outside of the blinking lights of Geneva, outside of the ethos which brought him up. But it may be also coming back somehow to some ultimate truth, since he wakes up; the weight has lifted itself from his chest. And if that's the case, then maybe he would be able to perceive Geneva for what it is, merely another didactic symbol from which one should grow out and seek an appropriate perspective—across the lake, blinking lights, that's all. It doesn't have to be any specific interpretation; it's a story for what it is. If one wants to dismiss it, one can just say, "Well, there's Jonathan back in Geneva, if he had ever been there, or in Geneva recovering from his cure; he may now be back in New York and starting the whole thing again."

# A Nation of Videots

David Sohn/1975

Published in *Media and Methods* April 1975: 24–26, 28, 30–31, 52,
54, 56–57. Permission granted by *Media and Methods*.

The interview took place during last year's NCTE convention, in a
setting that was a media nightmare. In the lobby of the International
Hotel—lots of noise—no coffee—Kosinski just back from a stunning
lecture at the Secondary Section Luncheon (more about that later)—no
outlet—the recorder running on batteries of unknown vintage—fingers
crossed. He suggests we talk about media and communications. We
begin.

In a matter of moments, all the distractions and difficulties fade into
oblivion. Here is a man with a whiplash mind, a stiletto wit, a vision
that fires off devastating perceptions probing the human condition to
reveal startling ironies, jolting absurdities. Electrifying language spouts
from him with the intensity of a jackhammer. I find myself in awe of his
intense presence, blinded by the staggering brilliance of his darting
asides, intent on the lean language that strips bare the kernel of each
thought. It's like sitting quietly through the San Francisco earthquake.

Adding to my amazement is the fact that he has just delivered the
most passionate speech I've ever heard at a teacher's conference. It
happened by chance. The scheduled speaker was ill and Kosinski
generously agreed to fill in. His words stunned the teachers, assaulting
them with brutal facts: The average American watches about 1200 hours
of TV each year, yet reads books for only five hours per year. There are
200,000 functional illiterates in New England alone. Gallup's research
shows that more than half of us have never read a hardbound or paperback book, except for the Bible and textbooks.

America, he said, has a "middle-class skid row," students living in
"a mortuary of easy going." They seem incapable of reflecting: "Even
though their stomachs are full like the exotic fishes of the Amazon, they
swallow indiscriminately, quickly ejecting all as waste."

He concluded by underscoring the validity of the English language.

"This search for inner strength," he said, "is mainly conducted through the language—literature, and its ability to trigger the imagination, that oldest mental trait that is typically human. It is finally the teacher of English who day after day refuses to leave students emotionally and intellectually disarmed, who forces them to face their very self and to cope with the unknown—their own existence. Because of this rescue mission that takes place every week in the classroom, the teacher of English is this country's major missionary force."

The audience leaped to a prolonged standing ovation. They had, by sheer accident, been profoundly shaken. Many may not have known Jerzy Kosinski before the pot roast and peas, but they surely knew him now: an extraordinary and eloquent human being who cares about humanity and its survival, and communicates his feelings even while he acts on them. The room emptied, each listener carrying a spark of inestimable value, a new depth.

I had hardly recovered from the lecture when we began the interview. I needed some respite, the gracious lull of small talk. It never happened. Kosinski, I immediately discovered, was just warming up.

**Sohn:** Edmund Carpenter, the noted anthropologist observed that every medium has its own grammar—the elements which enable it to communicate. McLuhan also—with his "the medium is the message"—talked about how a medium communicates.

**Kosinski:** I tend to think in terms of a medium's recipients, not in terms of the medium itself. In other words, it's not the church which interests me, but the congregation. I would rather talk about "the grammar" of a perceiver, the grammar of an audience. A television set without viewers doesn't interest me either. Yet the role television plays in our lives does interest me very much.

**Sohn:** Isn't that related to what you were saying in your book, *Being There*?

**Kosinski:** The main character of *Being There*, Chance, has no meaningful existence outside of what he experiences on television. Unlike the reader of fiction who re-creates a text arbitrarily in his imagination, Chance, who cannot read or fantasize, is at the mercy of the tube. He cannot imagine himself functioning on anything but the particular situations offered him by TV programs. Of course, Chance is a fictional archetype. On the other hand, a number of teachers have told me that many of their young students resemble Chance. A child begins school nowadays with basic images from "his own garden" —television.

Children have always imitated adults, but "TV babies," with access to a world beyond that of their parents and siblings, often mimic TV personalities. They behave according to TV models, not according to their moods, and their actions reflect patterns they have picked up from television. They're funny à la Don Rickles or Chico or Sanford; they're tough like Kojak or Khan.

The basic difference, for me, between television and the novel as media is that television takes the initiative: it does the involving. It says, "You, the passive spectator, are there. Stay there. I'll do the moving, talking, acting." Frenetic, quick-paced, engineered by experts in visual drama, everything from a thirty-second commercial to a two-hour movie is designed to fit into neat time slots, wrapped up in lively colors and made easily digestible.

While viewing, you can eat, you can recline, you can walk around the set, you can even change channels, but you won't lose contact with the medium. Unlike theater or cinema, TV allows, even encourages, all these "human" diversions. TV's hold on you is so strong, it is not easily threatened or severed by "the other life" you lead. While watching, you are not reminded (as you would be by a theater audience, for instance) that you are a member of society whose thoughts and reactions may be valuable. You are isolated and given no time to reflect. The images rush on and you cannot stop them or slow them down or turn them back.

Recently I heard of a college class in media communication which had been assigned to watch two hours of television and record the content of those two hours. They were asked to describe each element—including commercials—in as much detail as possible, classifying every incident and every character in terms of its relative importance to the story. All these students had been raised in front of TV sets and were accustomed to being bombarded by TV images; many of them hoped to be employed in the communications industry after graduation. Yet, not a single one could complete the assignment. They claimed that the rapidity and fragmentation of the TV experience made it impossible to isolate a narrative thought-line or to contemplate and analyze what they had seen, in terms of relative significance.

**Sohn:** Have you ever noticed when you go to someone's house, that very often the television set will be on and it continues on? In fact, people leave it on all day.

**Kosinski:** Many of us do. I watch it a lot. In my apartment, for instance, my visiting friends often get very jittery around seven p.m. They want to see the news. I turn the television on and, for an hour, we all cruise around it. We're still talking to each other, or drinking with each other, but we have been disconnected—we are not *being there*, in that other world "brought to you by . . ." —the medium's crucial phrase.

Yet the viewer knows that he is not Columbo or Captain Kangaroo. He is separated from the stars not only by his patently different identity, being *here* while they are *there*, but also—and this is far more important—by the very process of watching, of having been assigned the role of spectator. In this process, the spectator occupies one world, while what he views comes from another. The bridge between the two is TV's absolutely concrete nature. Every situation it portrays is particular: every descriptive detail is given, nothing is implied, no blank spaces are left for the viewer to fill in.

Now, literature is general, made up of words which are often vague, or which represent many classes of things: for instance, "tree," "bird," "human being." A novel becomes concrete only through the reader's own imagining or staging-from-within, which is grounded in his memory, his fancy, his current reality. The act of reading mobilizes this inner process. Above all else, literature orients us towards our own existence as we individually perceive and define it. The child who easily imitates Don Rickles' "meanness" could not possibly imitate the Boy of *The Painted Bird* without having first fleshed out that character in his own imagination. To see that Boy, the reader must keep on *inventing* him in an internal imaginative process. The printed page offers nothing but "inking" ; the reader provides his own mental props, his own emotional and physical details. From the infinite catalog of his mind, the reader picks out the things which were most interesting to him, most vivid, most memorable as defined by his own life.

Because it is uncontrolled and totally free, this process offers unexpected, unchannelled associations, new insights into the tides and drifts of one's own life. The reader is tempted to venture beyond a text, to contemplate his own life in light of the book's personalized meanings.

Television, though, doesn't demand any such inner reconstruction. Everything is already there, explicit, ready to be watched, to be followed on its own terms, at the speed it dictates. The viewer is given no time to pause, to recall, to integrate the image-attack into his own experience.

**Sohn:** I'm intrigued by your analysis of how television influences our self-perception and behavior.

**Kosinski:** During the years when I was teaching, I invited several seven- to ten-year-old children into a very large classroom where two video monitors were installed, one on the left side and one on the right side of the blackboard, TV cameras were also placed on either side of the room. I sat before the blackboard, telling a story. Suddenly, an intruder from outside rushed into the room—prearranged, of course— and started arguing with me, pushing and hitting me. The cameras began filming the incident, and the fracas appeared on both screens of the monitors, clearly visible to all the children. Where did the kids look? At the event (the attacker and me), or at the screen? According to the video record of a third camera, which filmed the students' reactions, the majority seldom looked at the actual incident in the center of the room. Instead, they turned toward the screens which were placed above eye-level and therefore easier to see than the real event. Later, when we talked about it, many of the children explained that they could see the attack better on the screens. After all, they pointed out, they could see close-ups of the attacker and of me, his hand on my face, his expressions—all the details they wanted—without being frightened by "the real thing" (or by the necessity of becoming involved.)

At another time, I showed short educational 16mm films on the video, while telling the children—again from seven to ten years old—that something fascinating was happening in the corridor. "Now those who want to stay inside and watch the films are free to remain in the class," I said, "but there's something really incredible going on outside, and those who want to see it are free to leave the room." No more than ten percent of the children left. I repeated, "You know *what's outside is really fantastic. You have never seen it before.* Why don't you just step out and take a look?" And they always said, "No, no, no, we prefer to stay here and watch the film." I'd say, "But you don't know what's outside." "Well, what is it?" they'd ask. "You have to go find out." And they'd say, "Why don't we just sit here and see the film first?"

There it was: they were already too lazy, too corrupted to get up and take a chance on "the outside."

**Sohn:** That's an incredible indictment of television.

**Kosinski:** Not of television as much as of a society founded on the principle of passive entertainment. And young viewers have been affected by TV far more than we care to know. Once, I invited students (from ten to fourteen years of age) to be interviewed singly. I said to each one, "I want to do an interview with you, to ask you some very private and even embarrassing questions, but I won't record our conversation or repeat to anyone what you tell me. To start with, do you masturbate?" And the kids, quite shocked, usually answered, "Well, you know, I don't know what you mean." Then I asked, "Do you steal often? Have you stolen anything recently?" Again, the kids all hedged, "I don't know, uh, uh . . ." more mumbling. The girls were invariably more embarrassed than the boys.

When I finished, I said, "Now, I'll tell you why I asked you all those questions. You see, I would like to film the interview and show it on television for thousands and thousands of people to see." When they heard they would be on television, an instant change of mood occurred. They were eager to be on TV. I installed the monitors and the camera, and told the kids, "I want to make a show for the community, for everybody *out there*. Your parents, your friends, strangers, the whole country will see it. Do you mind if, once again, but this time for television, I ask you the same questions?" All the students assured me they were willing "to try harder" to answer them.

Once the equipment was installed, I started the video camera and addressed an invisible and, in fact, nonexistent technician, "Bob, will you make the picture sharp, because I want every one of my interviewees to be recognizable." Each child was then asked to introduce himself or herself: full name, age, and address. They all answered without hesitation. "Is the picture clear, Bob?" "Perfectly. Everybody will recognize your guest," came the prerecorded assurance from "Bob." It was time to address my first "guest." "Now tell me," I asked Tom, "do you masturbate? If you do, tell our audience how and when you do it."

The boy, suddenly poised and blasé, leaned toward me. "Well, yes, occasionally I do. Of course I'm not sure I can describe it. But I can try . . ." An inviting smile stolen from "The Mike Douglas Show."

After Tom described all, leaving nothing to the public's imagination, I
changed the subject. I said, "Since we are going to show this interview
on television, Tom, I want you to be very careful what you say. Now,
everybody will be interested in your experience as a thief. Have you
ever stolen anything?" Pensively, as if recalling a pleasant childhood
incident, Tom said, "Every once in a while when I go to the five-and-
ten, you know, I like to pick up something."

"Now, Tom" I said, "you realize that you are speaking to a very large
public. Your parents, your teachers, your friends are out there. And I
don't know how they will react to your admissions. Are you sure that
you're not saying anything on the air that only you should know?" "No,
no, no, it's alright," he reassured me nonchalantly, "I don't mind." I
broke in, "Should we arrange it so your face doesn't show?" "No, why?"
"Well, if you want to describe your experience as a thief, maybe we
should . . ." "No! I can talk about it. Honest, I don't mind," he insisted.

From about twenty-five kids, I got similar reactions. I don't think
there was one boy or one girl who refused to be interviewed about the
most incriminating subjects, ranging from less common sexual experiences to acts of violence, thievery, betrayal of one's family, friends,
etc. This time, the girls seemed even less inhibited than the boys. As
long as the camera was on and the students could see themselves on
the monitor they talked and talked and talked. Often I pretended to be
embarrassed by what they said. But, trained in the best talk-show
tradition, the guests were not put off by their host.

Their manner was so familiar: the easy posture of the TV conversa-
tionalist, the sudden warmth and openness, the total frankness. Every
interviewee answered candidly, looking directly into the camera with a
straight face, mumbling a bit, pretending to reflect, but in fact covering
up for a deeper verbal clumsiness. Suddenly, these youngsters seemed
too old for their years: each one a blend of actor, author, professor,
clown, talking with a bizarre ease about real or invented "forbidden"
acts. Yet, judging by their manner, you'd think I was asking about
yesterday's weather.

**Sohn:** Did you conduct any other experiments?

**Kosinski:** I did not think of these few *ad hoc* sessions as experiments. Rather, they were crude attempts to find out a bit more about the
young. I don't know whether I "tapped" anything. And, since this took

place some years ago, I don't know whether my results would be valid today. Still, I was very upset by some of them. When I was attacked by the intruder, for instance, the kids were less interested in the actual assault than in what the TV cameras were doing—as if they had paid to see a film, as if the incident had been staged to entertain them! And all during the confrontation—despite my yelling, his threats, the fear that I showed—the kids did not interfere or offer to help. None of them.

They sat transfixed as if the TV cameras neutralized the act of violence. And perhaps they did. By filming a brutal physical struggle from a variety of viewpoints, the cameras transformed a human conflict into an aesthetic happening, distancing the audience and allowing them an alternative to moral judgment and involvement.

**Sohn:** Did you question the students on their reactions?

**Kosinski:** Yes, later on I interviewed them about what had happened in the class. Most of them said, "Well, you know, these cameras were set up, and then, you know, this guy came and pushed you, and well, it was kind of, uh, you could see him and you on these screens very well. You looked so scared and he was so mean." I asked, "What do you mean, you could see it very well?" "Well, you know, you could see *everything* on those screens. They are great. How much does it cost to buy one of these videos?"

**Sohn:** That's eerie. What does it all mean?

**Kosinski:** I can only guess. It's obviously related to the fact that so many kids prefer to stay home and watch TV than to go to a museum, explore the city, or even play with their peers. They can see close-ups, and commercials, and when bored, shift to another channel. We've reached the point now where people—adults and children alike—would prefer to watch a televised ballgame than to sit in some far corner of a stadium, too hot or too cold, uncomfortable, surrounded by a smelly crowd, with no close-ups, no other channel to turn to. Uncomfortable— like life often is.

**Sohn:** Again, it's the idea of the passive spectator, lounging, half-distracted. What else did you find?

**Kosinski:** After a while, I also turned to "another channel." I guess I just did not want to know kids anymore. They are, to me, a sad lot. Occasionally, I do talk to them and I try to engage them in an imaginary play, but for how long can I—or anyone—compete with all the channels? I haven't done any more "sessions." Many of my anthropologically inclined friends were critical of my "tricking" the children, of "exploiting" them in a non-scientific experiment. As if they could possibly be exploited more than they have already been as "viewers," or as if I wanted or needed to be scientific! Go into any high school and see how limited students' perception of themselves is, how crippled their imaginations, how unable they are to tell a story, to read or concentrate, or even to describe an event accurately a moment after it happens. See how easily they are bored, how quickly they take up the familiar "reclining" position in the classroom, how short their attention span is. Or talk to their teachers. They know more about youth's ener-vation than any parent ever will.

**Sohn:** Did you see any of the episodes of "An American Family?"

**Kosinski:** Yes, I've seen most of them.

**Sohn:** I was thinking of that in relation to what you were saying about television. Here are these people doing something similar. It was fairly frank. They were revealing their lives week after week, on TV.

**Kosinski:** You mean they were making acceptable the bigotry and the incriminating private stuff of their lives by performing it for public consumption. If thirty million viewers love it, it cannot be harmful, right? Well, that's where my "experimental" kids get their training, from "An American Family" to "All in the Family." Despite the dif-ferences between the Louds and the Bunkers, the two shows have a lot in common. "All in the Family" is about an American family that, the show claims, is fictional, but still a composite of us all. "An American Family" was about a "real" American family that ended up as a TV show, though it disintegrated as a family through the process that I'd call "television."

**Sohn:** Right. Which is the reality and which is the fiction?

**Kosinski:** For me, the unusual aspect of television is that, unlike any other medium, it doesn't state its relationship to "reality" and to "art." A TV weather report doesn't claim that it is an art form. It is not intro-duced, for instance, as a video essay with weather as its main subject, with a gentle man speculating about an ungentle climate. On the other hand, television does not claim to be a "reality report" either, even though it often passes for one. Unlike theater or painting or photography or fiction, television makes no claim to have one "true nature." There-fore the difference between "All in the Family" and "An American Family" is, to me, a very relative one. Both are recorded, both are

edited, both are TV shows. Reality? Of course not. Art? Not quite or
not yet. Once a man knows that the cameras are recording him, he is
turned into an actor. No spontaneity survives, except a "controlled spontaneity," a rehearsed one. We have become so accustomed to the presence of accustomed recording devices that even the Occupant of the
Oval Office did not realize how incriminating his own recording set-up
was.

**Sohn:** One interesting thing about "An American Family" is that they
were perfectly willing to do this, they went into it, they got into it. But
then, they became very upset.

**Kosinski:** Private reality catches up with us all. When the "show" is
"brought to you by" yourself, its consequences can't be changed like a
channel. Nor can the pain. The Ruthenian peasants among whom I grew
up used to say that "to those who only watch the stars all suffering
comes." How many of us are prepared for the encounter?

**Sohn:** What you're saying reminds me of a comment that McLuhan
once made. He suggested that taking a slice of the environment and
putting it into another medium—a novel, a television show, a film,
whatever—has the effect of enabling you to see it more clearly. Do you
think that has any validity?

**Kosinski:** Only in the sense that if it's really a work of art, then it—
a play, a novel, a film—can elucidate our otherwise unstated reality.
But the record of "An American Family" was not art; it was nothing
more than an average TV soap opera. Instead of clarifying the "family
environment," the show obscured it. Members of a family were turned
into professional family members, all trained as actors and actresses on
the spot through the process of being filmed.

**Sohn:** In regard to television and education, are there any beneficial
effects that you can put your finger on?

**Kosinski:** For me, the word "beneficial" doesn't apply to television.
TV is simply a part of contemporary life. I must confront it, think about
it, accept it, or reject it.

**Sohn:** It's part of the environment, and therefore difficult to perceive.

**Kosinski:** Yes, perhaps because it exists in a very uneasy relationship
with the environment. The medium is so overwhelming. How do you
assess the importance of an activity which accompanies you practically
all the time? The average working American apparently watches it for
1,200 hours per year while, for instance, book-reading occupies only

five hours of his time. How do you judge its role in our political life? The impact of its commercialism? Of its ordering of time? Of its ranking of what's important (therefore visible) and what's not (therefore left out)?

**Sohn:** You can notice certain things. For example, children coming to school these days have been affected by "Sesame Street" and "The Electric Company" and some of the other programs. When they come to kindergarten they already know their letters and numbers. In the same vein, older people suddenly have better access to the world, a chance to see much more than ever before.

**Kosinski:** Let's say better access to the world of *television*. In small European communities still without television, the old people remain physically active, mixing with the young, venturing out into the real world. Here, like their little grandchildren, they sit immobilized by TV. An American senior citizen once told me that his TV set gave him a sixth sense—at the price of removing the other five. I think that both young and old are acquiring, via television, a superficial glimpse of a narrow slice of unreality. I'm not certain how such "knowledge" is used, or what it does. Does it make real life more meaningful or individuals more active? Does it encourage adventure? Does it arm an individual against the pains inflicted by society, by other humans, by aging? Does it bring us closer to each other? Does it explain us to ourselves, and ourselves to each other? Does it?

For me, imagining groups of solitary individuals watching their private, remote-controlled TV sets is the ultimate future terror: a nation of *videots*.

One thing I am convinced of is that human conduct is primarily determined by human intercourse—by the relationship of one being with another being. So anything which is detrimental to that interaction, anything which delays it, makes it more uneasy, or creates a state of apprehension, is detrimental to the growing of society.

I look at the children who spend five or six hours watching television every day, and I notice that when in groups they cannot interact with each other. They are terrified of each other; they develop secondary anxiety characteristics. They want to watch, they don't want to be spoken to. They want to watch, they don't want to talk. They want to watch, they don't want to be asked questions or singled out.

TV also influences the way they view the world. On television, the world is exciting, single-faceted, never complex. By comparison, their own lives appear slow, uneventful, bewildering. They find it easier to watch televised portrayals of human experiences—violence, love, adventure, sex—than to gain the experience for themselves. They believe in avoiding real contests just as they believe in pain killers and sleeping pills. It was TV that first taught them to rely on drugs, that there was no need to suffer, to be tense or unhappy or even uncomfortable, because a drug would relieve all that. Even death is no longer a necessary part of existence for them. Its finality is gone because their hero, no matter how dead, would rise again.

So, they grow up essentially mute. As teenagers, they are anxious to join an amorphous group—a rock band or a film audience. The music or the film relieves them of all necessity to interact with each other—the blaring sounds prevent communication, the screen above their heads is the focus of all their attention. They remain basically mute: sitting *with* each other, *next* to each other, but *removed from* each other by this omnipresent third party—music or film.

Silence and the absence of entertainment are more than discomforts to TV generations—they are threats. They cause anxiety.

**Sohn:** My grandfather used to say, when he was angry, "All I want is silence, and damned little of that."

**Kosinski:** I think silence is an invitation to reflection or to conversation, the prime terrors to videots. One of the TV talk show hosts once said to me that "this is the only country in the world where people watch conversation every night."

**Sohn:** On the other hand, another thing I've noticed—and it amazes me each time I see it—is children studying or reading with the television or radio on.

**Kosinski:** The constant companionship of distracting devices.

**Sohn:** The need for silence, as far as they're concerned, doesn't exist. Somehow they've managed to cope with noise. Maybe.

**Kosinski:** I wonder how they really cope with anything. A lot of them don't cope at all. More and more parents leave their children in front of the TV as baby sitter, assuming that watching shows is safer than walking in the real streets outside their homes. But is it?

Unlike television, children grow older. For years they have been trained to control their little world by changing the channels when they were bored, and were accustomed to a simplified, unambiguous TV world in which everyone exists to amuse them. As adolescents, they are naturally threatened by the presence of real people they cannot control. Others push them around, make faces at them, encroach on their territory. And they can do nothing to stop this. They begin to feel that this real world unjustly limits them; after all, it seldom offers alternative channels.

Because this unpredictable real world doesn't function according to neatly ordered time slots and is full of ambiguities, children brought up as viewers naturally feel persecuted. Yet, even though our industrial state offers few situations that can be resolved in thirty minutes, and no clear-cut heroes and villains, video-addicts keep expecting an easy resolution. When it doesn't come, they grow impatient, then adamant or disillusioned. In this world of hierarchy and brutish competition and depression and unemployment and inflation, they are always challenged and often out-ranked by others. Soon they believe *they* are defective. Instead of coming of age, they're coming apart.

This process of creating weak and vulnerable beings seems to be a current general rule in America. Upper-class children have experiences that counteract TV's influence: they have opportunities to be involved with real horses, real forests, real mountains, things they can see, touch, experience. However, many middle-class and almost all poor children are at the mercy of television for many hours a day. For years now we have had a skid row composed of middle-class, college educated dropouts, or stopouts, as they often call themselves.

**Sohn:** When I asked you about silence . . .

**Kosinski:** For me silence and solitude are necessary for self redefinition, for daily reassessing the purpose of my life. Silence occurs when I consider *who* I am, when I read fiction or poetry. Reading and writing are part of my confronting myself and society. Of my own rages and resignations.

**Sohn:** It would seem, then, that television may be robbing us of our fantasy life.

**Kosinski:** A TV show is a product of people, many of whom are first rank artists, profoundly creative, inventive, concerned with their work and with its impact on the public. But, by its very nature, a TV show is, above all, a result of a *collective* (not individual) fantasy. It is subjected to various collective influences, collective editing, collective simplifying, collective sponsorship, etc. In other words, *"Brought to you by . . ."*

But television has another characteristic as well, one that we tend to overlook. It's a portable multi-theater. If, while viewing, you're upset by one of the programs, you don't have to get up, leave it, and walk the street to reach another theater and pay to see another show. You just press a button, and you are transferred to another place. Thus, at any time, you can step out of one collective fantasy and step into another. That effortless control over an activity that occupies so much of our time is profoundly affecting. After all, such effortless freedom doesn't exist in any other domain of our life.

Let's assume that, right now, in the middle of our conversation, you angered me and I decided to leave in midsentence, without warning. First, in order to define my anger, I would have to reflect, to decide why I don't want to sit with you anymore or why I should leave. Then I would have to decide how I should go about leaving: Should I push the table away and reveal my anger, or, rather, should I make up some excuse?

Should I tell you what I think of you and expose myself to potential abuse, or should I say nothing? It would be a conflict situation, complex, difficult to resolve and painful. Still, quite common to us all.

Yet, watching a similar conflict on television would in no way prepare me emotionally to confront and handle such a situation in reality. As a teacher, what can I learn from "McMillan and Wife"? As a foreign-born, can I really absorb the idiom of "McCloud"? As a novelist, can I benefit from the calmness and insight of "Columbo"? And as an officer of P.E.N., would I imitate the practices depicted in "The Name of the Game"?

**Sohn:** We've explored some fascinating insights into the impact that television is having on us. And it looks so innocent: the fine wooden cabinet, or the contemporary molded design. We hardly suspect what it's doing to us.

But there is another question I wanted to ask you. It's about Joseph Conrad and yourself. You're both authors of Polish origin, and yet each of you wrote in English. Why is that?

**Kosinski:** I make no comment for Conrad. Frankly, when I arrived in America, what fascinated me most about the English language was that everybody spoke it here.

**Sohn:** Part of the environment.

**Kosinski:** Like television.

**Sohn:** But I'm intrigued . . .

**Kosinski:** I was a bilingual child; my parents were Russian but I grew up in Poland. As a boy I was mute for several years. When I regained my speech, the country was Stalinist. It lost its freedom of expression. That's why I never wrote in Eastern Europe. I expressed myself through photography. English, the language that I learned after I arrived here in 1957, doesn't evoke any emotionally negative responses grounded in my past. I became aware very quickly that it was easier for me to express my emotions even in my then rudimentary English than it ever had been in my Polish or Russian. In English, I was not afraid to be myself, I didn't feel personally threatened by what I said and I still don't—when I speak or write in English.

**Sohn:** Unless you're an Occupant of the Oval Office.

**Kosinski:** But even in the Oval Office you're threatened only if you record yourself. And you are still free not to do it—or to destroy your own tapes.

# Jerzy Kosinski: Tapping into His Vision of Truth

## Lisa Grunwald/1977

Published in *Vineyard Gazette* 29 July 1977:1-A,2-A. Copyright ©
*Vineyard Gazette*, 1977. Reprinted by permission.

Jerzy Kosinski is the author of six novels and he is the author
of his experiences. In a *Gazette* interview last week, he spoke
of the importance of having both kinds of command.

Mr. Kosinski came to America from Poland 20 years ago,
escaping the Communist bureaucracy by literally creating
people who came to recommend his departure. His private
world is divided, almost equally, between New York's literary circles and its street life. Mr. Kosinski moves freely in
both worlds and has as much to say of the publishers, the
editors and the artists as he does of the drinkers and soldiers,
the pimps and gamblers with whom he talks.

He is a vigorous man with an ardent need for new experiences and new realms of thought. His novels dwell consis-
tently on his protagonists' needs to find autonomy through an
exploration of the self. His characters look to control other
people, and elements of society before they are controlled.

Mr. Kosinski was spending a short vacation with friends
on the Vineyard. Publishers, film scripts and a darkroom
were waiting for him when he left for New York. His sixth
novel, *Blind Date*, will appear in November. His others are
*The Painted Bird, Steps, The Devil Tree, Being There*, and
*Cockpit*.

What follows is an edited transcript of three separate
conversations.

**Q:** You have spoken about living in two worlds. How much of your
experience in these worlds is dictated by the fact that you will write
about it?

**A:** I once wrote that a writer takes from outside only what he could
imagine anyhow. Whatever I pick up from the outside world—a street
scene, an event—I use only because I would have used it anyhow,
without seeing it. To a degree I could say that my fiction doesn't really

follow the reality to which I am exposed; that the reality to which I am exposed follows my fiction.

**Q:** So you could write the same fiction without having the experience?

**A:** Absolutely. The experience triggers something that is already there.

**Q:** But don't you have to see something in order to write about it? I've just written a poem with an image of a beach, in which I compare the rocks and shells to a thousand eyes. I didn't stand on the beach thinking "that looks like." But if I'd never stood on a beach I couldn't have written the image.

**A:** How do you know that you couldn't have? To give you an example, in *Blind Date,* the forthcoming novel, I talked to a girl who was almost entirely a head. She was one of very few crippled beings who survived a dreadful childhood illness. Her whole weight was not more than 15 pounds. She had a head and the body of a three-year-old. One would think that her experience of the world would be extremely limited. And yet nothing that she said to me indicated that she was not imaginatively exposed to the world. She projected. I think the ability to project into is precisely what makes humans human.

**Q:** Is the value of your experience then a personal or a professional one?

**A:** A personal one. The only way for me to live is to be as close as I can to other members of the race. And nothing else interests me really. I have no other passions. The only moment when I feel truly euphoric is when I can either match my experience against the experience of someone else, or someone else's experience does to me what ideally I would want my fiction to do to others.

**Q:** Contact with people is then the basis of your experience?

**A:** Yes. It triggers in me something which is a moment of ultimate joy. This is what I love more than anything, and I'm willing to do a lot for it. My whole life has been centered around looking for such a moment, a moment in which my life is suddenly synthesized.

**Q:** Is this the same kind of feeling you have when you write?

**A:** Very much the same. It is a sudden feeling that however peculiar one's life might have been, there's someone else who understands it. When you create a fictional character, he becomes a bridge between your experience—extremely idiosyncratic—and that collective experience which you feel you have reached.

**Q:** By tapping into it in some way?

**A:** Yes. This is something of which I'm absolutely convinced. That if one writes, one writes not because one is different from others but because one feels an enormous kinship with others.

**Q:** Do you keep someone in mind as you write?

**A:** I don't have to. If I keep myself in mind, I already, by implication, keep a lot of others. My experience is really in no way peculiar. It's general, and from time to time it has to be merely stated, or restated, so that others can respond to it.

**Q:** But Jerzy Kosinski's stories are not your average, run of the mill stories. There is a universality in them, but you go out and find things that most of your readers never do.

**A:** I think that the nature of the middle class experience is basically to limit people to certain patterns of thought, certain patterns of belief, to certain exposure, no more. I think the purpose of fiction therefore is to tap what is already implicit in the culture but which the culture for some reason refuses to open.

**Q:** You feel that everyone could see, firsthand, what you see?

**A:** It is very often that they have not been exposed to it. They may not even have been alerted that all they have to do is step a bit more to the left or a bit more to the right or to pause for a while. They will find exactly the same thing.

**Q:** Is the purpose of your fiction, then, to make them pause?

**A:** This is the purpose of all art. It has always been the purpose of art. That's why we have a painting in the gallery, and we hope that those who pass will stop and look at it. I think the principle of art is to pause, not to bypass. The principle of true art is not to portray, but to evoke. This requires a moment of pause—a contact with yourself through the object you look at or the page you read. In that moment of pause, I think, life expands. And really the purpose of art, for me, of fiction, is to alert, to indicate, to stop, to say: make certain that when you rush through you won't miss the moment which you might have had, or might still have. That is the moment of finding something which you haven't known about yourself, or your environment, about others and about life.

**Q:** And this requires that you are perpetually looking for such moments?

**A:** In myself as well, since I'm no different, the tendency is to rush through. I'm already 44. This passed very quickly. Some of the passing was due to a marching column. It was not, perhaps, my fault. I did my very best to get out of the marching column, and I did at the age of 24. I regret that I wasn't able to do it earlier.

**Q:** How did you escape a police state when millions of people have not been able to escape?

**A:** Well, most members of my generation were exposed to an enforced contact with a certain reality that was not part of our natural upbringing: the second World War. Your nanny in a middle class family was replaced by solitude, by escape, by freezing, by hunger. You realize at the age of six or seven that you can do very well without your family. Two years later you don't even remember your parents. You begin to grab experience the way you grab food. It makes sense: new places mean safety, you're not known there.

**Q:** Did you share these sentiments with your generation?

**A:** We had, in common, the fear of regimentation, the fear of indoctrination, a fear of being limited in choices. These are all forces which I consider the most deadly. There's nothing I fear more than not being able to be myself. In this sense, I think I am very much like those I remember.

**Q:** You left many of them behind, though.

**A:** Many of those I remember wanted to get out but couldn't. They may not have been able to because they were not bright enough, or they were intelligent but in a very specific way that prevented them from exercising more general options. Or, they got involved—in specific conditions. They may have been married, or too attached to their parents, many were crippled. And the ultimate threat was that of a new society in which all the values you have known may not be valid at all. It was a fear of the unknown.

**Q:** That didn't bother you?

**A:** I was, like many others, willing to get out no matter what the price. We knew what was in store for us was not worth waiting for anymore. We had seen it, we detested it. It was the ultimate enemy of how we perceived ourselves. I'm asked quite often whether I left the Soviet orbit because I hated communism, and I quite honestly answer no. I hated myself in it. I felt my life was wasted, and so my duty was to get out.

**Q:** Do you think that having English as a second language has helped your understanding of it?

**A:** What an acquired language does, more than anything else, is it allows you to come to terms with yourself much more. The early experience of my life took place in Polish and Russian. When I was 25, I could communicate in English relatively easy and suddenly I discovered an enormous sense of freedom.

**Q:** I'm fascinated. You moved from one culture to another, and even within this one there are different worlds. Have you remained the same?

**A:** Well, I was greatly assisted by the German invasion.

**Q:** Granted. But you seem to be tapping into a very current theme. The thrust of the 1960s was a search for the absolute self through spiritual and meditational means. The religious revival, the Jesus Freaks, T.M., the Buddhists. If there's a comparable theme to the 1980s, isn't it that the absolute self is unreachable?

**A:** Because the absolute self exists only in relationship with others. Part of the American meditational culture of that period was that the self was perceived as some kind of independent ingredient, altogether outside of the supermarket. It's not outside of the supermarket. It's everywhere and it includes the supermarket.

**Q:** As the supermarket changes, do the people change?

**A:** I think the popular culture is a powerful force only for those who have given up already. I think the separation so many people feel from life, or from themselves, are basically very superficial covers. It doesn't take that much to get out of this, but not that many of us make an effort, I think. The popular culture runs away from the true condition. It tells us that the real threat comes from Jaws, or from the Deep, or from the Towering Inferno.

**Q:** Where is the real threat?

**A:** I'd say that the great thing about one's life is that the real threat is implicit in every moment. The purpose of art is not to do what the popular culture does but to undo it. That is to remind the man and the woman that we are temporary witnesses to our own life.

**Q:** You have talked about being euphoric when you come in contact with people, of enjoying the moment's threat. But your books leave your readers so often depressed.

**A:** The negative protagonist, the accident, the disaster, the illness, the menacing characters are far more important to make us perceive ourselves as we are than the very opposite. My books should make readers euphoric that, one, they are different perhaps from my protagonists; two, that they have met my protagonist only on a printed page, thank God; three, that if one day they meet someone like my protagonist they should welcome it, then avoid it.

**Q:** You're showing them something that could, or might, but hasn't.

**A:** Yes. If it crossed my mind, it may cross their life.

**Q:** God help them.

**A:** Not God help them, fiction help them. Being imaginative about one's life. Have I invented illness? Have I invented accidents? Have I invented terrorists? You might as well learn how to enjoy your own fear. The alternative is no better.

**Q:** How do you instill that sense of adventure in someone?

**A:** By reading an imaginative book, by being exposed to people whom you have no concept of. It takes an effort, and you take a chance. Good art prompts you to take such a chance, to make such an effort. You will make such an effort if good art tells you that your time is limited and that all that matters in life is perceiving yourself in a state of being alive.

**Q:** When you speak of a sense of adventure, then, are you really talking about pushing past a sense of fear?

**A:** Yes, or embracing it. Fear of rejection, of being unloved, of the unknown. But these are the very forces of life, the forces that do not threaten us after we are dead. Those who have not been exposed to it may have been born to unimaginative families. They may have not had an accident of any kind, no German invasion, no car crash, no sudden death, no being abandoned by a lover in the midst of what they felt was a rewarding relationship. It's enough to look around. I think most of the surprises, like most car accidents, happen just next to your home. It is the surprise of suddenly finding something that was not predictable in their existence.

**Q:** What is predictable?

**A:** That's just the point. The culture insists that there's a plot to one's existence. By saying that there is a beginning, a middle and an end, predetermined, it dismisses choices which we could and should make from day to day, from moment to moment. This moment is our life. I

am always especially upset when I meet someone—say a bridge con-
structor—who says he doesn't like what he does. I say, well why don't
you change it? He says, it's too late, I'm 33. We are, ironically, buried
in this kind of plot before any other.

**Q:** How does one avoid it?

**A:** When you are approached by someone who triggers the sense of
adventure in you, or the sense of life, I think you give in to it. It's just
that it doesn't happen very often. One has to work at it. It is like
reaching Martha's Vineyard. It's not a mere highway. You have to
change transportation. There's an effort involved: you do not arrive on
an island easily, and that's the whole point.

**Q:** But is there anything you would never do?

**A:** Yes. That stems from moral values. I accept the notion that
morality is to limit experience. I would never be imprisoned without
hope of escape. If I were to be used against others I would simply
remove myself, and I like to think I'm prepared to remove myself one
way or another from such an attempt. I would not consciously harm
anyone. I know that harming others means that eventually it comes back
at you. Our victim is in fact a replica of ourself. You start inflicting
pain, and eventually that means you lose the concept of pain yourself;
it means you are making yourself far more vulnerable.

**Q:** You would always have to be free?

**A:** Yes.

**Q:** Free from what?

**A:** Being free is actually to accept yourself as you are.

**Q:** Some people would say that that is the greatest kind of limitation.

**A:** Some people have a right to say it. This is still a free society. One
lives not by what some people say. As long as they are not free to arrest
me, I respect what they think, and I do what I have to do. It's my life.
Being free is accepting that regardless of what happens, one should
embrace it as part of one's condition. Regret and speculation are useless
complaints.

**Q:** Not because of any sense of fate.

**A:** No! Because of an absence of a sense of fate. The condition is
implicit. One is still free to feel free. To ponder. It could have ended a
long time ago. Who said it couldn't? But one becomes close to others
only when one is ultimately close to oneself. I always say to myself,
"Thank God that the critics are just as free as I am." Just as there are

many versions of human experience, there should be as many judgments pronounced upon it.

**Q:** What if *Blind Date* comes out and the critics say, "That's it, Kosinski's washed up."

**A:** Well, a lot of stones are washed up on the beach. They continue to function as stones. I'll be there, enjoying the sand, enjoying the waves.

# The Renegade Novelist Whose Life Is Stranger Than Fiction

Art Silverman/1977

Published in *Berkely Barb* 25 November–1 December 1977:8–9.

In order to appreciate the cruel, ironic, perverse yet oddly moral world of Jerzy Kosinski's novels, one must first come to terms with the random successions of joy and grief, fantastic wealth and dire poverty, human kindness and senseless brutality that have made his own life even more fantastic than his fictional creations.

He has lived under Nazi fascism, an orphan roaming the battlefields of Eastern Europe, surviving only by sheer luck and the natural grace of children (though now he claims to have never been a child). At the age of nine, in 1942, Kosinski lost his speech, not to utter a word for more than four years.

Rescued from an orphanage, half-mad, the young boy was reunited with his family after the war. He regained his voice while hospitalized following a serious skiing accident at age 14; then promptly worked his way through high school in less than a year.

He has also lived under Soviet communism. After finishing two masters degrees in Poland, Kosinski was dispatched to the Soviet Union as a promising scholar and photographer for doctoral studies. But his intellectual aptitude was coupled with unacceptable ideas, and the young man fell into political disfavor. In 1957, feeling himself close to arrest and imprisonment, Kosinski decided to escape to the West.

Using his photographic expertise he forged documents, created the fictional identities of four government officials, then used these officials to grant him a passport. He arrived in New York in December 1957— 24 years old, $3.80 in his pocket, speaking not a word of English.

Jerzy settled in the boiler room of the YMCA and taught himself the language in four months by memorizing a Russian-English dictionary and working as a projectionist in a movie theater. After short stints as a Teamster truck driver and chauffeur to a Harlem drug dealer, he

successfully applied for a Ford Foundation fellowship in 1958 and
enrolled at Columbia. In 1960 Jerzy Kosinski published his first book
under the pen name Joseph Novak. *The Future Is Ours, Comrade* was a
non-fiction critique of the Soviet Union. It was also an instant hit, serialized by *Reader's Digest*, and Kosinski was suddenly $150,000 richer.

But even that wealth paled when he received a fan letter and an
invitation to dinner from Mary Weir, the beautiful young widow of
Ernest Weir, multi-millionaire founder of the National Steel Corporation. They fell in love, married, and for six years Kosinski lived on
private yachts, chartered airplanes and in secluded villas. His own
considerable income was spent on clothing and tips.

During this time Jerzy wrote his first and most famous novel—*The
Painted Bird*, a fictionalized version of his own childhood and an
attempt to come to terms with his past. A second nonfiction work, *No
Third Path*, was also written shortly after his marriage.

Mary Weir Kosinski fell ill and died of brain cancer in 1966 after six
years of marriage. Kosinski's second novel, *Steps*, was near publication;
a "plotless" series of encounters between the protagonist and his environment in a variety of extraordinary circumstances. *Steps* won the
National Book Award, firmly establishing Kosinski in the front ranks
of American novelists.

But another tragedy was not far behind. On August 7, 1969, Jerzy
was preparing to return from Paris to visit the California home of his
close friend, director Roman Polanski. Polanski himself was filming in
Europe, but Jerzy was going to visit his old pal Wojciech Frykowski,
who was living at the Polanski house along with Sharon Tate,
Polanski's pregnant wife, hair stylist Jay Sebring and coffee heiress
Abigail Folger.

Due to an airline mixup, Kosinski's luggage was mistakenly sent to
New York instead of Los Angeles, so he remained in New York
overnight to straighten out the mess. That same night the Polanski
household was invaded in a horrible bloodbath by five of Charles
Manson's followers. Steven Parent, a bystander, was also murdered—
the police initially thought his corpse was that of Kosinski, who had
telegraphed his impending arrival.

Jerzy turned to teaching next, at Princeton and Yale. Under the terms
of Ernest Weir's will he was completely excluded from any of the family fortune after Mary's death.

In 1971 he published a third novel, *Being There*, the widely-acclaimed story of Chance the Gardener, a nobody. Through an outrageous series of events, Chance the Gardener becomes Chauncey Gardiner, industrialist, advisor to President Kennedy, and eventually himself a candidate for vice president of the United States. *Being There* is a book about the terrors of television and its subversion of our ability to think for ourselves. The critics thought it a delightful change of pace from his earlier, darker novels. Kosinski thought "it is the cruelest book I have written."

From 1973 to 1975, Jerzy Kosinski served as president of PEN, an international watchdog of writers' freedoms similar in purpose to Amnesty International. In 1973 he published a fourth novel, *The Devil Tree*, about the restless and rootless wanderings of Jonathon James Whelan, a young American of vast inherited wealth. His fifth book, *Cockpit*, appeared in 1975, concerning the adventures of a retired secret agent called Tarden.

No longer teaching, Kosinski winters between books in Switzerland, where he pursues his passion for skiing. Last week he came to San Francisco promoting his sixth and just-released novel, *Blind Date* (Houghton-Mifflin, $8.95).

*Blind Date* is the story of an American, George Levanter, a self-described "small investor" who travels the world in search of experience. When vengeance is required, he is a one-man judge, jury and executioner; but he is also a rapist who allows his closest friend to be punished for his own crime. He engages in blackmail; then is himself blackmailed into betraying his lover on behalf of her husband.

Many real figures appear in Levanter's life: Charles Lindbergh, French biologist Jacques Monod, Stalin's daughter Svetlana, the president of an African republic, the United States secretary of state, the late actress Sharon Tate and others.

We began an hour-long interview with Kosinski by inquiring about the way in which he interweaves fiction with the facts of his own life:

**Barb:** All of your novels have been autobiographical in the sense that they contain large elements of your own life, yet that element is always interwoven: both with your imagination and with the real world, in a way that's almost journalistic. How do you determine that balance between the public and private realms?

**Jerzy Kosinski:** The ingredients of my life that you mention, particularly in *Blind Date*, belong to all of us. Charles Lindbergh, for instance, is not only my property. He is an image: the image of a hero, of a tragic man, of a misguided politician, of a great aviator. An archetypal figure.

The same goes for Jacques Monod: a scientist, a philosopher, a discoverer of DNA, the substance of life. His book called *Chance and Necessity* has, by the way been very influential for me.

As for Sharon Tate, she represents the environment of murder. Manson. Again, a collective property. That I knew the victims personally is only of secondary importance. I included them in the novel precisely because they are a collective property, and can therefore serve as instruments of what I'm after. They are the dramatic components of the collective psyche.

**Barb:** And your wife?

**Kosinski:** That's exactly why my now-deceased wife is in the book. Think of it! An encounter of a newcomer to this country with a very rich widow; that's what the stuff of great Hollywood stories has always been made of. A refugee comes in, and look who he marries—one of the richest women in the country. It was your property long before it actually happened to me.

**Barb:** Does that mean that we, your readers, are actively considered when you work?

**Kosinski:** Absolutely. What I need more than anything else when I write is the conviction that others could have written the same thing, because they see the world in fundamentally the same way as I do. And, conversely, that I could change places with them. When I go back to my apartment to write my next novel, I see myself as representing a condition larger than my own. And I even censor myself: when I come across something in my own life, I ask "is this something marginal, idiosyncratic, individual?" If so, then I will not incorporate it.

**Barb:** I'm a little surprised to hear you say that you consider yourself as part of a community, albeit a small community. I'm even more surprised that you see yourself as responsible to that community. My impression of you has always been that of a loner, the intellectual cowboy; that your fondness of America, for New York especially— maybe in reaction to the early part of your life—was motivated by the wide open spaces, nobody messing in your business, freedom to come and go as you please.

**Kosinski:** Actually, the opposite is true. It is the totalitarian system which separates you from the human condition. It insists that your place in society is measured by other yardsticks than your actual life. The drama is imposed from the outside—the failure, the success, the pain, the pleasure are all given to you by the state. There I saw myself as an isolated cowboy. I was a photographer, a lonely man, locked in the darkroom by himself, for his own sake.

I don't like to part too easily with the image of the cowboy—it suits my threatened masculinity. But it is here that I can feel part of the human condition.

New York for me, like all America, is an enormous human factory. I love it. I go to it. I live in the center, because I love people and human experience. In fact, that's all that I like. I have no other hobby.

**Barb:** But as you yourself have often pointed out, Americans have no more free will than the Russians do. We are fed by the television instead.

**Kosinski:** But you make that choice.

**Barb:** Do we really?

**Kosinski:** Oh, yes. Most people here have lost their sense of choice, their sense of life even; they feel that they have been predestined to live a certain way. The idea that all it takes to change your life is the will to change it is probably very foreign to them.

**Barb:** But a cage in your own consciousness isn't all that different from a cage in reality, is it? Both are prisons.

**Kosinski:** That's very true. But they can still get out of it if they want to. Let them read my books, and maybe some of them will pop out of it.

**Barb:** What is there in your novels to encourage that kind of response? You seem to assiduously avoid that kind of moral instruction.

**Kosinski:** I don't provide easy moral judgments. Those judgments, in my novels, come to us as they come in life. You have to make them; I'm not going to give them to you. You judge the protagonist in one of my novels the same way you judge people in life—you observe their acts, you listen to what they say and you make up your mind.

**Barb:** On a slightly different subject, those of us who are writers are very interested in the way you work. Do you just churn it out, or do you rewrite and revise page after page?

**Kosinski:** I revise page after page after page, but I'm not a bleeder. I enjoy it. I change my galleys, and even change my page proofs, for

which they bill me and it gets very expensive. But I don't mind. I like
to change things. It makes my publishers unhappy, but I change them
often enough too.

Writing for me is no different than the rest of my life. It's the same as
what I'm doing here with you. Part of me is engaged in listening and
answering, and part of me is observing it happen.

I like to write, and I have completely incorporated it into the rest of
my existence. I can do it anywhere. I have no writing habits, no beloved
typewriter, no particular type of pencil.

**Barb:** Despite the critical acclaim your novels have received, you
have yet to achieve the mass market audience that many inferior writers
have. Does this bother you, and do you think it's inherent in the kind of
books you write?

**Kosinski:** I think that I am a marginal writer among novelists, and
that reading fiction is a marginal activity to begin with. It belongs to
those whose curiosity about society and themselves hasn't been easily
satisfied. It's also a very private enterprise: reading a novel is probably
the most private event known to our imagination. You have to recreate
something that doesn't really exist, except on a page, and yet there's a
whole world implicit in the language. It's highly abstract, and nothing is
set for you. You read it on your own terms.

Movies and television, they set everything for you. They render you
passive. The novel is completely the opposite activity.

**Barb:** Is that why you have refused to allow your novels to be made
into films? There is a rumor that your friend Roman Polanski bought the
rights to *Painted Bird* and is sitting on it.

**Kosinski:** That's not true. I own all the rights to my books, and the
reason that there are no movies is that I refuse to sell to the movies. My
novels are not meant to be films. They are meant to be decoded; they
are meant to be seen as you see things when you read them. You provide your own protagonist: I don't need Clint Eastwood.

Also, my protagonists are extremely internal characters. They are in a
process of continual self-definition. They are caught in various ambiguous situations—sexually, morally, economically—that cannot be
portrayed in one easy visual act. It's not a matter of entries and exits,
not even a matter of setting. The reasons for what they do are com-
plicated.

**Barb:** I know that you have had something like 1200 different offers for film projects, and it is a tribute to your integrity as an artist that you have turned them all down. But isn't there another reason? I read somewhere that you dislike the idea of filmmaking because it is a collective endeavor.

**Kosinski:** That's quite true. I like fiction because it is a private act. I'm never contracted in advance. I don't have an agent. If you ask me about my next novel I can tell you only what I know: I might or I might not write it. I'm free not to.

A movie is a collective endeavor: it's a studio; it's someone else's money; it's somebody else's talent, or absence of talent. I escape collective situations because they dilute responsibility, they corrupt in many ways and reward in many ways. I don't really like to go back to that. I might someday, but I hope I won't.

**Barb:** But what about your presidency of PEN? Not only is that a collective situation—running an international organization—but it is also decidedly political in nature.

**Kosinski:** I saw my function in PEN as one of service to the community which I use, the community of writers, a community of which, well, I'm a part. I saw myself contributing to this community the experience of one who has known the other side—the lack of freedom, the bureaucratic oppression—and who managed to counteract it. I saw myself as giving, in exchange for what I have very graciously received.

And I very carefully limited my actions. As the president of PEN, I didn't do anything that I wouldn't have done as an individual. Whenever there was something I found objectionable I took it to our board of directors—40 men and women—and they voted and made a decision.

This is a good example of creative collectivity, which in no way infringed or invaded my sense of responsibility for my own life, or what I like to think is my very specific set of moral convictions.

**Barb:** So why do you despair of political activity in a more general sense? You seem to be equally distressed by the excesses of the left and the right—although you are more ambivalent about this country . . .

**Kosinski:** No I'm not. I think America is more ambivalent about itself than most countries. Most of the other countries I know have already frozen their political makeup, their bureaucratic structure and economic hierarchies. America is fluid.

**Barb:** Between what and what?

**Kosinski:** That's difficult to say. I have the feeling that the U.S. is

moving in basically the same direction as the rest of the western indus-
trialized states: rigid control of the individual. Not so much for political
reasons as for economic reasons. Not by a total party, but perhaps by a
total corporation.

Those are the forces that terrify me here. Those are the forces that
I try to counteract. My fiction is basically about individuals who defy
social pressure, who insist on defining themselves in an act of being
alive—not in an act of being socially defined.

**Barb:** One element in the personality of many of your protagonists,
and it holds true for George Levanter as well, is an inability to give of
themselves, to form attachments. In fact, there is a fear of making those
kind of commitments to other people. Where does that come from?

**Kosinski:** It comes, I think, from the realization that human attachments are ambiguous. By their very nature they are crude symbols.
Marriage is a crude symbol. To become a lover—the phrase itself is
awfully dismissing. What does it mean? It involves a whole way of life,
a whole way of thinking. Endless emotions and emotional states.

My protagonists, mistrusting society and its ready-made formulas,
also mistrust relationships, just as they mistrust the apartments in which
they live, their neighbors next door, their credit cards.

This doesn't mean that they are negative about it. They are mistrust-
ful because they realize that human understanding doesn't come in a
*Magnum Force*, or in an *Encounter of the Third Kind*. It comes in an
extremely ambiguous form, known as an ambiguous social and human
condition—in which sexuality, morality and politics are profoundly
complex acts. They cannot be easily dismissed by forming an
attachment.

**Barb:** But the tenor of his relationships seems to be a desire for
surrender of the other partner to him, but complete detachment in the
reverse. A one-way street.

**Kosinski:** If, from time to time, some of my protagonists do exhibit a
manipulative trend, I think they get defeated. Take, for instance, the
man-woman relationships, even though there are many in my novels
that are homosexual.

Most of my female protagonists are just as menacing as my males.
They want to manipulate, and they also get beaten down. They get the
same kind of character back. So there is a democracy of motives on
both sides of the sexual spectrum, and everywhere in between.

**Barb:** Are you saying that you're a feminist?

**Kosinski:** To a degree. Yes. I think it's an extremely beneficial state of awareness, for men and for women. Anything which polarizes the spectrum, which renders it more ambiguous, which destroys the existing myths, should be welcomed with open arms. We are doomed, I'm afraid, by watching the three deadly channels of stereotypes.

**Barb:** So what about the future? You say that America is coming closer to the Soviet Union, dehumanization is on the increase every-where . . . and yet you preclude the possibility of organizing against it, because inherent in the idea of organization are the seeds of everything you oppose. Where are things heading?

**Kosinski:** Well, I think what is needed more than anything else right now is an individual aware of his place or her place in society. I find such a man, and such a woman, the only antidote to an oppressive state—whether it comes from a computer-oriented technology or a totalitarian political party. My mistrust of collectivity stems from precisely what you mention: it tends to dilute individual responsibility.

I think American society is composed of a great many individuals who have lost the sense of their identity, which makes them very likely victims of an oppressive corporate state; or or an oppressive popular culture, which replaces ideology in this country, but is every bit as betraying.

I see Americans traumatized because there is no aspect of popular culture which will arm them against the very conditions of their lives which render them incapacitated so easily and so readily.

There is still time for many of them to reverse the trend, to set them-selves on a different blind date, so to speak . . . but very few of them, I think, are capable anymore of finding sources which point it out to them. The popular culture promptly incorporates anything subversive—be it a Kosinski novel or anything else . . . and turns it into a fad, which means to turn it exactly against its own roots, which were to stimulate and encourage awareness. Once prepackaged and sold, it does exactly the opposite.

The enemy, then, is the total state and the total ideology in the Soviet Union. For me, here, the enemy is the popular culture: *The Deep*, the *Towering Inferno*, the *Encounters of the Third Kind, Mr. Goodbar*, or at least the movie version.

From this point of view the future is bleak. It's just like the American highway: they call it a freeway, but as you in California know better than anyone else, it's not free any more. And what a way to go.

# The Psychological Novelist as Portable Man

Gail Sheehy/1977

The spidery figure in the driveway is a weekend guest at a relaxed country house on eastern Long Island. He is in no danger. He is among friends. Yet once or twice a day he slips out to the driveway and half-buries himself in the trunk of his convertible. Pulling out a variety of items, he examines and rearranges them, handling each one with such reverence that one imagines the contents to be rare minerals or perhaps high explosives.

Upon closer scrutiny, the observer will note that the items are quite pedestrian: canned foods, a drop-legged bed, nonalcoholic beverages, notebooks to write in and novels to read, cash, weapons (or what the owner refers to as "relative protection systems" the "strength of character" being the only absolute one), and an odd-looking, charred, one-quart can with holes punched in its sides and a wire loop for a handle. This, the owner will explain, is an item essential to survival without human help: a comet.

Few Americans would be in a position to know that a comet, a simple can, when packed with moss, bark, and damp leaves, and lighted, will serve as a stove to roast birds' eggs plucked from the nest, will repel insects and snakes, and—when swung in a broad arc so as to spew menacing sparks like a comet—it can even drive away savage guard dogs and undependable human beings. The owner spent a great deal of time with comets on his childhood odyssey during World War II through the backwoods villages of Eastern Europe.

All this and more travels with our protagonists on even the most innocuous of outings. One never knows from second to second when the need might arise to escape.

Jerzy Kosinski is his own law and his own survival. Dedicated to outwitting society in its every attempt to impinge on the individual, Kosinski works at being the utterly portable man. The trunk of his car is one of his many exits. They are always ready.

Plunging into the back seat of Kosinski's mind, we are in for a swift and startling ride. The driver is one of the foremost psychological novelists in the world (as well as the author of two books on collective behavior). The route he chooses, the hopes and perils he sees on his sightseeing trip through the human landscape, are as instructive as more traditional teachers.

Kosinski was born of Russian parents in Poland in 1933 and raised in both Russian and Polish. He came to the United States in 1957 at the age of 24, speaking almost no English, and rapidly became fluent in his adopted language.

Today, with millions of his novels in print, Kosinski is primarily known as the author of *The Painted Bird, Steps, Being There, The Devil Tree,* and *Cockpit. The Painted Bird* earned him status as an underground cult hero in the 60s; official recognition followed: the National Book Award (for *Steps*), the Award in Literature of the National Institute of Arts and Letters. His most recent novel, *Blind Date,* will be published by Houghton Mifflin this month. In the following conversation, Kosinski talks about the underlying psychology of his work.

**Gail Sheehy:** I think there is something in your protagonists that we fear to see in ourselves. What do you think that might be?

**Jerzy Kosinski:** They represent the essentially tragic condition of life: the condition in which our own conduct is often a spectacular mystery to ourselves, as well as to others. The mechanics of society are equally unpredictable, and its mass-managed consciousness is hostile to man's real aspirations, fears, and joys.

In *The Painted Bird,* a war-torn society turns against a boy. In *Cockpit* Tarden, a middle-aged, supertrained ex-intelligence agent, wages irreversible war against a mindless state and some of its institutions. *Steps* centers on sexual and moral entanglements; *Being There*, on the emergence of Chauncey Gardiner, a retarded character, via media-induced charisma. *The Devil Tree* portrays the inability of Jonathan Whalen, a young American heir to a large industrial fortune, to sustain his totality in a world of fragmenting values.

And now *Blind Date,* the story of George Levanter, a small investor who leads his life eminently aware of the overwhelming role of chance in each of his life's encounters. I realize that these are not readily digestible situations, but I would consider myself a fraud if I were to give my characters any other philosophy of life.

And yet I feel that putting an individual on a constant moral and emotional alert has a positive effect in that it heightens the sense of life, the appreciation of its every moment, the sheer miracle of existence in a basically hostile environment.

**Sheehy:** Do you have to experience threatening situations, as you did as a child, in Eastern Europe, to have that sense of "moral alert"?

**Kosinski:** I refuse to perceive myself and my life as threatened. Rather, I tend to see my life as being challenged by the forces which are implicit in the process of being alive.

**Sheehy:** But you intensify those challenges.

**Kosinski:** I intensify only my awareness of them. As a human being, I answer not only to reality but also to plausibility—to the plight of my imagination. Nothing bars me from perceiving my life as a series of emotionally charged incidents, all strung out by my memory—all dictated by chance, nature's true fantasy.

**Sheehy:** Why incidents?

**Kosinski:** An incident is simply a moment of life's drama of which we are aware as it takes place. This awareness and the intensity of it decides, in my view, whether our life is nothing but a barely perceived existence, or meaningful living. To intensify life, one must not only recognize each moment as an incident full of drama, but, above all, oneself as its chief protagonist. To bypass that moment, to dilute it in the gray everydayness, is to waste the most precious ingredient of living: the awareness of being alive.

That's why in my fiction I stress an incident, as opposed, let's say, to a popular culture, which stresses a plot. Plot is an artificially imposed notion of preordained "destiny" that usually dismisses the importance of life's each moment. Yet, that moment carries the essence of our life.

**Sheehy:** You've spoken about your six novels as part of a cycle exploring the relation of the individual to society. It would seem that if you were to create your own world, you would want to give the individual the greatest amount of power of will and of freedom and reduce the power of the state, the restraints of collectivity. Yet, many people want the various protections that society offers; so they often submit to restraints and relinquish many freedoms in exchange for such a collective protection.

**Kosinski:** This collective protection does not remove the threat of chance. With or without it, we are on a blind date with society, and the society promises a mutually rewarding encounter. To me such a promise is a lie. The institutions of society are objectively there, no doubt, but in terms of our private drama, they are nothing but a backdrop. We play our drama by ourselves, and when we finally exit, our play has come to an end.

**Sheehy:** Still, society is an immensely powerful illusion.

**Kosinski:** It certainly is. Most of us, by the time of adolescence, carry in our head a veritable totalitarian state of illusions and most of them suppress us. Take the sexual arena: our inner censor is far more powerful than all the combined real-life censors of the Western world. The two lovers on the solitary lover's lane more often talk and answer to their inner censors than to each other.

**Sheehy:** Your protagonists seem to call all the shots in their own lives.

**Kosinski:** If they do, it is because most of them are desperate to find out who they are. And if this requires freeing oneself from an outer oppression, then some of them have trained themselves to fend off the threat of society using complex bureaucratic means as well as camouflage, disguises, escapes, and so forth.

**Sheehy:** Those are all methods you yourself use.

**Kosinski:** Why not? I need the examples of my protagonists as much as they seem to have needed mine. Yet, my protagonists do not isolate themselves. They are adventurers but also self-appointed reformers of an unjust world: they interfere on behalf of the weak and the fallen and the disfigured. I see this as an important part of the philosophy of the self: you cannot be faithful to your own sense of drama in your life if you disregard the drama in the life of others—those right next to you.

**Sheehy:** Your novels ingeniously catch us in the trap of our knee-jerk attitudes to those born deformed, and the new novel is no exception.

**Kosinski:** George Levanter, the protagonist of *Blind Date*, is about to fall in love with a woman who, after surviving an early-childhood illness, had a normal-sized head, but whatever little was left of her body was shrunken to the size of a baby and disfigured. Well, I knew such a woman once (she is dead now), and I found her, her vision of the world, her entire experience, fascinating. She was one of the most wholesome, most alive, beings I've met. Because of her joy of life, she was able to acquire and to convey a range of feelings, fantasies, and observations few of us have and all could benefit by. But, in the eyes of popular culture, this woman and her experience would be, at best, out-landish and rudimentary.

**Sheehy:** You spoke once of the necessity of embracing your fears. Can you give me an example?

**Kosinski:** I think you start by imagining yourself in the very situation which frightens you. Hence, the enormous importance of imagination, our ability to project oneself into the "unknown"—the very "blind dates" of our existence. For instance, you are in the midst of playing tennis and suddenly you see yourself as not being able to play it ever again—a victim of a car accident, a crippling disease, old age . . . all possible, after all. In the moment of such a projection, you are at peace with both your own current condition and with a change this condition implies. You're true to yourself, and, by implication, to all of those who have failed—and who will never play tennis. You intensify your joy of the moment—your game of tennis—and you ready yourself for whatever might be, for the innumerable contingencies you might have to face in your life.

**Sheehy:** What do you think is the primary influence in your life that has caused you to feel a special compassion for those who fail?

**Kosinski:** Possibly growing up in Poland and the USSR, societies so ravaged by the war that during its five years, Poland, for instance, had lost one-fifth of its entire population. And if one out of five people died, bombed, murdered, exterminated, think of the remaining four—how many of them survived maimed for life, wounded, traumatized? All of Eastern Europe and Soviet Russia was, during and after the war, a battlefield populated almost entirely by incredibly damaged human beings. Throughout my school years, most of my fellow students were one way or another crippled by the war and its aftermath. Most of them suffered from serious physical and mental problems. I was no exception: from the age of nine, I was mute for several years.

**Sheehy:** No other functions were impaired?

**Kosinski:** I like to think they were developed to make up for the imposed silence. But when I look back at the years of that imposed silence, I have no complaints. They might have reinforced in me my belief that I should write: fiction is a silent process. Confronted as an adolescent by human misery of such staggering proportions, I found myself feeling privileged to be alive, to feel, to think, to be among people, to seek friends. I am 44 now, and I don't recall one single moment in my life when I saw myself as a victim chosen by fate, even though I remember being beaten, molested, ridiculed, punished, pushed around. I remember bleeding and vomiting and crying and suffering a lot of pain and looking for God to help me out, but what I remember above all is that in the midst of my misery, I kept seeing myself as merely one of a majority of people who suffered and were not happy— my oppressors included. Happy men don't waste their time beating and punishing others, I thought, and I kept imagining how unhappy those who caused my pain would be the day they realized how uselessly they lived the only life they had.

**Sheehy:** I wouldn't be the first to observe that next to the protagonists of your novels, you are probably your most interesting character. First of all, I wonder what you would have faced if you had not left Eastern Europe for America in 1957 when you were 24?

**Kosinski:** As a social scientist I would have continued to aim at preserving the sense of self in a totalitarian society which objects to such preservation. I would have tried to maintain an active inner life by becoming an artist, a photographer. I remember I used to call myself an inner *émigré*. I would have remained such an inner *émigré* all my life. For artistic expression, I would most likely have continued actively with the work I was doing as a photographer—never as a novelist.

**Sheehy:** Could you tell me why you chose photography?

**Kosinski:** It offered a temporary escape from politically infested social sciences—and a darkroom I could lock myself in. Also, as art, photography was less ambiguous than fiction and more open to general scrutiny.

**Sheehy:** When after you came to America and began writing in English, did you feel less, or more, articulate?

**Kosinski:** It was a great surprise to me, one of many surprises of my life, that when I began speaking English, I felt freer to express myself, not just my views but my personal history, my quite private drives, all the thoughts that I would have found difficult to reveal in my mother tongue. It seemed that the languages of my childhood and adolescence—Polish and Russian—carried a sort of mental suppression. By the time I was 25, an American, my infancy in English had ended and I discovered that English, my stepmother tongue, offered me a sense of revelation, of fulfillment, of abandonment—everything contrary to the anxiety my mother tongue evoked. Come to think of it, there is something ominous even in the phrase "mother tongue" and I utilized some of this linguistic experience in *Blind Date*.

**Sheehy:** "Mother tongue" appears to carry all the prohibitions and directions of one's infancy. . . . Have you ever heard of anyone else who has exchanged languages in a similar way?

**Kosinski:** I have. I have talked with some of my compatriots, writers, film-makers, and other artists who in midlife emigrated from Eastern Europe and have been forced to embrace English, French, or German as their second language. Like me, most of them profess to be creatively freer in the adopted language.

I have taught at Princeton, Wesleyan, and Yale, and I advised some of my students that to free themselves from that inner oppression they felt in English, they should consider settling in a foreign country and start to write in another language.

**Sheehy:** What is the purpose of fiction?

**Kosinski:** To engage the reader in a drama that is much more condensed and crystallized than the drama of our daily existence, yet made of the same ingredients: human beings in a state of interaction, of conflict. I believe that through this process, the reader's awareness of his or her life—as a drama—is increased. As we tend to perceive our life in a "diluted" way, fiction—good fiction, anyhow—counteracts that by "dramatizing" it. It insinuates that we, like the fictional characters, can also have a position of relative importance, of certain mastery vis-à-vis our life.

**Sheehy:** Suppose the reader rejects your vision of life as drama?

**Kosinski:** The purpose of fiction—of any art—is above all to evoke a concrete dramatic response: to accept the artist's vision *or* to reject it. My fiction aims at acceptance very democratically; it does not place itself *above* the reader by insinuating the novel's "moral" and providing the judgment. As in ordinary life, it is the reader who, in the act of reading, judges the fictional events and the characters as they come by. The moral is, of course, implicit in any encounter—whether with a fictional protagonist or with real heroes or villains.

Fiction doesn't propagandize or advertise—it merely evokes; thus, to generate a moral judgment in a reader is yet another didactic purpose of literature.

**Sheehy:** Isn't your fiction, then, rather demanding on the reader?

**Kosinski:** If it is, so is life. After all, life is not only demanding but, like a novel, also ends. To me, the formidable purpose of life is to perceive it as drama plotted not by design, but by chance concurrently with each event of life (not prior to it), and oneself as its central protagonist. That's why the importance of strong fiction that mobilizes imagination, calls forth emotion. The popular culture renders us passive; most of our novels, television, and films tend to distract rather than to confront us by being true to our emotional and physical environment. And how often these days does anybody shake us up? I think literature is the last surviving awakener, the last form of art which still requires a profound effort from within.

**Sheehy:** Do you think of yourself as having a spiritual life, having a belief?

**Kosinski:** I guess I simply worship feeling alive.

**Sheehy:** But you would not feel uncomfortable calling it a force given by God?

**Kosinski:** I'm not preoccupied by the giver; I am preoccupied with the gift. And I'm immensely grateful to the previous owners, my parents, both of whom are, sadly, dead.

**Sheehy:** In the last few years can you evoke a time, a moment, when you felt most intensely alive?

**Kosinski:** I have such moments during most days of my life. I think the advantage of the imaginative life is that when reality slackens, at any time you can summon up some of these strong images—memories, fantasies, stories by other writers—that can speed it up.

**Sheehy:** You can be lying on the beach and you can summon up these images?

**Kosinski:** Certainly. Today, for instance, on the beach, I tried to recall all the beaches I lay on in the past. I wondered why is it that three of my novels end with an image of a large body of water. . . .

**Sheehy:** Water is not a comfortable element for you.

**Kosinski:** I guess the world has not been created as my water bed. I wondered about it today: I was traumatized by water many times. Once, as a child, I was pushed under ice and barely survived. I recalled a lot of other moments of panic and terror when suddenly submerged. In the moment of recalling these moments, I was petrified again—and promptly reassured that I was on the sand, quite safe, and among friends, all very good swimmers, none of whom would want to drown me. I guess that's what I meant by summoning dramatic images, a fusion of memory, fantasy, and emotion, without which that might have been a dull hour in the sun next to a terrifying ocean.

**Sheehy:** Some people say that the protagonists of your novels are so preoccupied with death, terror and violence that they must be paranoid.

**Kosinski:** If paranoia is a delusion, a broken bridge to objective realities, then to me the culture that systematically refuses to be realistically concerned with the place of terror and violence in our proper life is paranoid, not a character who chooses to acknowledge its dimension in our life.

The leading causes of death in America today are heart disease, motor-vehicle accidents, cirrhosis of the liver, and suicides. Yet, do you know of any major film, TV series, or a fictional potboiler that would address itself to those subjects? Is heart condition so much less dramatic than *The Deep?* A motor car, America's most potent killer, less frightening than *Jaws?* Isn't alcohol our real-life *Omen?* Cigarette smoking the *Towering Inferno?* No wonder only 24 percent of the total U.S. population knows what hypertension actually means! Of people with hypertension, only 33 percent knew what it was. And is it a wonder that over 22 percent of Americans believe in astrology? That one-half of all hospital beds in the United States are devoted to psychiatric patients! And that, in some of our mental hospitals, the ratio of patients to psychiatrists is over 200 to one!

As it goes along, popular culture develops its own audience. People who enjoy certain shows are going to enjoy these very shows in an even cruder form when they grow older: the stuff of imagination diminishes faster than all other natural resources and is progressively so diminished that to satisfy it, even cruder and cruder entertainment is needed. If you look at the content of most of the television shows and popular films as opposed to the films of the American 30s and 40s, you will find a staggering reduction of true concern for what makes life human.

**Sheehy:** You have looked at the world from both ends of its ideologies: Soviet totalitarianism and American capitalism. Also from both ends of its class ladder. When you first arrived in this country, with no English, you were scraping ships, cleaning bars, parking cars, chauffeuring in Harlem. You were a truck driver and lived in the YMCA. By 1962, in four short years, you became a known author, you met and married a woman who was one of the largest taxpayers in the United States. Then, until her death 10 years ago, you lived in the environment that this tax bracket provided. At which end of your experience of fear or freedom, rich or poor, did you find the greatest sense of being alive?

**Kosinski:** At both ends—and in between. As I have no habits that require maintaining—I don't even have a favorite menu—the only way for me to live was always to be as close to other people as life allowed. Not much else stimulates me. I have no other passions, no other joys, no other obsessions. The only moment when I feel truly alive is when, in a relationship with other people, I discover how much in common we all share with each other. Money and possessions—I care little for the first, hardly for the second—were never necessary to experience life as I live it. As greatly as my wife, her wealth, and our marriage contributed to my knowledge of myself, of America, and of the world, they contributed just so much—no more, no less—as all other moments have contributed to my curiosity about myself, others, society, art—and to my sense of being alive.

Of course I've always known moments of loneliness when I felt abandoned, rejected, unhappy—but, in such moments, I also felt alive enough to ponder my own state of mind, my own life, always aware that at any moment this precious gift of awareness of the self might be taken away from me. That state of awareness has always been, to me, less a possession than a mortgage, easily terminable.

Perhaps that's why, in the 60s, in the midst of the affluent existence my marriage had provided, so much removed from the misery I'd once known, living in secluded villas, flying in private planes, floating on custom-built boats that turned the world into one's playground, I sat down to write *The Painted Bird,* a novel of an abandoned boy in the war-ravaged, small pocket of rural Europe, which I remember so intimately.

**Sheehy:** Perhaps the picture you had of the world inside and outside at the age of 12 continues to supply your picture of yourself as an adult.

**Kosinski:** The war was my kindergarten, my introduction to modern society and its capacity for a senseless destruction and terror. What I witnessed and lived through as a child and then as an adolescent in a Stalinist society might have been responsible for the respect I have for the individual—total state's first victim. All my novels, really, are about conscious or unconscious victimization—our mental traits, our customs and mores—by the institution of society and the individuals who fall prey to them.

**Sheehy:** Do you think that Americans are used by corporations, by educational systems, and by our governmental institutions in ways they don't recognize? Or that we submit to being so used because the rewards are so plentiful?

**Kosinski:** Not the way they would be used in a totalitarian state but, to a degree, yes: we are all used. One recent poll established that about 70 percent of American businessmen admit they have been expected, on occasion, to compromise personal principles in order to conform to corporate standards. Almost 30 percent said that increased strain and business tension have hurt their health. Some of these businessmen are undoubtedly victims of a popular culture that for years has insisted that one's career is one's only "given" plot, a sure way to counter and even to avoid unpredictability in life, the dangers of old age, and so forth. In dismissing the possibility of many choices which these businessmen could and should make from day to day, by discouraging change, by playing up fears and insecurities of growing old, the popular culture has helped to dehumanize their predicament even faster.

**Sheehy:** How can we start cleaning up our own psychic cupboard from the unholy influence of the popular culture?

**Kosinski:** A very difficult task. Whenever an authentic quest for life's meaning spontaneously emerges on the margin of American life, the popular culture—whether political, social, psychological, or literary—in pursuit of an easy box-office success or best-sellerdom or high ratings, packages and sells it. The guest becomes yet another entertainment commodity, as dispensable and replaceable as merchandise, and in time is replaced by another effortless cultural fad. Many Americans seem by now no less indoctrinated by the Pollyanna values of their popular culture than are, let's say, their Russian counterparts by the decades of dehumanizing ideology of omnipotence of the Party.

**Sheehy:** As a result of entering your 40s, have you noticed certain changes in your perspective?

**Kosinski:** I certainly have, thanks to practicing sports—skiing and, more recently, horseback riding. I constantly notice my body's inability or refusal to carry out certain sustained or more elaborate efforts, even though my brain seems to be quite capable of projecting and demanding them in great detail.

**Sheehy:** Do you find you are becoming less dispassionate as you grow older?

**Kosinski:** More compassionate, more attentive to the voice of life and more forgiving of its various failures, in myself as well as in others, but also more critical of a society so cruel to the old, sick, infirm. And I begin to perceive certain periods of my past, like certain skiing tricks I used to perform, as not available to be reproduced by me anymore. From now on, they will reside in me only as memory—and as a play of my imagination. Nostalgia and sentimentality—this is new.

**Sheehy:** Sentimentality?

**Kosinski:** Yes. Once, I considered it merely a mood undefined. To be sentimental was not to be clear about oneself or others. Now I feel it as a minor but necessary shade, a mixture of regret and of desire.

**Sheehy:** In *The Painted Bird,* you presented a wandering boy whose demeanor caused others to believe that he possessed magical powers, that he was able to cast evil spells on others. In your own life, you sometimes take on this persona and like to convince others that you are casting spells on dogs you don't like, children who invade your privacy, or adults who betrayed your trust.

**Kosinski:** Art is about casting spells. Every artist should believe in his or her power to spellbind us long enough for the work of art to slip new awareness into our commonplace existence. If there is magic to art, there must be—shouldn't there be?—a mystery to the artist. I am very possessive about my powers to cast spells and if indeed I cast them, I do it seldom—at a misbehaving horse, a playful friend, or an unsuspecting but willing reader.

# Conversation with Kosinski
Patricia Griffin/1978

Published in *Texas Art Journal* 1(1978):5–11.

This world unwinding on its reel is composed of sounds: constant clinking, metallic clatter, the fitful crash; broken syllables, an intermittent mechanical rasp. From this babble voices detach themselves. Fragments of distant conversations emerge. A loudspeaker makes its pronouncements about cars and telephones. An interview is in progress. This world has no voice, but speaks in many tongues, not all of them intelligible.

"What are you doing now?"

"Talking to you."

One voice is hesitant, a little shy; it occasionally trips over words or subsides into the inaudible. The other is energetic, intense, impressively articulate. Much of the time one need only listen.

"You were saying that speech is an event."

"I am aware when I write that speech is a dramatic unit; even in *The Painted Bird* where dialogue doesn't appear, speech is an inner dialogue. The external being is silent. The child is both mute and muted— and ambiguous in the sense that he claims to himself that if he would *want* to speak he *could* speak, but really he doesn't want to because that is how he presents himself to himself. And when he meets the Silent One, the ambiguity between —the willingness to speak—and the muteness imposed by an accident—is habitually undenied, since the Silent One does not speak and does not want to. Isn't it so?"

In *The Painted Bird* Kosinski writes:

> The Silent One was older and stronger than I. At first we avoided each other. I felt that by refusing to speak he was mocking boys like me who would not speak. If the Silent One, who was not mute, had decided not to speak, others might think that I too was only refusing to speak but could do so if I wanted to.

Kosinski's concern with this kind of ambiguity persists in the other novels.

"*The Devil Tree* is a muted novel with various, highly fragmented, dispersed voices that form the narrative. Each dialogue is set as an independent event—external even to the participants in the conversation. In *Steps,* the man and woman exist as man and woman. The relationship exists on several levels, one of which is the language they use. This is stressed once again somewhere in the novel when the protagonist willingly abandons his idiom to become more natural and closer to other people who speak another language. But whether they speak to each other or not, he always feels that his language, his accent, his idiom set him apart from the sheer humanity of action—from the events of life as opposed to the events of speech imposed by language itself, by the syntax, by the vocabulary, by the collective thought implicit in each phrase, and so forth.

"In terms of the use of dialogue in my novels, *The Devil Tree,* I think, is the most complex of them all, and probably the most difficult to read. The speech serves occasionally merely to identify certain characters. We know them only by how they speak, not by who they are; the cemetery attendant, people who encroach on Whalen, are known to us only by how they phrase certain things. This can be connected back to *Steps* and back to *The Painted Bird.* Speech as a separate dramatic unit contains all the other ingredients, contains all society already in it. All social order is already implicit in how people address each other. *Being There* is almost entirely devoted to the ambiguity of our communications with each other."

For Kosinski language often indicates impotence, separation from either full engagement in one's own experiences or full participation in the human community. Jonathan Whalen, the protagonist of *The Devil Tree* insists "My impulse is not to speak or write, but to remain elusive;" for him language opposes freedom. "It [language] brings its own ordering," says Kosinski. "It brings ordering of emotion, ordering of time."

"And the whole impulse of the novel is toward the 'far side of communicable thoughts?'"

"Yes. To go to the origin of one's interests. Whalen says to somebody he'd like to return to the place beyond the words where the experience first occurs. That's the preoccupation of all my main characters, actually."

Hence its ending.

Likewise at the end of *Steps* the protagonist acts as a deaf-mute in
order to become closer to those whose language he doesn't know; again,
language is seen as separating him from the community. This use of
language obviously diverges from the traditional view which maintains
that speech is necessary to make the biological organism fully human,
and I try to think of an instance where Kosinski uses language to unite
people rather than to indicate their separation.

"Oh, I know! What about at the end of *The Painted Bird* where the
boy says it matters little if one is mute because people do not understand
one another anyway. But then his last act is to speak."

"Ah! Speaking on the telephone!

"And again the voice stands on its own outside of action and outside
of the people. The voice, leading to *Steps* then, becomes a fragment of a
connector, on its own, an independent existence. A fatherly love for the
son does not have to be expressed on the phone—and it's the father who
calls. His father calls, right?"

"I don't think you identify the caller. I think it's just a man's voice."

"Oh. In life it was my father."

"Did you refuse to speak when you were mute?"

"No, I couldn't. But I always pretended to myself that I didn't want
to. After all, who could tell? I was in charge of my own voice, hence I
was also in charge of my own muteness. I tried to avoid circumstances
in which I would be tested, forced to admit I was mute. I was selecting
situations where I wasn't, where gesture or silence would suffice."

I did not ask Kosinski how much of his life has gone into his fiction—or vice-versa. Certainly incidents in his fiction recall incidents
from his life (for example, his childhood muteness), but the extent to
which he uses his life as subject matter or the ways in which his life and
fictions connect remain for his biographer to analyze. Meanwhile stories
abound.

Many people, struck by the cruelty which is the most obvious
characteristic of Kosinski's writing, mistake the events he describes for
the man. Kosinski mentions he has heard of people refusing to attend a
dinner party on learning he was to be among the guests. At the party
following his public lecture, a man listened to him recount an incident
in which he killed a cat. The man spoke as if he were horrified, but his
real response was fascination; he sought out his companion, brought her
over to Kosinski, and asked him to repeat the story.

Was the story even true? Possibly, but when I listen to him I wonder where fiction begins. If his fiction sometimes follows his life, his life may in turn follow the fiction. Thus the protagonist of *Cockpit* has some military uniforms made for himself; the uniforms bear no insignia which would identify them with a particular nation or even with a definite rank, and yet when he wears them people step aside, defer. Kosinski also had some uniforms made for himself; he wears them occasionally, but only when he is in Europe. Life imitates art?

Then there are the squirrels. When he was teaching at Yale, students would, of course, come to his office to discuss their work, and sometimes he would find it awkward to end these conferences. Therefore he trained two squirrels. He brings a ruler to his forehead, and one squirrel leaps out of the bookcase, lands solidly on the desk, and disappears into the opposite wall; he raps his pen sharply on the desk, and another repeats the performance, only it leaps from a different position. By then the student believes he is beseiged by squirrels and leaves the room. Truth? Fiction? It makes a good story.

"I have another theory which you reminded me of. You said in one of your previous interviews that the purpose of your novels is moral; that it's to take everydayness and turn experience into adventure."

"Yes. The incident of daily living. The hour as the event of life. To intensify the reader's awareness of himself or herself and of the uniqueness of the time which passes by. The blind date with chance: the next moment."

"And the question I had was, do you believe in such a phenomenon as a Self because most of your protagonists aren't Selfs, they're different selves."

"The role of the protagonist is to trigger the sense of Self in the reader. Hence they cannot be overpowering. For one thing, they exist only indirectly; they exist through the reader's perceptions . . . they borrow a self from the reader to bring them to life. They have no existence outside of the printed page other than in the reader's mind, clearly. It is the reader who, ultimately, dominates the protagonist. Not the other way around."

"But what I'm getting at—I realize a character cannot have a self in that his identity is no more than the words on the page; and it seems to me that language, not speech but language, is what creates a character's self for the reader. But you seem to be working against yourself."

"I'm suppressing the over-exaggerated self of the author, but trying not to act against the self of the reader. The idea is to use the language in such a way as to draw the reader into the conflict of the characters— conflict which is not necessarily a conflict in the negative sense, a *relationship with* characters, perhaps—by making the character as idiosyncratic as possible and the text, the events, inner languages, the silence of the reader—to make the reader respond, to facilitate such response. I try to achieve this by suppressing *the text as fiction* (the voice of the author) and aim at *the text as event* (the voice of the protagonist). By silencing myself I bring the product of myself much closer to him."

"But do you silence yourself?"

"In the novels, I do. The characters and the action are deliberately defined only by the most essential means; by verb, not by noun; not by adverb or adjective; it's a highly verbal style which stresses action, not on adornment—a sort of a triggering rather than portraying. There is a constant paring down of the voice of the author—and of his presence."

"If one were to imitate your style, I think he would concentrate on images."

"Possibly."

"You wouldn't talk about the protagonist. In fact, the protagonist would be almost anonymous."

"That's precisely the point. By making each incident so visible, I want to invite the reader to become the protagonist. *He* has to identify himself with him. Hence the visibility of the situation—of the incident—serves to bring the reader *via* the protagonist into the incident. He is the voyeur watching the animal in *Steps*. *Cockpit*, for instance, addresses itself plainly to the reader; it starts with 'you.'"

Although Kosinski specifies that the setting for *The Painted Bird,* or *Cockpit,* is "Eastern Europe" or "Ruthenia," (not "Poland"), his readers will try to see his novels as, at least in part, autobiographical accounts of his own wartime and post-war experiences. At the panel discussion held the afternoon following our conversation, a young man asked Kosinski whether *Cockpit* did not in fact take place in Warsaw. "Warsaw!" Kosinski was incredulous, and the young man hastened to explain his reading. "Well—it does for you!" The reader makes his own novel from the text given him.

Moreover Kosinski accepts the reader's freedom to make of a book what he will; indeed, he exploits that freedom. "There is no morality other than the morality provided by the reader," he had said earlier in that afternoon's discussion. "I provide the situation to be judged— that's all. And in judging the situation, the reader judges himself." The artist's responsibility is finally moral; Kosinski regards himself as a didactic writer. Redemption, if it comes at all, will be found not in the work but in the reader.

"There are two things. One is that writing fulfills certain roles in my own private life, regardless of whether it is published or how it is received. This is something which I intend to keep; I like to write. It's a moment of manipulating my imagination, of manipulating my thoughts, the language. It's like playing backgammon for some people or bridge for others or gambling or developing photographs; I used to photograph when I was younger. And so it's a game between certain parts of myself and other parts of myself: Kosinski's temperament, which is basically disjointed and rather uneven, struggles against the structure of the language, which imposes discipline. This is the *agon* I keep for myself.

"When I was at the university in the U.S.S.R., there was a game we used to play. I don't remember who instigated the game—I would like to think that I did but I'm not sure. We were always travelling, twice or three times a week, on a train which would take us to a community where we had to talk to workers and entertain them; this was the Party's attempt to bring the students closer to collective farms. Now on this train peasants would travel to the marketplace, and when we—the students, the *intelligentsia*—talked to each other, the peasants, most of them, didn't understand what we were saying; the student's jargon was not readily accessible to the simple peasant. But from time to time I would start telling a story, and the peasants would listen. And eventually the peasants listened so much that they would occasionally forget to leave the train at their station.

"Someone then devised a game: we would bet on how many peasants would miss a station for a good story; if on a seven-station run we would start telling a story, I or someone else, who could keep the peasants from getting out at their station? It could be any story, but it had to be told, of course, in such a way that it would be of interest to us as well as to the peasants; some sort of common language had to be found. And I remember that I enjoyed this game very much. For one thing, I was curious about people and their relations to each other, I always have been. And I think because of my childhood, I had more in common with these peasants than with my fellow students. Later I didn't know, I couldn't tell whether I regretted that the peasants would miss their station or whether, in fact, I thought they benefited by learning something about themselves from the stories they had listened to.

"This is, I think, the other aspect, that in my relationship with people all I really want is to get their *incidents of life*. What fascinates me about you or about anyone is the same thing which makes me curious about myself. What is it that makes me afraid to die? What is the inner force that makes me want to go to tonight's interview or tomorrow's panel? What are and where do they come from, these forces which are often not even named or perceived by us, which are dormant. Now they can be hinted at and evoked only in an act of storytelling. When I ask you, where have you been studying, or what do you want from life, for an answer the culture provides either the silence or an answer-as-a-story about yourself. Or whatever you provide, you provide not in terms of a plot, but in terms of incidents in your life. There's simply no other way for us to communicate. Hence, the role for the artist—or a novelist— is to make visible a moment which without him or her would be less visible, or more often nonvisible. I would write regardless of whether my novels would be published or not. When I walk, when I listen to people, that's exactly what I do. I try to engage them in an exchange of what amounts to storytelling about themselves, about their life—their Self."

"This explains the form of your novels."

"Absolutely. I'm after incidents. I don't believe there is a central destiny to one's existence. I think a notion of such a destiny is a philosophical fraud. I think a plot is a device; a plot is a fraud of the same caliber to me as the statement, 'you will always live a happy life.' or 'learning a profession will make you a better man.' Statements of this sort are absolutely fraudulent; they mean nothing. They may be true, they may not be true; there's no way to verify them."

Literature's function, then, is predatory and redemptive; it captures the reader to restore him to himself. "I see the purpose of fiction as concentrating on the moment." Why? Because we tend to dismiss ourselves too quickly, says Kosinski. Art returns us to the moment, any moment, which is all the life we have.

"Do you see your place in American letters?"

"No. I don't see my place in even the building in which I live. I don't have a private address, I don't have a place where I live; I hardly have any belongings. I don't relate myself—I don't exist by connecting myself to anything as concrete as that. Rather, I exist by cutting myself off."

"And defining yourself in relation to?"

"Defining myself in relation to my own inner life. And, indirectly, to the community which is manifest, implicit already, in my life. And in the language I use."

"So you wouldn't be an American novelist, you would be a man who writes books?"

"I wouldn't even pause to think about such plots."

"I was just thinking of that collection *New Fiction,* which includes you among others."

"Well, I'm also listed in the Manhattan directory, and as an incorporated entity in the yellow pages, and with the I.R.S. I think one of the reasons I left Eastern Europe was precisely the very conscious denial to be forced to orient myself towards preexisting units, ideological units, societal units, political units, and that sort of artificial ordering of my existence."

"You're not at all a political novelist; and yet you're very much a political novelist."

"I am a political novelist in the sense. . . . "

"I was thinking of you as isolated in the sense that a storyteller is isolated."

"I'm isolated perhaps also in the sense that I'm very much preoccupied with the individual, the only unit of life I know. I don't think there is such a thing as families. A family is a group of individuals, and each one of them carries his own or her own life. Our families belong to us, not we to our families. And the only instances of anger I notice in myself when I am with people is when people are not aware of what is happening. When they dismiss their own life. And I will never show this. And I will never tell them this. But I feel the way I would feel, say, at a sight of a senselessly dying tramp—it's anger combined with a hopeless sense of loss. And I was very angry at my students very often; again, not willingly have I ever revealed it, but I had a sense that they were not aware of the hours which were passing by. I may be isolated in the sense that I refuse to deal with larger units; they are of no interest to

me, the individual is. That's the only carrier of life I know. And of
death. When the individual dies, the family doesn't die with him. The
tribe doesn't die with him. He or she definitely does die, though."

"One is not important enough not to be oneself. One might as well be
oneself—and after all, who cares?"

"My view is that to recoil, to reject, that's just as didactic as acceptance. The more you recoil, the more you withdraw to yourself. If my
fiction makes you rebel against it, you rebel against certain components
in yourself, and then you might be able to define yourself more clearly.
Thus, the purpose of art, of my art, is to a degree fulfilled. But it's not
enough just to read the title page or an outline. You have to go through
the entire story and then reject it."

"Your books call for an emotional involvement on the part of the
reader."

"And moral judgment—as a reader, involuntarily, you perform an act
of judgment. But that is the purpose of art anyhow, to purge the man of
dangerous emotions. One could add that today the purpose would be to
bring the emotions forth, to counteract the popular culture that systematically deadens them. Men may not be aware that there are emotions of
this sort anymore."

There is not much time.

"What are you doing now?"

"Talking to you."

"Do you find writing is a very slow process?"

"For me, very. But I don't complain, I think it ought to be. It's
organizing one's own psyche in a way. It cannot have the speed of a
thirty-second commercial. How do you spell relief? 'Rolaids'? A true
relief requires more than Rolaids.

I note that Kosinski uses skiing in many of his books.

"I think it is a natural activity. Skiing lends itself to my vision; that
is, it is societal to a degree, and yet it is solitary and it is mute. It's a
sport in which you usually don't talk or listen to anyone. Unlike many
sports which require some special knowledge, this one really doesn't—
it's generated by the law of gravity. You slide down. Which is in no
way man's invention really—you slide down even when you walk down
the hill—unlike baseball or rugby, which are invented and where nature
doesn't provide anything. Skiing is noncompetitive in a sense that you
don't collide with other human beings physically, you don't face

another being. Skiiers don't run into each other, the way rugby players do, say.

"Skiing is closest to walking. It's walking downhill really. Of all the sports I could use, skiing fits my fiction very well. This is, in fact, why I have chosen it in my own life as well, I guess. At the time I started to ski—I was thirteen—I probably didn't know it, but subconsciously or semiconsciously I embarked on it when I was a mute myself; by chance I've then chosen skiing as the only sport that fulfills me for the same purpose I select it now for my fiction, for some of my protagonists."

After the panel discussion, one of the students present came up to the instructor to show her Kosinski's signature slashed across his copy of *The Painted Bird*; beside the name was a face drawn in profile. "I wouldn't have known what it was if he hadn't told me." The young man was pleased.

"Frankly, I see my characters as being rather typical, and that is how I see myself as well. I know now some of you don't think we are—but wait a few years. You never know."

# My Books Are Weapons, A Blind Date with Jerzy Kosinski

Tom Teicholz/1978

Published in *East Side Express* 2 February 1978:11, 16–17. Reprinted by permisson of Tom Teicholz.

"What do you do, Mr. Levanter?" he asked.
"I do as I please." —from *Blind Date* by Jerzy Kosinski.

The door opened. I was surprised to see a woman at the door. Jerzy Kosinski's secretary. She explained that he would be right in and motioned me to sit in the study. His study was unpretentious and comfortable. On the walls I recognized the artwork that had served as covers for Kosinski's novels and photographs which I later learned Kosinski had taken at 17 on an emulsion of his own fabrication.

He entered, looking tan and well dressed in brown turtleneck and suede jacket, albeit a bit thin. He resembled the pictures on his dust-jackets more than I had expected. I asked permission to use a tape recorder. He refused:

"I feel more articulate when we just talk. With the machine you have a long transcript to work with, to edit . . . this way we just talk."

I was, though, encouraged to take copious notes. And if Kosinski's novels are unsettling, their author is the opposite. Throughout the interview I found him at ease and eager for me to be at ease, engaging, funny and helpful.

Too many of Kosinski's reviewers and interviewers are obsessed with the similarity between the man and his fiction. They talk of his childhood during World War II, like that of the protagonist in his first novel, *The Painted Bird*, 1965: of how he grew up in Communist Poland and studied in Russia, like the protagonists of *Cockpit*, 1975 and *Blind Date*, 1977: of how he escaped from Poland (see *Cockpit*) and came to America, at first doing odd jobs like scraping ship's hulls and parking cars (see *Steps*, 1968): of how in 1962 he married Mary Weir, the widow of the founder of the National Steel Corp (See *Blind Date*) and soon after began to write the novels we know him for. (Mary Weir Kosinski passed away in 1968.)

But of his books Kosinski says: "My relation to my books is no different than my relationship to my skis. I am responsible. There is no metaphysical relation. Whenever I re-read my works . . . I do so reluctantly. It makes me uneasy. Today I might have written certain things differently but . . . no apologies. I am responsible."

Control-taking, responsibility, is a major theme in Kosinski's work. Kosinski: "My novels are largely concerned with ambiguity: characters pondering motives . . . inner decision makers faced with moral and ethical decisions." His characters are free men living in the present. Free from economic want, in control of their potential, yet open to the unpredictability of human experience—they pass from one moment of heightened perception to another in a continuous fashion like a skier who glides from mogul to mogul making his way down the slope. They are Cartesian characters who say: "I am, therefore I act."

*Blind Date,* Kosinski's latest work, is the story of George Levanter, a small investor, an idea man. The novel is composed of "dramatic units" brief situations, encounters, anecdotes, stories. We see Levanter as rapist; extortionist; assassin; photographer; seducer; deceived lover. Charles Lindbergh, Henry Kissinger, and the Nobel Prize winning philosopher Jacques Monod—each figure as 'blind dates.' A large section of the novel is devoted to the Sharon Tate murder which Levanter (like Kosinski) narrowly misses attending.

Kosinski's protagonists do not live above the law: "My characters take the law into their own hands—in situations where no law exists . . . look at the hotel clerk in *Blind Date.*" (The clerk refers East European visitors to rooms in the hotel which are bugged and later relays the tapes back to officials in the East European country. For innocent conversations in hotel rooms, the visitors are later arrested, punished and imprisoned.) "What was the clerk's crime? Not so great. He gave out rooms, mailed tapes. But look at the consequences . . . The fencer, I call him JP in the novel, a national hero, imprisoned for 25 years! That is why Levanter acts."

Kosinski served for two years as president of the American Center of P.E.N., an international association of writers. Was his work frustrating? "Yes, of course, very frustrating. But I am allowed to make my

characters in my novels do what I, as president of P.E.N. could not do."
He smiled and added, "Maybe."

"In this way, my novels can be seen as weapons. Whenever a deputy
minister of a country like Indostran (in *Blind Date* Levanter, at a ski
resort, assassinates the deputy minister of Indostran, a fictional country
made to resemble any one of several republics where torture is common
fare) receives a complimentary copy of *Blind Date* with a beautiful
inscription, I've already sent out a few, and then reads the section
describing the deputy minister's assassination he will say 'This man is
crazy' but perhaps he will be a bit more careful when he goes skiing."

But even if Kosinski's characters are not above the law, they are
always free of a need for money. Why? "The advantage of being a child
of war is that war takes away predictability, takes away savings . . .
There is a democracy of destruction. For those of my generation of like
circumstances, life is not based on a cumulative notion, but rather a
notion of condensing experiences and relating it to the present.

"Money is a common artifact and so can't be difficult to obtain. My
message has always been: be creative. Extract enough freedom to work
as you wish and from work extract enough money to be free. Jonathan
Whalen in *The Devil Tree* says: 'I am my own event.' Tarden in *Cockpit*
says, paraphrasing Blake: 'I make my own system so as not to be under
any one else's system.' And George Levanter in *Blind Date* says: 'I am
an idea man. I do as I please.'

"Feudalism has never disappeared. It is still rampant. Any man who
gives eight hours of his day to someone else and must make excuses if
he is absent is a vassal. The emigrés of my generation came to America
with the idea of being free."

But what of the emigrés who became more American than the Americans themselves? They cry out for Law and Order, strive for material
wealth, and send their kids to Harvard.

"For them, the United States is the land of no war. This is the land
which has never been invaded, the land of continuity. You can invest
here. In a sense, they are all small investors. For them, this is the
mythical land, the escape from the blind date with history. Here they
can take root.

"Early this morning I was taking a walk. I started a conversation with
a woman who said she was going to visit relatives. I told her I had no
relatives. No relatives? I explained that I had no relatives, no family,

they'd all been killed. All? The woman wondered how that could be possible. Did they all die in an accident, in a hotel gathered for a reunion, a convention? (Kosinski and I laughed at the vision of a family version of *Towering Inferno*.) No, I told her, they had died in one of three wars. Then, she concluded, they must have all been soldiers. She couldn't understand."

Who can understand Kosinski? His novels are not so much difficult, as difficult to bear. In his novels we switch from comical anecdotes to scenes of unbearable cruelty. His characters lead us through a maze of moments of heightened perception, through scenes of revenge and fascinating perversity. The effect of Kosinski's books is so strong that his first novel, *The Painted Bird*, was once "banned" as a 'psychological drug.' The sexual descriptions are so graphic and perverse in their contextual implications they have turned many a reader away. Hence, I was surprised to find out that Kosinski's books sell best in the midwest. "Over 60 per cent of my books are sold there . . . I've learned a great deal from the cross-country promotional tours I've done, the blind dates I've had with my readers in supermarkets and bookstores. Many of the blue collar workers I've met have a perception sufficient to have written my books and many could have written them. I find this very reassuring, that although one writes alone, you have a spiritual electorate. Balzac, Stendhal, Faulkner might have expected such an electorate, but today we have the means for verification (mass media) that they could only hope for."

But are the great number of recognizable characters in *Blind Date* there to trigger the reader's perception of everyday events and of the novel? "The real events of our lives are . . . an emotional kindergarten . . . Characters such as Henry Kissinger or Charles Lindbergh, whom I've met and know personally are as well known by the general public, by you, as by me. You know them better perhaps because you see them in terms of the way they are seen, in terms of the collective fiction in which we all participate."

Are TV and the movies which make the real seem more unreal, a parallel to Kosinski's work, in that just as in his novels one changes from one moment of perception to another one can change from one TV channel to another? "TV does not stress the moment of perception . . . it chops up the continuity. In my work, there is a continuity of separate moments . . . They are dramatic units by which I seek to convey didactically that to lead a rewarding life you must dramatize each separate moment and perceive it all at the same time." The Sharon Tate murder is a perfect example: Hollywood . . . the American movie dream . . . Beverly Hills quiet compound. What could be more American and what could be more unexpected than the horror that was to follow.

Then that's why your last two novels, *Cockpit* and *Blind Date*, have both had at their conclusion scenes from the novel's beginning. What might have appeared to be a gratuitous act if presented at the novel's beginning is revealed in its full intensity at the novel's end because of the intervening "moments of perception." "Yes. That's it," Kosinski laughed. "In fact you said it better than I could have. From now on I'm going to use your words as my own."

In a sense you could say Kosinski is accustomed to using other people's words as his own: Kosinski has never written in his native tongue. Writing in a foreign language may be more of a benefit than a detriment. It is possible that although he has been credited with being outspoken on issues of morality and as having described sex in a manner few of his contemporaries have dared to equal, Kosinski's boldness may be explained by the very fact that he writes in English rather than Polish. "My originality may be nothing more than a lack of cultural prejudice," Kosinski admits. There is a scene in *Blind Date* where Levanter invites a Russian actress up to his apartment in New York and realizes that he cannot seduce her:

"The more he searched for the appropriate Russian words and phrases, the more apprehensive he became. The mother tongue had turned into an uninvited chaperone, guarding his passion from getting out of hand."

Kosinski: "Yes, as the saying goes, 'The Mother Tongue is the Father's whip.' But the philosophical implications may go far beyond that. Were you to write what I do, your friends, parents, school would ask you, Have you done these things? Right away it is a punitive matter. While if you were to ask me the same questions it would be more out of curiosity than to reproach me."

Has he ever returned to Poland? "No, I have no desire to. I have no relatives there and when I left I was 24 and I took my memories with me." Are your novels published in Poland? "No, they are banned there.

But I have heard that they are actively traded on the black market. One of my books, a paperback, goes for about a pair of Levi's." Does Kosinski, like many emigrés, still count in his native tongue? "No, when I came to America I sought to lose contact with my past. In a matter of weeks I was speaking English. . . . You see, Woytek in *Blind Date* (a childhood friend of Levanter's whom Levanter persuades to emigrate to America and who is one of those who died at Sharon's. He is modelled on Voytick Frowkowski), Woytek is the perfect emigré dream. He came to America convinced that he would connect with history—and he did—as Gibby does (Abigail Folger) as I did myself by marrying Mary Weir. But it is never as one thinks. As one character says in *Blind Date:* 'It was and it was not."

*Blind Date* is different from all of Kosinski's earlier work. It is and it is not. The ideas common to the body of his work have been discussed above: the protagonist's taking the law into his own hands, the moral and ethical questions, the fragmented exposition, the sexual adventures. These are still the same in *Blind Date,* yet they are subtly different because now Kosinski's orientation with regard to Philosophy, Love and Life has changed.

Kosinski: "None of my characters adopts a particular philosophy, except Levanter who accepts the philosophy of Jacques Monod. But Monod's philosophy discredits itself; it is a philosophical blind date you may or may not pick up. There is no moral implication."

*Blind Date* is prefaced by the following quote from Monod: "But henceforth who is to define crime? Who shall decide what is good and what is evil? All the traditional systems have placed ethics and values beyond man's reach. Values did not belong to him; he belonged to them. He now knows they are his and his alone. . . ."

Kosinski is seeking to fight predictability, to extend our perception of the Possible. "War takes away predictability," he said earlier in the interview, but there is one system all too predictable and impossible to control: Aging. In *Blind Date,* Kosinski speaks of aging as "Becoming conscious of what he knew he had done once and what he could do now." Does Kosinski feel that there is also an aging of the mind? Does he feel differently about his subject material now than he did when he began writing?

"Yes, there is a definite difference: The perception that life is running out makes the intellect more insistent on not letting go—you concentrate your focus; you are less diluted. In the past I have been interested in various issues: moral, sexual, aesthetic, etc. But now the accent becomes, how do these relate to the maintenance of life? How can you soften the impact of old age, illness, death? Old age, illness, death, these are all themes I've dealt with before, but now they are focused, tied to the theme of maintenance."

Does it take longer now to write, because the effort is more concentrated? "No, it is easier. I am more determined, more obsessive, less scattered in direction." But *Blind Date* has a certain looseness about it not evident in his earlier work. "The focusing allows more liberty with that scheme. Also, although I'm not becoming sentimental, there is a certain sentiment in *Blind Date*, a love Levanter displays for the pianist that Tarden of *Cockpit,* for example, would be incapable of feeling . . . "

I also noted that *Blind Date* is different from most of Kosinski's work in that it touches upon the theme of Jewishness, a theme first mentioned in *The Painted Bird* (we are never sure whether the protagonist is a gypsy or a Jew) and then left aside until *Blind Date*. Toward the end of Kosinski's latest novel he tells of a game played in his childhood called, "Finding The Jew." Levanter refused to participate and had to be saved from his classmates by Woytek.

"You know, you're the first one to pick up on that. And yet everyone reads the book (pointing to *Blind Date*), don't they? They read but they don't read." Kosinski then called my attention to Arnold Lustig's review of *Blind Date* in the Washington Post (12/27/77) and this passage: "In stressing these questions of human consciousness (as Adolph Hitler put it, 'a Jewish invention which cripples the human being just as circumcision cripples his body') Kosinski is a very Jewish writer reminding us in every story in *Blind Date* that human invention is in Jeopardy." "That," said Kosinski, "is precisely the point!"

Earlier Kosinski had ventured, "My best audience is enlightened middle class. Enlightened about their condition, their aspirations and their failures. My worst audience is Italian, Jewish, sentimental New York readers." Now he elaborated. "There are two Jewish responses on the one hand, what I call the "Moses" response, a need to know the truth of the condition . . . a highly moral vision, the tragic vision and on the other, the "Fiddler on the Roof" response which is a reflection of radical isolation from what they perceive the world to be, but what is just predictability and sentimentality—devoid of real life."

But what about alienation? "The Jewish condition is not alienated by virtue of history. Its all embracing condition, the mentality of the victim makes them able to fit in anywhere." But even if they fit in, will they ever really feel at home? Will they ever be allowed to feel at home? Levanter joins the elite of WASP society by marrying Mary Jane Kirkland, but one of her friends asks: 'What does Mary Jane, your own wife, really know about who you are?'

"It is funny that you see this as Jewish alienation. I see it more as the issue of the wanderer. My characters are always in the state of becoming, of perpetual redefinition. They are wanderers. Even Jonathan Whalen, whose self documentation is obsessive, he even saves his father's cigarette butts, is cut off from his roots by his wanderings . . . Just like a Devil Tree."

" . . . I received a great deal of complaints from Jewish groups about the scene where the girl is raped (In *The Painted Bird*, there is a scene where a young Jewish girl escapes from a train headed for the concentration camp only to be viciously raped by a gang of peasants). They said 'Why should this Jewish girl be raped?' But what should I have done? Showed her in the gas chamber? Wasn't it better that she died desired, wanted as a woman, raped as all women would be raped, than killed as a Jewess?"

Kosinski disappears to get some clippings that he feels will be helpful. The secretary reappears saying that she is sorry to rush us but Mr. Kosinski has another appointment and he is leaving the country soon. Suddenly, the interview is over. I asked Kosinski where he is travelling to. "Switzerland." To ski? "To finish my new novel. I've been working on it for about a year now and hope to finish it in four months of intensive work." Is it different? Kosinski smiles: "I am experimenting. It is braver."

I don't say anything, but wonder what "braver" could mean. I think back to the beginning of the interview. I had been told that Kosinski prized himself on having an excellent memory. About eight months ago, I had seen Kosinski on the street, coming out of a movie. I had introduced myself and we had talked for a few minutes. Now at the interview, I said, "You know, this is not our first blind date. We've met before." Kosinski did not hesitate. "Yes, in front of a cinema."

Who can predict what is possible from such a man?

# An Interview with Jerzy Kosinski on *Blind Date*

Daniel J. Cahill/1978

Published in *Contemporary Literature* 19 (Spring 78):133–42.
Reprinted by permission of University of Wisconsin Press.

Jerzy Kosinski's most recent novel, *Blind Date,* (1977) is a chilling examination of the adventures of George Levanter, a free spirit who recognizes that destiny is written concurrent with event, not prior to it. In this interview Kosinski expands upon the idea of what it means to become a personal "event" in a modern society that insists upon a predestined future. The interview took place on September 22, 1977 in New York City.

**Q:** In various places, you have stated that your previous five novels constitute a cycle—a special exploration of society and the individual's capacity or incapacity to survive in modern civilization. Do you still view your previous fiction as a cycle and is that cycle completed with *Cockpit*? Is the reader to interpret your most recent novel, *Blind Date,* as a continuation or a redirection of the cycle?

**A:** Although each novel of this cycle reflects and comments upon the motifs of the others, only *The Painted Bird* and *Cockpit* concern themselves with its full archetypal spectrum. In *The Painted Bird* society refuses the individual (the Boy) a place within itself by waging a war against him; in *Cockpit,* it is the individual (Tarden) who, refusing the place society insists he occupy, wages a war against the institutions of society.

*Blind Date* is a redirection of these previous concerns; here the modern character George Levanter is engaged in the Socratic quest—one's oligation to examine and assume responsibility for *one's own* actions regardless of the societal framework in which they occur. Whereas in *Cockpit* Tarden is preoccupied with the impact of his own camouflage on others who either accept or reject his altered truth (and so does *Cockpit* as a novel), in *Blind Date* George Levanter reveals his unfulfilled longing to be able to examine one single human being, one single truth at a time. *Blind Date* examines the concerns of George Levanter. The question posed by Socrates, about righteousness and sacrilege "with respect to murder and to everything else," is at the core of *Blind Date*.

**Q:** Do you view *Blind Date* as a radically different novel—in intent, structure, philosophical impact—from *Cockpit*?

**A:** Yes, I can repeat after Browning that "my stress lay in the incidents in the development of a soul: little else is worth study." The development of the soul of George Levanter in *Blind Date* is of a different sort than that of Tarden in *Cockpit* or, let's say, the hero of *Steps*. Tarden perceives and lives his life as if it were a cumulative process. In *Cockpit's* opening sentence he sets up his predicament: "Although we have known each other for a long time . . . ," and the novel continues as a confessional *summa* of Tarden. To Levanter, life is composed of moments, each one commencing with one's awareness of its beginning. *Blind Date* opens with "When he was a schoolboy, George Levanter had learned a convenient routine," but for the rest of his life Levanter will rebel against routine. In *Cockpit,* it is Tarden's language, his narration that is the sole dramatic agent that recasts what the protagonist claims had been his life's experiences. In *Blind Date,* objectively narrated events of Levanter's life provide the novel's outward expression.

**Q:** You have used two mottoes—one from Jonathan Swift and one from Jacques Monod. First, can you comment on the Swift quotation: "Remove me from this land of slaves. . . ." Who are the slaves and fools in *Blind Date*?

**A:** To Swift, the land of slaves and fools meant Ireland. To George Levanter, it is Eastern Europe, the land of totalitarian oppression that he had left behind. Swift, by the way, has always been among my favorite writers, a master role creator with a universal imagination, able to comprehend and to portray the totality of societal forces that condition men's daily lives and thoughts. The author "reports" to the reader what George Levanter, like Captain Lemuel Gulliver, has seen and done— in "the land of pygmies and in the land of giants"—and he does it as a storyteller who claims to have had no share in what he tells. His stress is on the characters and on the incidents, his language simple and evocative enough for the average reader, and his vision "the art of seeing things invisible" (Swift).

**Q:** With respect to the Jacques Monod quotation, I know (as you make clear in the novel) that he was a warm and affectionate friend, a man whose mind and ideas you valued greatly. What special force or shadow does he cast over *Blind Date*?

**A:** Like Jonathan Swift, Jacques Monod is a historical figure and his philosophical work *Chance and Necessity* (1970) is, like Swift's, a historical document written by one of the greatest scientists of this century. [Jacques Monod received the 1965 Nobel Prize in physiology and medicine for demonstrating how the living cell manufactures the substance of life.] The scientific discoveries of Monod and of other biologists led him to postulate a fundamental theory that there is no plan in nature, that destiny is written concurrently with each event in life, not prior to it, and that to guard against this powerful feeling of destiny should be the source of our new morality. George Levanter, the hero of *Blind Date,* is dissatisfied with Marxism because he feels betrayed by the Soviet society that preaches "objective destiny," proclaiming, in a travesty of scientific discourse, that Marxism offers access to the "scientifically" established "objective" laws of history which man has no choice but to obey, and that the State and the Communist Party have a moral duty to enforce at any cost to the population. Thus, Levanter embraces Monod's scientific postulate that forces man to acknowledge his isolation, to utilize each moment of his life as it passes rather than to dismiss it as a minor incident in a larger passage or zone of time. This philosophy, derived from and based on modern science, presupposes an ethic which bases moral responsibility upon that very freedom of choice an individual exercises in each instance of his life, an instance being dictated entirely by chance, and not by necessity.

Levanter's friendship with Monod is merely a consequence of Levanter's profession: he is a successful small investor whose activities are not limited to one country or any particular field or endeavor. In the course of his life he has met and been befriended by many men of accomplishment—Jacques Monod among them.

**Q:** While all of your fictional work has contained intermittent auto-biographical elements, these were always submerged or welded to the dramatic episodes of the novel. *Blind Date* strikes me as more frankly autobiographical. Is this a fair representation of the novel?

**A:** *Blind Date* is neither less nor more autobiographical than my other novels. The inclusion of "real life" characters—Lindbergh, Jacques

Monod, Stalin's daughter, the U. S. Secretary of State, the Soviet poet, the victims of the Manson murders—makes the novel in my eyes more, not less imaginative and perhaps less "subjective." In any case, these "real life" heroes are no more or less real than the novel's other "real life" characters: President Samael of Lotan, the Arab diplomat, Impton's Chief of Police, Mme. Ramoz, the beautiful wife of the President of the Republic of Deltazur, J. P., the tragically punished greatest saber-fencer of all time, the corrupt court officials from Indostran, the Foxy Lady, the henchmen from PERSAUD, Weston of Pacific and Central. They all inhabit together the imaginative space of the novel that, by its nature, abolishes the ranking of "real-unreal."

The so-called "historical figures"—Lindbergh, Monod, the Manson killers—influence the way we perceive ourselves in a society, our moral and ethical values, our concept of justice, our fear of evil. And don't they influence us pretty much the same way fictional characters do—Hamlet, Robinson Crusoe, the Brothers Karamazov, Julien Sorel? Like World War II in *The Painted Bird,* television in *Being There,* or the financial trust in *The Devil Tree,* the "real life" personages of *Blind Date* only reinforce for the reader the novel's "objective referrals," providing the general climate for the personal story of George Levanter, the American small investor.

**Q:** As a novelist, are you concerned that your reader will or should recognize these passages as actual elements in the life of Jerzy Kosinski?

**A:** Whatever the reader "recognizes" in the act of reading the novel belongs, by virtue of his imagination, to *him,* not to the author. By its very nature language fictionalizes our "real" experience. To me, "recognition" by the reader—the semiconscious power of projection into another time, place, and identity—is fiction's foremost principle.

The stress on "what's autobiographical" in fiction (as opposed to what's imaginative) so dear to our popular culture has, in my view, its source in the Hollywood-made preoccupation with the life of the actor (as opposed to his ability to portray various roles). The popular culture shifts the source of celebrity from talent to that of simple visibility. Such attitudes applied to imaginative fiction simply mean its death.

Aiming for the greatest involvement on the part of their audience, Shakespeare, Swift, Milton, and Browning already realized the importance of the literary manipulation of masks, identities, inherited

historical scenarios, dramatization—and the protective characterization
of the authorial persona.

**Q:** Few readers will know of your fateful escape in the Sharon Tate
murders. Your account of that murder scene in *Blind Date* is both real
and personal drama. Can you say how your dramatization of this
tragedy served your novelistic intentions?

**A:** Popular culture "immortalized," of course, the murderers—they
are the best-selling heroes—not so their victims. My preoccupation
has been with the victims. In *Steps,* published shortly before the Tate
tragedy, I wrote: "many of us could easily visualize ourselves in the act
of killing but few could project ourselves in the act of being killed in
any manner. We did our best to understand the murder: the murderer
was a part of our lives; not so the victim."

The victims of Manson typify, to me, the terrifying randomness of
our modern existence. By including the fateful encounter of the victims
with their killers, I wish the reader to be able to visualize, to recreate
an atmosphere of serenity, peace, and prosperity brutally invaded by a
gang of murderers who come to the house by chance to kill everyone
in it.

**Q:** There are certain sexual scenes in *Blind Date*—the rape of
Nameless, the highly graphic and violent sexual episodes with Jolene,
the bizarre encounter with Foxy Lady—these are all graphically intense
scenes in which Levanter imposes his will on another person. Is he a
dramatization of Monod's criminal without a definable crime?

**A:** The only instances in which Levanter imposes on another person
took place when he was a boy (the rape of Nameless) and a student (the
kidnapping of Robot, the girl from China). He was willing to suffer the
legal consequences for the first act, but the authorities refused to believe
he was the rapist. Robot, of course, never felt abused by the two men:
she had long before lost her capacity to acknowledge her self.

As a mature man, Levanter is increasingly given to acts on behalf of
others—Weston, the shareholders, PERSAUD, the tortured intellectuals, Mme. Ramoz, the imprisoned journalists, and many others. Even
killing the hotel clerk is not only an act of revenge for what was done to
J. P. the fencer and to countless other unsuspecting visitors from behind
the Iron Curtain, but a way of breaking the chain of further denuncia-
tions and misery for them (as it was with getting rid of Barbatov,
Levanter's Commander in the Army).

Even when Levanter is blackmailed and used—by Jolene, his out-of-town blind date, by Impton's Chief of Police, by Serena—he does not respond with malice. He makes no attempt at revenge—as soon as he is free, he merely steps away.

**Q:** In an echo of *Being There,* George Levanter frequently acts as an invisible assailant in an atmosphere of nameless, faceless violence. Is *Blind Date* a warning against this future of violence?

**A:** If *Blind Date* contains such a warning, it is not against our future but our present. It is a warning that, given the staggering proportions of violence in our society, life is, at best, uncertain—we might not live through the very next moment, our next blind date, so to speak.

**Q:** One function of your fiction is to prompt "awareness" of self and the world. Today we see the fantastic popularity of "guides" for living, such as *Your Erroneous Zones,* and "religious literature": they are outstripping the usual top-ten best sellers. All of these books seek a continuity of human experience and they all represent a tremendous "search" for "totality of experience."

**A:** In the parlance of popular culture, "totality of experience" is simply another label for a sort of popular religion, which is to people who feel lost in the midst of the so-called free economy what a Soviet version of Marxism is to the masses hopelessly locked behind the Iron Curtain. The popular religion's elements are all there: one's destiny is somehow "predictable"; just as one's life can be psychologically computerized, one's destiny can also be predicted, or, at least, "not escaped." For me, this trend represents a further repression of the development of an awareness of life as it happens in each of its moments, and that man must treat each of those moments as unique.

But, I guess, the society of parrot-like trained "consumerists" demands an easy assertion of the continuity of its psychological "spending" habits, emotional "investment" routines, sexual "wheeling-dealings"—briefly, a Master Charge attitude to life.

**Q:** One of your critics has commented that the figures in your fiction have "a great capacity for barbarism" such as Levanter seems to possess. Yet he is also guided by contrary impulses—friendship, concern, affection.

**A:** This is the kind of frivolous judgment that spokesmen for our Pollyannaized popular culture easily dispense against literature that portrays our everday physical and moral reality, thus threatening their propagation of happy-go-lucky, life-banalizing philosophy, without which our rampant consumerism could not flourish. What consumerism needs more than anything else is the idea of the predetermined, predictable life that obviously invites predetermined investing and buying. Thus, popularization of the notion of a central plot to one's life does, to a degree, encourage the philosophy of the installment plan, long-term credit-based investing. . . .

A serious novelist's effort to confront a reality that is anything but rosy is quickly labeled "morbidity," "pornographic imagination," "lonely rituals." My novels and I get our share of such labeling. In most cases, though, such reviewers are not really critics; they are, rather, "cultural Kapos." They don't bother to examine the novel's (and the author's) point-of-view, they simply reprimand; they denounce, and all they seem to miss is an opportunity to kill his vision and put the writer in jail. Their counterparts in Eastern Europe do just that. . . .

To me, a serious novelist's task has always been to take society to task: he is no more answerable to his critics than to his publishers, family, lovers, or neighbors—he is answerable to the plausibility of his vision, to his construction of dramatic imaginative reality that intensifies readers' awareness and confronts the very areas steadily deadened by the popular culture, which, in its essence, is fundamentally hostile to man's real aspirations, fears, and joys. Thus, imaginative literature not only dramatizes life; above all, it enhances man's ability to perceive his own condition for what it is: a drama of which he is the protagonist, but a drama of particular, clearly delineated moments. Each moment is his blind date.

**Q:** In the parlance of American dating patterns, a blind date is generally an innocent and harmless affair—two people brought together by well-meaning friends. Perhaps you will elaborate on your title and its implications in the novel?

**A:** In Aristotle's terms, the most moving elements in human tragedy are *peripeteia* and *anagnorisis*: the first can be freely interpreted as working in blindness to one's own defeat; the second, the opening of the eyes. The American "blind date" is, philosophically, a complex invitation to both. It presupposes an invitation relying on chance; it postulates a willingness to go through an encounter arranged by a "third party" (who is, even if for a short moment, placed in charge of the destiny of the two other people who are about to meet); it reveals optimism—a

belief that "the unknown" other might, in fact, become our "partner"—
and also the fact of our isolation—a human need for an encounter, even
with a stranger. . . .

Jacques Monod once told me that *Blind Date* would have been a
perfect title for his philosophical book, with "An Essay on Chance and
Necessity" as its subtitle. But the French don't go on blind dates; they
don't have a corresponding phrase for it either. For that matter, only
Americans seem to have the blind date custom—and because nobody
else does, I have to come up now with another title for my novel in
foreign languages. So far, the Dutch, French, and Germans will call it
*The Unknown Partner.*

**Q:** How is the reader to respond to the central character, George
Levanter? Is he a creator of values or is he a clever opportunist who
preys upon, and is preyed upon in return by, others?

**A:** A reader must "decode" George Levanter on his own terms. After
all, Levanter's acts are open to the reader's scrutiny and they invite
moral judgment, which is implicit in any encounter—whether with a
fictional protagonist or with a neighbor next door. The novel is written
in the third person, past tense—"tragic tense." If Levanter was happy,
he is no more; if he was unfulfilled, he can't relive his life better. This
stance places the reader in a relatively superior position: unlike
Levanter, he can still attempt to be master of his character, of his
"moment," and thus, to a degree, of his fate. In terms of my own
reading of *Blind Date,* I can't see anything in the novel that would
suggest George Levanter is "a clever opportunist." Rather, many
incidents suggest that he is a true, self-appointed protestant.

If in life we're finally betrayed by what is false within, then I
perceive George Levanter as free from such falsehoods—a man who,
having learned some harsh lessons in his boyhood during World War II
and as an adolescent in Stalinist Russia, has emerged greatly concerned
with moral issues. As a small investor active in America, George
Levanter is a classic "permanent reformer," preoccupied with counteracting social injustice. That's why he executes the hotel clerk and
blows up the henchmen of PERSAUD, and why he exposes abuses of
political power. He is aware and critical of the fraud and sterility
implicit in the concept of morality perpetrated by the popular culture.

**Q:** I have tested the ending of your novel on several readers—some
were merely puzzled, some felt Levanter drifted in his mind and died

on the cold ledge—a final blind date. Does Levanter "sell himself for naught"? Does his death become useless because he has exceeded the limits?

**A:** Levanter dies with an image of a boy who wanted to hear the end of the story that Levanter has started to tell him. But the boy's American divorcée mother and her British suitor disapproved of the stories Levanter was telling the child, "an old experienced sinner instructing a young beginner. . . ." That's from Swift. Thus, perhaps Levanter feels his life—if its lesson cannot or will not be conveyed— has been wasted: "And since thy essence on thy breath depends/Thus with a puff the whole delusion ends." Swift again!

**Q:** The reader of your novel is directed by the general flow and sequence, yet the novel dislocates time: for example, on page 92 we read, "It was Levanter's fifteenth Christmas in his new country." In a different episode in the same chapter, we read, "A few years after Levanter's arrival in America." What artistic purpose or authorial intent is served by keeping two or more time-frames operating?

**A:** The novel has the order of a painting or a work of music. Its order is both circular and spiral, corresponding to the different parts of Levanter's memory. Its philosophical basis is the chance selectivity and randomness of our memory and our ability to say why we remember certain events and not others; and our reluctance to look for the principle of such ranking. The randomness of one's memory is an indication that unless each moment of life can be assisted by an emotional awareness of it, the moment simply flows in the stream of lost time. Perhaps one's personal history is indeed mainly the creation of others; perhaps we have been trained to see ourselves as we have been—not as we are. Unless one is consciously armed with a philosophy to undo this, a philosophy which refuses the notion of natural preordaining, one be-comes entrapped in the best-selling notions of one's own predictability. The current fad of popular culture is selling the alleged predictability of life's patterns as opposed to the proven unpredictability of life's moments. This leaves man at odds with himself: he remains maladjusted and he waits hopelessly for the newest "maladjustment correction course." With a true sense of the randomness of life's moments, man is at peace with himself—and that peace is happiness.

# Sellers and Kosinski—Alliance for the Absurd

Tom Zito/1979

Published in *The Washington Post* 2 February 1979:D1, D5. ©
1979, *The Washington Post*. Reprinted by permission.

"Circles that I mix in seem to be well inhabited by nuts," declares Peter
Sellers, creator of the mixed-up supersleuth Inspector Jacques Clouseau.
He is recalling certain Eaton Square suppers, the London equivalent of
Cleveland Park dinner parties.

"They close in on you. The worst part is that after dinner the ladies
retire and the host begins to forge ahead . . ."

He starts creeping forward from his chair like a feeble, fading noble-
man, " 'Have you got a good story?' " he asks very slowly, mocking the
style of his host. "And you tell something dreadful and they're all
tapping the sides of the table, mumbling 'quite good, quite good.' It's
enough to make you a real manic-depressive."

He's just beginning to break into vintage Sellers, after a half-hour of
chit-chat now hitting the kind of zany humor that's delighted fans of
more than 40 movies, including the Pink Panther films, "Dr. Strange-
love," "What's New Pussycat!" Now—GONG!—he's interrupted by
novelist Jerzy Kosinski.

"Of course, in England," says Kosinski, "I've said the most amazing
things at parties and people will say, 'yes, you're absolutely right.' "

"Yes, you're absolutely right," deadpans Sellers.

This is an unholy marriage, although it has lasted eight years, ever
since Sellers read Kosinski's *Being There* and decided it would make a
wonderful movie. And so they met in London eight years ago, to talk
things over in an Italian restaurant.

"I have a photograph of us," says Kosinski, who is rarely without a
camera around his neck, ever ready to document the tenuous reality that
surrounds him.

"Ah yes," says Sellers, "Myron Lorenzo's on Beauchamp Place."

"A friend of yours," asks Kosinski in mock surprise. "He was responsible for the worst diarrhea of my life!"

Sellers laughs and stares through his smoked lenses, out the hotel window. He crosses his legs and his black trouser cuff rides up to reveal a white sock under his black loafer. He's very low key. Sends his wife off to the room to get his "pink morning pill." She exits, trailed by her Lhasa apso.

Kosinski and Sellers have a sort of mutual admiration society that has come to fruition in the filming of Kosinski's *Being There,* with Sellers in the lead role of Chauncey Gardiner, a meek fellow addicted to television and gardening who just happens to become the president's most important adviser. The film is being shot partly in Washington, and Kosinski has flown in for the event, having just finished his seventh novel two days ago.

"I do not know who will publish it," he announces in a heavy Polish accent that 21 years in this country hasn't homogenized. "I have no editor, no contract, no agent. I invite publishers to come to my apartment and read the manuscript and if they like it they can buy it. If not, at least they get a free drink."

"When I read *Being There,*" says Sellers, "I could tell that it would adapt perfectly to movies."

"Yes, it is completely visual," Kosinski concurs.

"We started chasing Jerzy," says Sellers. "He's a terribly difficult person to pin down."

"I am always in the movies," says Kosinski. "I learned English from going to the movies. I saw 'The World of Henry Orient,' two times and once on television. When my English publisher told me Peter had called, I was wild. It was a chunk of Anglo-Saxon culture I was going to meet."

"So that's what you thought of me," says Sellers.

"A character actor," says Kosinski, waxing philosophical. "A character actor teaches a foreigner that you can become someone else, which is what being a writer is all about." And then he shifts gears.

"Ah, the seduction of Kosinski by Peter Sellers was very clever. We're in Beverly Hills, mind you, and Sellers has ordered champagne and the waiter comes to serve it and Sellers is staring at a television screen that isn't turned on. And he says to the waiter, 'Would you mind not stepping in the way,' and the waiter is walking around half the room so he won't block Sellers' view of the screen."

Sellers and Kosinski laugh in unison.

Sellers begins to talk about his creation of the Pink Panther's Inspector Clouseau roles, and Kosinski hurries into his own bedroom. Even as Sellers is in mid-sentence, Kosinski is pulling out newspaper articles pasted on index cards, emphasized with yellow highlighter. When Sellers stops to breathe, Kosinski yanks the conversation in his own direction.

"Do you know how many people voted for Congressman McCloskey because they knew his views?" asks Kosinski. "This is from a survey his own campaign took. Five percent said they knew his views. Eighty-four percent said they voted for him because he appeared serious on television. And do you know who introduced the president at the Bicentennial celebration in Philadelphia? 'A man you know, love and believe in,' the announcer said. It was Charlton Heston. Not an astronaut, not a businessman.

"I have more facts," Kosinski says. "They cost one dollar. Insights we charge five dollars for.

"Life," he adds—as Sellers gazes off into space—"is very tyrannical."

"Quite good," says Sellers, and he begins himself to discourse on similar matters.

"I once had a real nut case say to me, 'dddddddddddo . . . dddddddddo . . . ddddddddo . . . you have a real job as well as this acting you do?'" And he starts mimicking a British horseman who's dressed to the nines, all ready for the big hunt, when Peter Ustinov happens by in the course of shooting a movie. And of course the huntsman offers the services of the entire hunt:

"We're with you all to a man," Sellers intones, in perfectly clipped Queen's English.

But just as the familiar Sellers' style is about to get rolling again, Kosinski interrupts again.

"Relations are difficult," Kosinski says. "I love renting things. It's a free relationship. When you send it back, no one gets hurt. . . ."

# Life at a Gallop

Daniel J. Cahill/1979

Published in *Washington Post Book World* 16 September 1979:10.
© 1979, *The Washington Post*. Reprinted by permission.

In *Passion Play* Jerzy Kosinski has done for polo what Hemingway did
for bullfighting, and made a sport into a literary metaphor. His choice of
polo was not dictated merely by his own private passion for the game.

"Polo is the oldest organized sport in our recorded history," he says
from his two-room Manhattan office located midway between Tiffany's
and the Russian Tea Room. "In its make-up, polo is antiquity's answer
to American rodeo—the polo player appears as a sophisticated fusion of
the Hollywood swash-buckler and the Wild West's cowboy. In spite of
several super-American ingredients, polo has yet managed—for various
social reasons—to avoid having ever to perform for a mass audience
and be turned, like other sports of controlled collision—hockey and
football for instance—into spectacles of purposefully ugly violence
and vulgar conduct that benefit neither the players nor the viewing
audience—but keep TV ratings high."

Both as an avid player and a trained observer, Kosinski was able to
survey the U.S. polo scene quite sufficiently to use it as a backdrop for
*Passion Play,* a novel which, he explains, "is, like polo, about 'controlled collision'—between life's passion and life's play."

The preoccupation with time and its impact on one's emotion and
memory—more than merely on one's body—is another recurring theme
of *Passion Play*. It is thus appropriate that, after writing, photography
should be Kosinski's other form of artistic expression. As a young man
he had important shows in Poland of his own photographs. He was, for
instance, the youngest artist ever to have a one-man show of photography sponsored by the city of Warsaw in the state-owned gallery of
modern art.

In his New York apartment several large albums of photographs taken
of Kosinski (photographs *by* him are kept in rented storage) unreel the
documentary of his own life: as a child in Poland; as a boy of six, at the

outbreak of World War II, shortly before he was separated from his parents and was sent to spend the war years in the remote peasant villages of Ruthenia and the Ukraine. As if to keep for himself the visual record of this "camera-less" chapter of his life, his albums also contain the photographs of these villages—and even of the huts that sheltered him—taken there shortly before the war by a group of American anthropologists and geographers.

The photographs in the albums also show him: as a ski instructor in the Polish Tatra mountains; as a student in Poland and in the Soviet Union; as a truck driver soon after his arrival in New York; with Mary Weir, his late wife. They portray him in his travels on horseback, playing polo, his years as a professor of English at Wesleyan, Princeton and Yale, with his friends, in his encounters with diplomats and heads of state when he was a president of P.E.N., the association of writers.

Says Kosinski: "Recently, I realized that, quite likely in the last 30 years not a single month, often not even a week, passed without my taking pictures of others, who in turn would photograph me with my own camera. No head of state has ever had more pictures taken than I of the state of my head," he quips.

Like *Passion Play*'s Fabian who traverses this country in his Van-Home, Kosinski has wandered widely in Europe and the United States. As an emigrant from Poland at the age of 24, Kosinski began his American odyssey as a truck driver, "transporting hats—one object that I have never worn," through the hot states—Wyoming, Utah, Arizona, Nevada, California, and like Fabian, "enthralled by so measureless a domain."

To become a trucker he had to borrow a lot of money to ease his way into the union. To pay it back he moonlighted as a Kinney parking lot attendant, a cinema projectionist, a chauffeur and racing driver for a black nightclub entrepreneur. "By working in Harlem as a white, uniformed chauffeur I broke a color barrier of the profession" he recalls.

After two years in the United States he learned English well enough to write in it. He obtained a Ford Foundation fellowship and, as a student of social psychology, wrote *The Future is Ours, Comrade*, the first of his two nonfiction books on collective society, published under the pen name "Joseph Novak." The book was an instant best seller, was serialized by *The Saturday Evening Post*, condensed by *Reader's Digest*, and published in 18 languages. He was firmly set on a writing

career. "When you're a student you're supposed to read serious books—
not publish them. The pen name allowed me to conduct my studies
uninterrupted by the controversy that my books triggered among my
fellow students and professors. A side benefit of a pen name is that it
allows you to recommend your own books, to those who don't know
you've written them, as the very best on the subject—without ever
feeling immodest."

During his publishing debut he met Mary Weir, the widow of a millionaire steel magnate from Pittsburgh. They began dating, and, two
years later, after the publication of *No Third Path*, a study of collective
behavior, the second "Novak" volume, they were married.

During his 10 years with Mary Weir (which ended with her death in
1968) Kosinski moved with utmost familiarity in the worlds of the steel
industry, big business and high society. He and Mary traveled a great
deal—there was a private plane, a 17-crew boat, and houses in Pittsburgh, New York, Hobe Sound, Southampton, Paris, London and
Florence. He led a life most novelists only invent in the pages of their
novels.

"During my marriage, I had often thought that it was Stendhal or
F. Scott Fitzgerald, both preoccupied with wealth they did not have,
who deserved to have had my experience. I wanted to start writing
fiction and, frankly, was tempted to begin with a novel that, like *Passion Play*, would utilize my immediate experience, the dimension of
wealth, power and high society that surrounded me, not the poverty I
had seen and experienced so shortly before. But during my marriage
I was too much a part of Mary's world to extract from it the nucleus of
what I saw, of what I felt. And as a writer, I perceived fiction as the art
of imaginative extraction. So instead, I decided to write my first novel
*The Painted Bird*, about a homeless boy in the war-torn Eastern Europe,
an existence I've known but also one that was shared by millions of
Europeans, yet was foreign to Mary and our American friends. The
novel was my gift to Mary, and to her world."

In the years to come—and in his other novels—*Steps, Being There,
Cockpit, The Devil Tree, Blind Date*, and now *Passion Play*, he would
draw on the experience he had gained during his first American decade
when once a "Don Quixote of the turnpike" he had suddenly become a
"Captain Ahab of billionaire's row."

Until just recently besides his own active writing and teaching career,

Kosinski was also the president of P.E.N., the international association of writers and editors. According to the American P.E.N.'s resolution, made at the end of his two-term tenure and inscribed on a plaque that hangs over his desk, "he has shown an imaginative and protective sense of responsibility for writers all over the world. No single writer can possibly be aware of the full extent of his efforts, but it is clear that they have been extraordinary and that the fruits of what he has achieved will extend far into the future."

In addition to P.E.N., Kosinski has been active in the International League for Human Rights, the American Civil Liberties Union and other American human rights organizations. During this interview he was constantly on the phone trying to help a Connecticut poet who wrote to him asking for help in countering a legal action instigated against him by a reader who claimed to have been libeled by one of his poems.

Kosinski is proud to have been greatly responsible for freeing from prisons, helping financially, resettling or otherwise giving assistance to at least 80 writers, political and religious dissidents and intellectuals all over the world, many of whom have thanked him publicly for his role in their liberation. One has even written a book about it. "Whenever I learn of yet another journalist imprisoned, novelist silenced, teacher suspended, I feel implicated by their fate. Here I am, once a dissident myself, free to write, to teach, to travel—and they—men and women of my profession—are not. Their plight spoils my own freedom—I have to do something for them, something that would improve their condition—and restore my peace of mind. Thus, I do it as much for myself as for them."

Critic Geoffrey Wolff once said of Kosinski that he "writes his novels so sparsely as though they cost a thousand dollars a word, and a misplaced or misused locution would cost him his life." He was close to the truth: Kosinski writes slowly and rewrites massively: he took almost three years to write *Passion Play*, and he rewrote it a dozen times; later, in subsequent sets of galley-proofs, he altered most of the novel's text, condensing it by one-third. "Writing is for me a constant crystallization of the very essence—of characters, and of the setting that the reader needs to recreate it. It is not the mass of details but the clarity of vision that forms the basis for such recreation."

As the author covers the cost of the type re-setting above his 10 per-

cent publisher's allowance, Kosinski's corrections produced the highest
bill of his writing career: a large chunk of his advance royalties. But he
does not complain, "Writing is the essence of my life—whatever else
I do revolves around a constant thought: could I—can I—would I—
should I—use it in my next novel? When I face the galley-proofs I feel
as though my whole life was at stake on every page and that a messy
paragraph could mess up my whole life from now on. As I have no
children, no family, no relatives, no business or estate to speak of, my
books are my only *spiritual* accomplishment, my life's most private
frame of reference, and I would gladly pay all I earn to make it
my best."

# A Passion for Polo

George Christian/1979

Published in the *Houston Chronicle* 7 October 1979, 18,22. Reprinted by permission of the *Houston Chronicle*.

Jerzy Kosinski surfaces like a dolphin and propels himself onto the edge of the Hyatt pool. "It's cold," he mutters, a cheerful Polish-accented mutter. Around him downtown Houston rumbles and grumbles and in the center of the pool five lodge auxiliary ladies, arms locked, are smiling for a photographer and jumping. Kosinski wraps a towel around his lean sinewy athlete's frame and leads off for his room. There's an extra pair of trunks, he says hospitably, and sunglasses, but instead we order sandwiches and settle down to talk about his new book. It's called *Passion Play* (St. Martin's Press) and it has to do with a traveling polo player named Fabian whose passion is both the game, at which he's an expert though disputatious player, and the young women he meets in the course of his travels. The two are inextricably knit.

As it happens, Kosinski is himself an ardent polo player, and he's often asked to ride with teams throughout the country, San Antonio's among them. Noting the parallel between Fabian's life and his own, a parallel not uncommon in his novels, I wonder what corner of his psyche Fabian sprang from. Kosinski switches on. Energy flashing out of obsidian eyes. Intense! Articulate! The locutions just skewed enough to remind you that he's Polish. Or was, a couple of decades ago.

The new novel is a turning point for him, he tells me. Then he explains where's turning from.

"I think in a way," he says, "it starts an entirely different set of concerns. All my novels until now dealt with a character who perceived himself denying society entry to the private sphere. Or who perceived himself as the surviving psyche against the oppressive forces of others."

Kosinski reaches into his earlier novels for examples.

"For instance, in *The Painted Bird,* the child oppressed by the situation of abandonment or persecution. In *Steps* a man divided between two different political systems who's now trying to find his

167

whole, himself, in the United States. Who defends himself against influences of *both* cultures, trying to extract from it what it is that he really is.

"*Being There,* at the center of that cycle of six novels before *Passion Play,* portrays a condition very important. That is, a man without self, a man with no notion of himself, and how such a man is used by society for various purposes. *Being There,* standing in the center of the six novels, addresses itself to the condition that the remaining five novels actually elaborate. Then *Devil Tree,* the next in line, the predicament of a young American who has to define himself again against the tradition of his Protestant heritage and a strong father who even though he's not alive his presence of course is very much there through the family trust. Jonathan in *Devil Tree* is basically in a defense position. His act of self-definition is arrived at by trying to sort out what is his, what is roots, what is branches? And is he still part of the tree or is the tree reversed?

"Then *Cockpit,* a man trained to survive, a professional agent once in the service of a large corporation and now alone. And how does he manage it? A man *trained* to survive. Is his *self* any better? Is he any fuller? Are his dimensions any different? And finally George Levanter of *Blind Date,* the last of the cycle, in which the character is a small investor who defines himself in terms of each moment as the moment comes by.

"So this closed the cycle of the threatened self. Or not so much the threatened self as individuals so much conscious of their condition they would defend it in various ways and at various times."

Kosinski offers a wedge of salmon and carries on fidgeting almost fiercely with his sunglasses. He is wound up. His right index finger describes a circle clockwise on the table.

Is he saying goodbye, then, to search for himself? Kosinski nods but wants to put it another way.

"We start something different now, which is closer to what I am right now. Fabian is a good messenger of this new truth. Or perhaps a truth which now is the time to write in my life. And here is how it works in my head: Unlike the other characters, Fabian discovers and identifies himself by that sacred flame which he feels is his very essence. *That essence is not be modified.* It's not be proven or abandoned. The essence rests in his ability to be what he is. To hit that ball in a game. That's the gift of life he has."

Is that the self? He shrugs.

"Well, it's as good a self as any. That's his *essence*. That is what he has. To deny this presence of that gift would be in fact for him to deny that there is more to him than what meets the eye.

"What meets the eye is a ruin, a man falling apart. A man without estate, without family, without traditions. This self is not to defend itself but to redeem itself. There's a difference. To redeem itself by finding those in whose eyes he's a heroic figure. Who will overlook this Don Quixote and who will instead see in fact Captain Ahab."

Captain Ahab?

"As he sees himself. Of course! To others he's a vagabond, he's a hobo, not that different from that beggar in the beginning of the book. In American society the only people who can redeem him for what he is, a heroic figure to himself, the only ones who can perceive him in heroic terms, in romantic terms, are young women."

Kosinski rests the fingers of his left hand on his temple.

"Because to *them* he is in fact a knight riding from another sphere of life, bringing the knowledge they like, knowledge about horses. Young women who are preoccupied with horses simply because horses offer them the first initiation into the control of something larger than oneself. And of course Fabian comes from the world of horses and equestrian art which he writes about.

"Fabian's search for young women is only because they can see him as a romantic figure, an image which he needs to survive."

He pauses, walking his fingers across the table, and explodes.

*"Which we all do!"*

"They perceive him as heroic simply because they have no background to compare him with anything else other than equestrian art. In this equestrian art he is a master. Therefore they can see him as a hero. And as a figure of fantasy almost. A figure free of repressive society, free of home, of school, of community, all the forces which young people somehow identify with the forces that lock them in."

What does this mean, I want to know, in terms of his own life. Does he need to be seen as a romantic figure? "Of course." But he returns to the novel.

"What happens then is with the young women when he arrives for the first time he is a romantic figure. When he arrives a second time two or three years later they're already grown up women, but still they don't have anything else but the memory of the romantic past. So he arrives now as a romantic figure. As a potentially romantic lover.

"And in such a way he's redeemed twice. Once as a man of a profession. And then as a man Fabian also writes books about equestrian art. Obviously they are not popular, but through these books Fabian also confronts his conditions as a *professional* man. And the matter now is clear. The resemblance now between Fabian and Kosinski becomes very obvious.

"Toward the end of the book Fabian is confronted by the change of life Vanessa (a female character) is willing to make for him. He doesn't accept it because again, unlike my other characters, his life does not depend on its change. In fact his life depends on a sense of calling. That sense of mission, of inner unity, and of inner substance, is not be exchanged, is not to be modified. It's to be merely *lived* until the end only he can see will take it away."

Fabian really knows who he is? Sharp agreement.

"Oh, yes! Much more than any other of my previous characters who basically defended themselves. And part of their definition would go into the acts of defense."

Is this true of Kosinski, that he knows who he is?

"I think this is true of myself *now*."

He delivers the table a karate chop.

"Because like Fabian I think that I have a sense of destiny now which I didn't have before. Because I have the books that I have already written—they form my destiny as it has been lived until now. There is a pattern. It is a destiny that I have defended which I could have abandoned it. Or when I was offered a gift of a different life during my marriage to *one of the richest women of this country.*"

There's an unaware pride in the way he says it. I get a flash of the Polish war waif inducted into the American noblesse. He continues the thought.

"Who actually could have changed my life by offering me some other thing to do."

I interrupt to ask about his polo playing. Is he good at it like Fabian? Goals on 60 out of a hundred shots?

Kosinski smiles.

"Twenty. By Polish standards I'm the best. At my age. On borrowed horses. You know, doing other things, after all."

Back to his point.

"So like Fabian I didn't surrender what I thought to be the essence of my life. Confronting what it was in my life that gave a sense of unity to me and that was *writing*. Now one could make a further analogy by pointing out that my fiction, in its components, should be actually quite popular. It isn't but it should be. It deals with the condition of man in a modern American environment, a man who's divided between different cultures as many Americans occasionally are. But basically it deals with a sense of self which Americans used to have—in fact the expression *self-made man* exists only in American English. It doesn't exist in any other language.

"It's interesting how the phrase betrays that that self was made by a man, by himself or herself. Polo, in which Fabian excels the way I excel in my particular kind of fiction, polo is an ultimately American sport. It came from outside, but in its components it's an ultimately American sport. Only in this country can it be completely understood, for this reason. It is played on a western-trained horse. It involves a horse and a rider in the country of the cowboy. In which *everyone* knows who the cowboy is. The polo player is a supercharged cowboy. Moving freely in the saddle. Free of any restrictions. With style and grace. The mallet like a lasso extends seven feet from the shoulder to hook the other player or a moving object, a ball. Stick and ball are phenomena ultimately American.

"And that final element, the collision of two teams, a violent collision, a principle of organized violence which you have in your hockey—and football. And roller derby. We in Europe do not.

"Fabian is engaged in a profoundly American sport. Just as I am engaged in a profoundly American fiction. His sport is no more popular in spite of its all-American ingredients than my fiction is.

"That's why I picked it up as a sport. I loved polo from the minute I arrived in this country. You have a sport which didn't make it because it is not conveyed in terms of popular entertainment. It's too direct, it's too serious. Polo is not hockey. It's not a bruised shoulder.

"There's an interesting analogy between my fiction and polo in a way. My fiction also does not lend itself to easy portrayal on a film or television. And therefore it has a limited audience."

Would he like to reach a larger audience?

"I think the way polo players would, so would I, of course. Why not? It has all the human American ingredients. My life in the United States has gone through all the shades of the American ethos, from a truck driver in the beginning, a chauffeur, student, a writer of nonfiction books. Graduate and postgraduate studies in the United States. My marriage which allowed me for 10 years to scrutinize the American society in all its powerful components. Heavy industry, finance, Republican politics. After my marriage, teaching the sons and daughters of the American middle class for seven years. As if to recapture the sense of growing up in a country which I didn't grow up. And also writing novels about all that. The way Fabian writes his books about equestrian art as he perceives it in the United States. Of course this doesn't get him more readers."

"And it doesn't make him popular with his polo playing friends either."

Kosinski toys with a match book.

"The sentimental *Fiddler on the Roof* crowd that looks at my fiction—they object to it on the same level that people who like writing would object to Fabian's. They want to be reassured rather than threatened and confronted. I think there's a sentimental trend in this country, very powerfully involving literature as well. You're not supposed to make the reader uncomfortable. He's your customer. Be nice to him. Puzzle him, don't confront him. Amuse him, don't disturb him. Don't talk about an accident as an accident. Talk about an accident as a memory of an accident or an impression of an accident. You are not threatened by it any more. Distance, distance, distance.

"There's no distance in my fiction. *Time* magazine's review reprimands me for what I would have been praised for 15 years ago."

He quotes with indignation: "His characters search their souls to the limits."

"You're not supposed to do that, apparently. The second is: 'His characters are prototypes.' How can you understand a character if he's not a prototype? I think 15 years ago I would have been praised for making characters search themselves to their limits. And certainly for trying to extract from our condition what is prototypic in it. What it is in a man who fears death. You can't describe it by a clown telling jokes about dying on a stage."

Aging is an issue in *Passion Play*. I wonder if Kosinski, whose big shock of black hair has no hint of gray, is afraid of aging.

"Aging means that there's a signal, that nature is trying to tell me something. Not society this time. That's why this book is about aging. Because the agencies of society are not involved here any more. Now we have discovered a certain wisdom in ourselves. The wisdom is that we are going to die. We begin to know that. That's why this book is also about age and youth. That's another reason Fabian cannot accept Vanessa, because how is she going to deal with his background. He dismisses the whole war in one sentence. She says, how did all of your relatives die? He says, "In a fire. An arson, one of the biggest."

# Old Man River Lures Literary Giant to City

Jeanie Blake/1979

Published in the *Times-Picayune* 21 October 1979:sec. 3:8. Reprinted by permission.

Author Jerzy Kosinski says he wants to live near a river and so he is moving to New Orleans, adding his name to an already illustrious list of literary figures.

Kosinski has great respect for Southern authors—Tennessee Williams is a good friend and Flannery O'Connor is his favorite writer—but it's the Mississippi River that is drawing the Polish-born author of starkness and the darkness to this city. "As a child, I grew up near two big rivers and rivers have always been important to me," he states simply.

Kosinski says he will be here for an indefinite period. He's looking for a modern apartment, one which will be easy to maintain and is centrally located. "I'll use New Orleans as a point of arrival and departure to see other parts of this area. New Orleans may be the setting for my next book," he volunteers, without volunteering into any details about his eighth novel.

Arriving this week for the opening of the new Dalton bookstore on Canal Street, Kosinski's first two nights were spent in a downtown hotel where the "service was lousy," he complains. "The trays outside my door are from last night," he points out, but not bitterly.

The receptionist at the hotel, a young woman with a fresh-scrubbed face and gently waved hair that is still clinging to its girlhood blondness, was pleasantly shocked when she heard that Kosinski was one of the guests, "Oh, is he *really* here?" she beamed. "I had to read one of his books in high school. Can't remember which one it was, but it impressed me more than *The Snows of Kilimanjaro*. But maybe that's because I was an adolescent then and things shocked me more.

"Can't remember what the book was about either," she confessed, repeating for emphasis: "But it sure did leave an impression."

And Kosinski's books, if nothing else, leave a haunting imprint that life promises nothing, especially longevity.

His works are scars that continually remind you of your vulnerability. He is the protagonist at the cocktail party talking about survival and despair and infidelity and violence while everyone else is trying to figure out why the canapes are so good. His books twitch at the reader's nerve endings like a toothache and some people say they are as undesirable. And when he talks he frequently taps at the television set accusingly and says TV lulls his audience into inactivity.

Four flights up from the bubbly receptionist and light years away in experiences, Kosinski sits in his small hotel room. The window is open and the sounds of the Central Business District, filtered through the curtains, enter the room. His lean figure is now even leaner, hungrier, after a rapid succession of promotional tours drained 12 pounds of nervous energy from his taut athletic frame. His tailored checkered shirt is monogramed and his ankle boots are highly polished. For someone who's suppose to be weird, he sure looks dapper.

Kosinski's stare is direct; his handshake, quick and firm; and his manner is pleasantly methodical. For someone who's an artist, he sure is businesslike. He appears to accept the task of promoting his works without prima donna sniffles.

Interviews, he shrugs, are all part of his job as a novelist. His books are his wares, as well as his art, and, like all good merchants, he listens to criticisms and praises and answers questions about his product. He takes great pride in his work and eagerly invites conversations with his readers.

"Any person who has read a novel by Kosinski is in a position to judge Kosinski," he believes.

But Kosinski separates students, who viewed him as a school assignment, from his readers or—as he prefers to say—his "spiritual community."

And so, if that same sweet bubbly receptionist skipped up to him and rat-a-tatted about her required reading of one of his novels, the master of despair and distortion, might surprise his followers, who know him only through his writings.

"I get embarrassed when people come up to me and tell me about a book of mine they read in school," he says. "I feel disjointed. I don't belong to my own past and suddenly I'm placed in someone else's past."

Kosinski says he quit teaching because his students (from Yale,

Princeton and Wesleyan universities) were unchallenging. Kosinski is also mildly annoyed at the various "M.A.s and Ph.D.s who specialize in my works." He gets the results of their literary contributions and just shakes his tightly-woven dark mass of hair.

"I could have saved them months of work, researching articles written about me," he says. "But they never think of calling me, asking me questions. It's as if I were dead."

Then, he continues, there's another group, the "the historical gossips," who practice "celebritizing" and only write about Kosinski and not his books. That's also frustrating. As he huffs: "It's as if I were alive but my books were dead."

Kosinski's past was the subject of his first novel, *The Painted Bird*, which won him France's Best Foreign Book Award and catapulted him in the mid-sixties as a cult figure.

The young boy in *The Painted Bird* is nameless but he is very much Kosinski as a child. Like the orphaned waif who wandered through villages, suffering tortures and extreme deprivation, Kosinski was separated from his Russian parents and left to survive by his wits in his native Poland during World War II. When he describes the child as looking like "a Gypsy or Jewish stray," a younger Kosinski comes to mind.

Kosinski is now 46 the author of seven books (*Being There, Blind Date, Cockpit, The Devil Tree*), a recipient of the Award in Literature of the National Institute of Arts and Letters, a Ford and Guggenheim fellow and author of two nonfiction books on social psychology, which he wrote while he was a graduate student at Columbia under the pen name of Joseph Novak. He is also past president of the American Center of P.E.N., the international association of writers and editors. His books are used in psychology courses as well as by English profs. Not bad for a Polish emigrant who arrived in New York in 1957 with a $2.80 bankroll.

Kosinski was married to Mary Weir, the widow of a millionaire steel magnate from Pittsburgh, Pa., for 10 years. She died in 1968 and they had no children. His first book carries this tribute to her: "To the memory of my wife, Mary Hayward Weir, without whom even the past would lose its meanings." Kosinski now travels with Kiki von Fraunhofer, a friend who—when the need arises—doubles as his secretary. They have been together 10 years.

People today are living separate sentimental lives, he says, and find his novels too disturbing, too threatening. Beauty and serenity are transitory experiences, he asserts. But pain and terror underline man's mortality and, therefore, linger, cling to the soul.

"Tragedy and brutality bring man closer to life," he says.

"When you are watching television, you are in control of the images. It's an actress up on the screen who is experiencing everything. It's passive. But literature does the opposite. You have to see yourself in what you read.

"The books I write go after the reader's values, question his lifestyle, say 'you're not living life as you should.'

"But I have no right to impose my judgment on my readers. I'm not selling my point of view. I see myself as a storyteller.

"I don't prejudge my characters or the events. The reader decides. Was the violence invited? Was the violence justified? Was the violence inflicted gratuitously?

"My novels do not have a tight plot. I think plots are a fraudulent seduction. You have to continue reading until you reach the very end to find the purpose. You read my books for the given moment, with no promises.

"Novels bring us closer to life. Unless there's something menacing, there is no sense of drama. We must realize that life might end at any moment and the only moments we have are the ones at our disposal."

Man, according to Kosinski's philosophy, must know the dark side of life to appreciate its joys. Life is a Yin-Yang affair.

Journalists have written about Kosinski, the nocturnal wanderer, the guy who walks catlike through the streets, looking like a "tough Puerto Rican, so people usually cross the street when they see me." But Kosinski is quick to quell the macho image. When he plays polo and emotions of team members overcome judgment, he says he stops. "I tell them I'm afraid."

Both nightlife—minus the discos—and the daytime interest Kosinski and so he is a divided man, sleeping four-hour shifts. That way, he says, he encounters both lifestyles.

"I'm a sportsman," he says proudly. "Skiing and polo (which was a pivotal part of his seventh novel, *Passion Play*) as well as my writing take up a lot of energy and all three of these activities require rest in the afternoon."

During the interview, Kosinski fidgets, jumps up, sits down, paces back and forth, talks in hurried spurts and then pauses as if to give his words a little space. He opens his suitcase and quickly closes it, almost absentmindedly.

In his suitcases are stacks of black and white photographs of polo games. Many of the pictures were taken by Kosinski during the matches with a camera strapped to his side. He also carries copies of stories about him, which have appeared in other newspapers. And it's rather charming and a bit disalarming that Kosinski, the rugged-looking man who writes of sadomasochism and deprivation, hands these articles out to interviewers to be helpful.

Kosinski jokes that if he stopped writing maybe he'd become an "aging ski instructor." But then, if he stopped writing, maybe he'd just stop living. He says his mind really soars when he's working on a novel. Now, he's enjoying a respite; but when he's writing, his hawk eyes photograph nonstop.

He keeps a little notebook and jots down character types, little personality features and fragments of conversations. He observes, interacts, records and then recalls and creates. He has no writing patterns, he says.

In 1968, Kosinski wrote *Steps,* which received the National Book Award in Fiction. This year, a would-be writer, to illustrate the difficulties of getting a novel published, retyped the *Steps* manuscript word for word, and submitted it to all the publishing companies in New York City. The work was rejected.

Kosinski views the unanimous dismissal of his 11-year-old novel as a commentary on today and not on his writing. Once again, he cites passiveness and television as the culprits. "That book was published during Watergate and Nixon. People then accepted reality as menacing. But now, they want the easy stuff like 'Manhattan' by Woody Allen or 'Fiddler on the Roof.' The publishers said *Steps* was too stark, too uncomfortable."

Kosinski has neither a set publishing company nor an agent. He accepts no advance money for a novel for two reasons: He's insecure about his writing and says he never knows if his most recent work will be his last and he doesn't want to be commited to writing a novel that just might not come.

And he is a man of few, if any, commitments. He is a man without a family or a permanent home. "My readers are my community," he says proudly. "They are my spiritual community and are very important to me. They give me fuel to go and write another novel."

His source book, he says, is his surroundings, which are varied as he has no ties. Where he is, at the moment, is where he lives. He is pure present tense. Neither perfect, nor past.

And for the near future, New Orleans will be his home base. He'll keep an apartment here as long as it is used. He'll be close to the river and then he says New Orleans is appealing to him.

"In many ways New Orleans is the only American city that is secure in its own past. So am I. Both New Orleans and I have been accused of being decadent," he smiles.

# *Being There* and Staying There: Jerzy Kosinski
Tom Teicholz/1980

Originally published in *Interview* February 1980:34–35. Reprinted by permission of Tom Teicholz.

Jerzy Kosinski's recently-published *Passion Play* (St. Martin's Press) concerns the adventures of an errant polo player. It is already a best-seller. An earlier work, *Being There*, is the first to be made into a film. Directed by Hal Ashby with screenplay by Kosinski, *Being There* stars Peter Sellers and Shirley MacLaine. It opened in New York and Los Angeles at Christmas to qualify for Oscar consideration and will open in the rest of the country in February. Kosinski's other novels are: *The Painted Bird, Steps, The Devil Tree, Cockpit* and *Blind Date.*

I ran into Jerzy Kosinski at the 90th Annual National Horse Show at Madison Square Garden. We walked around the Garden, watched the International Jumping Competition and made plans to meet the following weekend.

*At Madison Square Garden, during the jump-off of the International Jumping Competition, sitting with Katherina von F.*

**Jerzy Kosinski:** The foreign riders restrain the horses. The Americans don't. Watch! You see the necks. This is a mean course. Look at that stupid ass pushing the horse with his hand. What does he think he's doing? Horses know more about jumping than men do. They've been doing it much longer. You'll see, the best riders take a natural pace and let the horse do the work.

**Thomas Teicholz:** Who first introduced you to polo?

**JK:** I saw a lot of polo with my first wife, Mary Hayward Weir. But I think it was Averill Harriman who first introduced me to playing.

**TT:** And you had never played before coming to the states?

**JK:** Where? In Poland? No, but it was easy to pick up. It's great exercise. Very good for the cardiovascular system. Riding the horse loosens you up, too. The spine. It's the best; that's why there are so many older players. Polo gives them life.

*We approach a stall for H. Kauffman & Sons Saddlery Co. where a large sign advertises signed copies of Kosinski's* Passion Play. *Mr. Kauffman sees Kosinski.*

**Mr. Kauffman:** Hi, you're just in time.

**JK:** That's my talent to be in the right place at the right time.

**MR. K:** There's a woman here about to buy your book and she was just telling me that she's read all of your works. Excuse me (*to an attractive blonde woman standing waiting at the cash register*), this is Jerzy Kosinski.

**Woman:** Oh! Mr. Kosinski.

**TT:** How are the books selling?

**Mr. K:** Very well.

**TT:** Do you think the people who buy the book know it's a novel?

**Mr. K:** I think many are buying it as a horse book. The others, they just like dirty books, eh Jerzy?

**JK:** A good customer always finds what he wants.

**Mr. K:** I think we're running out of signed copies. Would you mind signing some more?

**TT:** Now that with *Passion Play* you're getting so much attention from the horse world, have you been tempted to write any serious non-fiction pieces on horsemanship?

**JK:** I've had a lot of offers. Especially from Canada. They have the best horse magazines there.

**TT:** I saw the story in *People* magazine.

**JK:** It was terrible. But again, I had no choice. They called me up and said they were going to do a story about me; and that they would do the story without me if I didn't want to be interviewed.

**TT:** I thought it was pretty funny: the picture of you playing polo on an exercycle.

**JK:** That was my idea; we set up right on my terrace. But what I didn't like was this: I said that people often come up to *me*: men, women on the streets. We talk. And *People* wrote that *I* often approach men and women on the streets and talk to *them*. I didn't want to make a big fuss. I had my own record of the conversation. But I called up the

journalist and said: Listen, how come you didn't say that if they refuse
to talk to me, I follow them and then murder them? Why not?
[*The journalist in question denied that this was the case or that Kosinski
was in any way displeased by the story.*]

*A young woman approaches Kosinski*

**Young Woman:** Mr. Kosinski? You don't remember me. . . .

**JK:** Of course I do, but you've changed a bit.

**YW:** Mr. Kosinski is a friend of the family. He took photographs of
me when I was five years old. I still have the photos.

**JK:** Did I tell you about *Being There*?

**TT:** Yes. Is Hal Ashby in town? Is the film finished?

**JK:** Yes. I saw it last night. It's very good. I'm very happy with it.
It's very beautiful, visually. Peter Sellers and Shirley MacLaine are in
it. Melvyn Douglas turns in a great performance.

**TT:** And Jack Warden?

**JK:** He plays the President of the United States.

**TT:** Where was it shot?

**JK:** In Washington, D.C. and in Asheville, North Carolina. At the
Biltmore house built by Vanderbilt. There's some irony in that the
house was built in the 18th Century style, and the inspiration for Chance
Gardiner comes from Shakespeare's Richard II. So at least architectur-
ally there's that connection. The making of the film was painless. I have
no objections.

**TT:** What about Peter Sellers? You were unsure about him?

**JK:** No, I wanted him from the beginning.

**TT:** But didn't you originally object?

**JK:** No, except for his age. But Peter Sellers underwent plastic
surgery for the film. I had thought of only two types of actors for this
role: a total unknown, or else someone who could become unknown.
But Peter Sellers is faceless, he has no definite camera persona.

**TT:** Any difficulty writing the screenplay?

**JK:** Anyone who writes a novel can write a screenplay.

**TT:** Fitzgerald had problems in Hollywood.

**JK:** Fitzgerald's problems were not in writing screenplays. They
were perhaps in *who* he was writing screenplays for. Fitzgerald's problem was that *he* had problems. I had complete screenplay control. It was
all written into the contract. The screenplay had to be bought first before

the film would begin. I wrote it in three versions: telephoto, medium-wide and wide-angle, philosophically speaking.

**TT:** And you find the film comes close to the novel?

**JK:** Yes, it's very true.

*The following Saturday I went to visit Kosinski at his office on West 57th Street. We talked about his new book,* Passion Play, *at length and then adjourned for lunch. Afterwards we walked over to Doubleday's on Fifth Avenue where he signed books and then over to his office, by which time it was night.*

**TT:** The novel's title, *Passion Play,* what relation does it bear to mystical passion plays of medieval times?

**JK:** The original plays always had a strong sexual content. Remember, these plays catered to the public and they needed the strong sexual content to draw them into the system of enclosure.

**TT:** Traditionally a Kosinski hero is a "free man" who does as he pleases, who travels throughout the world and in all strata of society unfettered by past, home, friends or need for gainful employment. He is at war with society and with Life itself. But Fabian of *Passion Play* is different in many respects: he is in constant need of cash; he is a sportsman getting older, he is the first Kosinski character to be capable of pity and the first that can be pitied. In your last two works, *Blind Date* and *Passion Play,* there seems to be a softening of the core. Levanter is capable of a love and nostalgia unprecedented and Fabian, in your own words, is a "pathetic figure."

**JK:** You see, it's funny. I find Fabian the strongest and least vulnerable of my characters. Everyone says to me, Kosinski is getting mellower. Why? Because Fabian says, "I love you"? A lot of people say I love you. So what? Fabian is the least giving, the most uncorruptable. Fabian faces the obstacles, and the barriers. He is unable to part with what he is. He takes the fact that he can only play polo and builds himself around the polo mallet. It becomes his strength. Fabian is rigid. Fabian makes an issue of his age.

**TT:** Isn't getting older the one obstacle he can't avoid?

**JK:** Yes. He confronts the issue, observes the process, watches the graying of his hairs and acknowledges them. In fact, most of my characters' ages are uncertain. They act as if they will never age. Tarden, in the final scene in *Cockpit,* visits an old age community in

Florida. He visits the old as if he were spying on their condition; as if
ageing would never be a part of his life. And Fabian is a sportsman.
He's the first of my characters who lives entirely as a sportsman.

**TT:** It's lucky then that he chose polo. Aren't there many polo players who continue to play into their sixties?

**JK:** Even seventies. In polo, the horse gives the energy and the man
is the strike. The horse stays young and the horse is 80% of the game.

**TT:** But what is it about Fabian that needs a horse, that needs that
partnership?

**JK:** He needs the horse but a moment. The horse is an extension of
one's flesh. As simple and as unpredictable as that.

**TT:** In your first published book, the nonfiction work, *The Future Is
Ours, Comrade,* you describe horses in the Soviet Union as objects of
fear.

**JK:** When I was growing up, horses were tortured and meant to in-
timidate. *Passion Play* is not the glorification of the horse. This book is
derogatory to the horse. Here (*Kosinski reads*): "Fabian knew that the
beauty, allure and menace of the horse rested solely in its anatomy and
not in a complex intelligence." This is the demystification of the horse.

**TT:** In *The Painted Bird,* your first novel, there was a strong
identification with the animal. In *Passion Play,* Fabian has two horses,
both, in your own words, "losers."

**JK:** Both losers and both crippled. Both have had imposed on them
society's notions of what they ought to be. They're both horses whose
identities have been stripped. Fabian brings them back, heals them as
polo horses. Horses on the run. The horses had been trained as show
horses, to parade step—which is like a goose step. Their whole upbringing is part of the Nazi nature, which says that you can't function
unless you've been trained to do so. The controversy between the
Tennessee Walking horse and the American Saddle horse has become a
philosophic debate. Scientists have written articles to prove that the
Tennessee Walking horses have "a natural inclination" for the running
walk. But they go on to say that the natural inclination needs training.
The horses were plantation horses and today in the South they need to
justify the terrible training the horses must go through. The whole idea
of a running walk is like the Aryan supremacy idea: the selected must
perform. Fabian refuses to have done to him what has been done to the

horses. He has the most soul of my characters. He is surrounded, enclosed by what he believes in. He has his Van-home.

**TT:** But if he's so independent, why does he need such a major constant, such a great support system?

**JK:** He's a polo player. How else could a polo player travel with horses?

**TT:** But that was your choice to make him a polo player. He could have been a tennis player.

**JK:** Yes, but the Van-home is important, because in a Van-home you do the driving. You're free from any outsider's gaze. When someone enters Fabian's Van-home, they enter the privacy of his world.

**TT:** You've described your parents' different personal reactions to the Holocaust: your mother busily taking notes, your father escaping in pure math, working at equations. In you, the Holocaust survivor, I find the two strains meeting: you were a trained social scientist but you now live as a fiction writer. How do you see these different strains at play in your work?

**JK:** There is pure math in terms of selecting the logarithm—in creating the mathematical equation. The Social Scientist provides the conviction that what I write is sufficiently typical so that it can be understood.

The Artist looks for the conception, the Social Scientist leases the space.

It works like this:

The Artist says: I'm going to write about sex; I'm going to write about war, I'm going to write it as a novel because it can't be done as a scientific treatise.

Next, the Trained Reader speaks up. As a novelist I must be a trained reader as well. He says: You've read this before, novels in which the characters are persecuted.

The Socially Responsible Reader says: That's alright, as a creative spirit you're not flying alone. There's Dryden, Sinclair Lewis, Upton Sinclair, Mark Twain, even Jack London we can lease you some space from. Space that hasn't been used since the Nineteenth century or space that's been underused. Like *The Confidence Man* by Melville for Tarden.

We lease the Tenement, the space, then we move in.

From Dreiser's *Financier* we lease a space he hasn't used sufficiently and we write *The Devil Tree*. And so forth. We leave Stendhal for Fabian. Remember in *The Chartreuse de Parme*—Fabrice? Fabrice, Fabian, it's interesting where we get names from. Anyhow, now the Social Scientist and the Anthropologist come in and furnish the apartment from our mental department store. No boutiques. No shop that's too specialized. It's between you and the common reader, that's how you must see yourself. Nothing over–idiosyncratic. Nothing that our department store wouldn't carry.

The Mathematician. . . .

**TT:** He's the interior decorator.

**JK:** Yes, he's in charge of rearranging the furniture. He's in charge of the formula. After all, novels are much alike. Even the most avant-garde works conform to basic notions of writing—we're moving in a Euclidian universe. Within the principles we alter the components to show different things, but it's still the same geometry.

In my case there's one more character which represents the intellectual in the industrial state, aware of inner forces. Aware of the police state on the left and the corporate state on the right and especially of the indifference in between.

This character defends the Tenement and installs the security system to protect the artist and his goods; to make sure the department store will not mislabel it. To guarantee control of the product.

**TT:** Isn't there also one more persona at play in your work: the alien? Always a stranger, always distanced. The Jew. The inner emigré.

**JK:** The inner emigré carries a passport from non-existing academicians. My life in fiction began when I created what was my most real fiction, the recommendations I forged which permitted me to leave Poland. Further, by having written novels which are "obviously auto-biographical" I have protected myself. By making myself so open to scrutiny that I am without a past, I'm a private person free to provoke the next step in my living by a conscious act; to be in charge of the Passion and the Play. In this way the notion of the heroic is defrauded. People can always say "Kosinski? He's a maniac." Because by saying openly that I know what I'm writing about I'm disguised, in camou-flage: A passport to leave my fictional country for the next experience.

**TT:** Fabian lives as well by writing books similar to those Jerzy Kosinski has written.

**JK:** If you substitute literature for polo in my book it works very well. There are only 1,500 players. It's a rough game. Though a team sport, it's moment of truth rests in the one on one, between the novelist and his reader. And you must gamble.

**TT:** What's the next facet left in the ontology?

**JK:** It will be about a corporate man.

**TT:** What about *The Devil Tree,* you mentioned something about revising it.

**JK:** Yes, that's the next project. But the problem is that it won't be a re-issue like Fowles' *The Magus.* I want to change certain circumstances. While I was writing the Devil Tree in 71–72 I was under treatment for an optic nerve problem. I had to give myself injections of an auto-vaccine—a vaccine made from my own cells to build up the immunities plus I was teaching full-time at Yale and this may have resulted in a narrative which could have benefitted from elements not included.

**TT:** New material?

**JK:** No, fragments I have in my notes of the time but which for some reason I didn't use. But the problem is to get a publisher to re-issue it in hardback, otherwise the libraries will continue to stock a *Devil Tree* which is not the one I wish read.

**TT:** While we're on the subject of economics, Fabian is your first hero who's in constant economic need.

**JK:** He tries to get the minimum he needs to keep up. He's a poor man who comes into connections. But perhaps my preoccupation with rich people is a remnant from my socialist past.

**TT:** You say your book attacks middle-class values so strongly and yet your books sell best in the Midwest.

**JK:** The Midwest is still the home of rugged individualism where they appreciate the one on one. It's non-Freudian, non-refractive. My novels are designed to assault the reader. So you can draw back. Out of this encounter you should extract something. Between the novelist and the reader you should reclaim the heroic that will allow you to match brain and wits with the author. One to one.

**TT:** What about the '80's?

**JK:** Very drab, slow time. Humiliating.

# Jerzy Kosinski Is the Zbig of Books

Nancy Collins/1980

Published in *The Washington Star*. 10 February 1980:F-1,8. Reprinted by permission of Nancy Collins.

"Brzezinski is to politics what my novels are to fiction: confrontation," begins Jerzy Kosinski on the subject of his friend and fellow countryman Zbigniew Brzezinski.

"Brzezinski, you see, is the modern corporate figure in politics. A prototype. But there'll be more of them. Kissinger belongs to the 19th century, to the Congress of Vienna, a marvelous figure but one who connects the present with the past.

"Brzezinski, on the other hand, connects the present to the future, and the future is going to be technocratic. The future is exactly where Brzezinski's vision is: China, Japan, the Soviet Union—confrontation."

It is early Monday morning and Jerzy Kosinski is already hitting life head on.

The night before at the Kennedy Center, the film version of Kosinski's novel *Being There,* for which he wrote the screenplay, premiered to raves from a black-tie audience. Washington loved it, as did New York, Los Angeles and Kosinski himself.

"It's a fantastic movie," he says as he stalks across the plushness of his hotel suite at the Four Seasons. Suddenly he stops. There is a mirror and he can't resist. Staring he takes himself in with eyes like ebony laser beams.

"And last night was great fun. It fueled part of my vanity, which is, *obviously,* enormous," he chuckles, shooting a last glance toward the glass. "That is why I look at the mirrors."

And does he like what he sees? Does he find himself attractive?

"I think attractive to . . . some," the 46-year-old Kosinski answers after an uncustomary pause. "And certainly very attractive to myself," he adds quickly. The laugh is cheeky. "I love myself when I ski and when I'm on a polo pony. For one thing I wear a helmet with a face guard longer than my nose . . .

"Actually, I like myself in uniform. I'm sure I selected those sports
for that, to add to the frail masculinity. There's never enough of me,
you see. So ski boots . . . the skis . . . the poles . . . the goggles . . .
the speed make it bigger. And a horse certainly does. Two thousand
years of macho right there with you."

Jerzy Kosinski is witty, brilliant and attractive. He is also enter-
taining—wonderfully so, in fact, possessing the sort of brittle, self-
deprecating humor that saves him from being caught up in his own
intensity.

"I think I am quite sentimental," he is now saying, bristling over a
reviewer's assertion that he has icicles in place of a heart. "But I know
what in me reacts. I also know there are parts of me I *don't* know. In
that inner kingdom, there are large white spots that I traverse very often,
knowing full well there are mine fields I do not know . . .

"Since I left Eastern Europe, everything I have done has been on my
own. A novel is a *very* individual act. In fact, except for this movie, I
am totally responsible fo every act of my life for the last 20 years."

Before that, before 1957 when he faked documents to escape Poland
and arrived in the United States with $2.80, speaking no English, there
was another life. In fact, there were even children. No, he says, he
never wanted a child, but, nevertheless, "I *had* two children. One when
I was a ski instructor. There was a maid in a hostel. We had a child and
I saw that child. But she married someone else. And then, there was the
law student in Poland. There was a child there, too. But I never saw it."

"There was also, I think," he adds moments later, "one in the United
States. But it was promptly—legally—adopted. No, they don't know
I'm the father, but I know the name of the family. They're on Long
Island."

Has he never been curious about the child?

"No. I am curious about grown-ups, not children."

Like the author himself, Kosinski's fiction is consumed by the inner
life. Combatting spiritual and physical destruction, his characters' lives
are fraught with dramatic, tortured encounters. "My novels are basically
about what it is we can get from life on our terms. Never mind the
Party, never mind the Master Charge. You are neither master nor in
charge of anything other than your own inner life. And there you reign.
I have to find out who are the enemies of my kingdom. Only I know
that. Once I know who I am, I'm safe to others and good to myself."

In all, Kosinski has written two non-fiction books and seven novels,
including *The Painted Bird*, an autobiographical account of his war-
torn childhood. Born in Poland in 1933, he was separated from his
parents at age 6 and spent World War II roaming homeless through
Nazi-occupied Europe. Traumatized by his experiences, he lost his
power of speech at age 9 and remained mute for five years. When the
war finally ended he was reunited with his parents and began his
formal schooling.

"In terms of my life, I am no wiser than I was at age 12," he says,
adding with great understatement. "And I was *very* wise then."

It was not easy getting *Being There* onto the screen. For years Kosinski swore he would never be corrupted, never turn his art over to
strangers, never allow any of his books to be made into film.

And then along came Peter Sellers.

In 1971, the day the *London Times* named *Being There* the book of
the year, Kosinski got a phone call. Identifying himself as Chauncey
Gardiner, the name of the protagonist in *Being There,* the man claimed
Kosinski had forever invaded his privacy and demanded to see him.
Figuring the caller to be a British eccentric, Kosinski agreed.

"He sent his car for me. It had TV antennae sticking out all over as
well as one gadget the driver said was radio communication with Mr.
Gardiner's plane. When we arrived at the restaurant, there was a man in
dark glasses and a hat who said his name was Chauncey Gardiner. He
also said I had opened him to permanent insecurity because he had spent
his entire life specializing in only partially incomplete characters.

"I thought he was a psychiatrist. So I said, 'Look, I have never been
analyzed. I know nothing about complete or incomplete. As far as I'm
concerned, we're all incomplete, but I never meant to portray you.'

"He then said he wanted the rights for my character. Now I *knew* this
man was crazy, wanting the royalties to my book, and I got up to leave.
But just then a little girl with a piece of paper came over and said, 'Mr.
Sellers. May I have your autograph?'"

Although his ruse was up, it still took Sellers seven years to seduce
his friend. "Every year Peter and I would meet in some restaurant in
some part of the world. He would play Chauncey Gardiner and try to
convince me. He said his whole life had been a partial portrayal: a lover
who's not a lover, an inspector who's not an inspector; a criminal who's
not a criminal. Chauncey Gardiner he said was the ultimate Peter Sellers

role because nothing about him is what seems to be. Which is actually correct. Peter *is* a sweet, innocent man who—never mind all those divorces—is in some ways as spiritually innocent as Chauncey Gardiner."

Two years ago Sellers finally won. "Peter was on a TV show. He has a heart condition, you know, and so he told the interviewer he expected to die soon. He was then asked what part he would have liked to have played. He said there was only one role in which he could ever really fulfill himself, and that was *Being There*. But he also said Kosinski did not want to make his book into a movie, so he, Sellers, would never be able to realize his dream. Then he promptly sent me a videotape. I, moved to tears thinking of Peter dying, naturally said yes."

Kosinski also said yes to writing the screenplay, his first. As for that experience? "Adapting your own book to the screen is like adapting your old wife to become a mistress."

Kosinski's external life is split between Switzerland and New York, where for 11 years he has lived with Katherina von Fraunhofer, American born baroness and businesswoman in her mid-forties. The two share an obvious mutual respect: He boasts of her polo skills, her skiing prowess, her unflappability; she takes his telephone calls, makes his appointments, organizes his life. Unlike himself, says Kosinski, "Kiki is very steady. No ups, no downs."

They have never married, because "it would be unfair to her. In traditional western society she would become Mrs. Kosinski when she is really a woman of totally independent character. Why fuse it?"

Yet there was one such marital fusion. Her name was Mary Weir, the wealthy American widow of steel magnate Ernest Weir. Kosinski found her when she wrote him a letter praising one of his books. In 1962 they married. In 1966 she died of cancer.

"We were a very good match," he says. "We had arrived at the same philosophy of life by completely different means. I was traumatized by World War II and she was a woman who had grown up in Pittsburgh, worked in a steel company and married the most powerful man in the business. That, too, is traumatizing. You begin to wonder what your life is all about."

Kosinski and his wife lived in a duplex on Park Avenue. When she died, she left him nothing. "I wanted nothing," he says matter-of-factly. "Did it bother me to marry such a rich woman? Not at all. I was aware that had she been a poor secretary somewhere, I'd never have been attracted to her. Her glamor was part of what was extremely seductive about her.

"In fact, throughout the marriage . . . this sounds sentimental . . . " he adds almost apologetically, "but in terms of my life . . . the relationship was . . . uh . . . out of the ordinary. Somehow too much given. I knew it couldn't last but somehow I thought I'd be the first to go."

According to Kosinski, 70 percent of his books are sold to—"thank God"—women in the Midwest and Southwest. "In that part of the country, they are not yet cheaply sentimental. And also my novels are not psychoanalytical. None of my characters has been psychoanalyzed. People do not come to you in life with a record of their psychoanalytical sessions so you know who they are."

In terms of his own "emotional origins," though, Kosinski sees himself as "one of many. My readers are now facing the same mental choices I once did myself: self-denial, reduction of expectations, hostility of environment, breakdown of moral dimensions, betrayal by the bureaucracy.

"Of course, confronted with my readers today, I'm a middle-class fraud and they are authentic. Look at me. Look at the choices I face now. Should I come to Washington to be feted? Should I go to Cannes? Should I go skiing or play tennis? What kind of choices are those?"

They are in fact choices of success, options only magnified now that *Being There* has worked. Because movies, Kosinski has decided, aren't so bad after all. "Novels show how a character thinks, while movies show how a character moves through life." So there will be another film and a book—both called *Autofocus* and both about the same character: a fashion photographer in New York City. Dustin Hoffman will star, Dick Richards will direct, Kosinski will write.

And will he also show up at the Academy Awards? "Are you kidding? Of course. Awards are important for artists. They flatter the ego, and the ego writes books."

Jerzy Kosinski thinks it is possible to design a life. He thinks so because he designed his own.

"And if it *is* possible that one designs one's life the way one designs a novel," concludes the author, "then a lot of people would do well to start reading Kosinski's books right away. Because it's all there."

# Jerzy Kosinski and the Writer on the Holocaust

David M. Szonyi/1982

Published in *The Jewish Times* 9 April 1982:69,79. Reprinted by permission of *The Jewish Times*.

The questions he posed came in an intense, rapid-fire staccato. When writing or speaking about the terrifying past, in this case, the Holocaust, he wondered: "Can we be vulgar, brutal, unkind? Is one supposed to hint at something rather than name it? What is the level of confronting one's past when it is the past of six million people? How secret can I be in this society? How honest? How direct?"

The Polish-Jewish-American novelist Jerzy Kosinski (*The Painted Bird, Steps, Pinball*) posed these questions before a hushed audience of over 600 people at an international forum of Holocaust survivors on March 21. Entitled "Coming to Terms With Our Past," the gathering was held at the Waldorf Astoria Hotel in New York and sponsored by the Holocaust Survivors Memorial Foundation.

For Kosinski, this was only the second time in eighteen years that he had spoken as a survivor and a Jew before a predominantly Jewish audience. "I have abandoned my past in a way," he said, it was a kind of "coming out." He called his fellow Holocaust survivors, their children and others whose lives have been directly touched by the Holocaust "almost a secret society," a group with its own illusions and emotional resonances.

For the writer-survivor, Kosinski pointed out, the question recurs: Should he address himself only to this "secret society," or also to those "merely here to listen"? The latter choice, he added, almost always involves "the compromise of the illusion that we can convey the experience."

By way of example, Kosinski recalled the last time that he had spoken as a Jewish survivor to other Jews—in 1964, before a largely American-born audience in Connecticut. After his talk, a woman came up and called *The Painted Bird* (his first novel, about a seemingly mute boy coming of age, and ravaged by history, in Poland during World

War II), "a terrible book." When Kosinski asked why, the woman al-
luded to a scene in the book in which one peasant had gouged out the
eyes of another. Kosinski retorted by noting that this scene took place in
the context of the novel's background, which was found on the "margin"
of the narrative: trains transporting Jews to the gas chambers. To this, the
woman replied, "we know about that, but gouged-out eyes . . . !?"

After noting how common such an assimilation of the terrible past is,
Kosinski commented, "Good art should be traumatic because it has to
convey a sense of reality—like the trains going to the gas chambers on
the margins of my page." He added that, if anything, his most autobiographical and Holocaust-rooted novel "should have been more direct,
more powerful, stronger." He recalled that his mother had found *The
Painted Bird* too much "a pastoral, bucolic tale."

But even a vivid representation of the past often is heard or spoken
in a very different spirit from that in which it was experienced. On a
Beverly Hills radio program recently, Kosinski was confronted by a
listener who spoke lightly of a scene in *The Painted Bird* in which the
protagonist is thrown into a manure pit. The author traced the scene's
autobiographical roots: In 1942, German posters appeared throughout
Poland depicting "typical Jewish faces," one of which was a boy who
closely resembled Kosinski. Fearful for his fate, Kosinski's parents
arranged for him to hide with a Catholic family, and he soon became
an altar boy. Because Kosinski's back was to the congregation, the
churchgoers rarely saw his face. But once, he fell on his back and was
recognized as a Jew. While Polish peasants during the Holocaust frequently drowned a Jewish child whom they discovered, the peasants in
this particular town threw the young Kosinski into a manure pit. "The
manure pit supported me," he recalled. While such a place was ordinarily utterly repulsive, in this instance, it represented a reprieve from
death. But then, the black world which produces such an association
may be incomprehensible to an American who always has lived in
comfort, he suggested.

Confronting the unvarnished past may or may not change one's own
behavior. Kosinski recounted having a convivial dinner with one of his
German editors, a seemingly sensitive and well-meaning man, along
with two of the editor's friends in Munich. After several drinks, the
editor revealed that the three Germans had been in the *Wehrmacht*
(German army) on the Eastern front during World War II. In fact, they
had been stationed in the same part of Poland where Kosinski was in

hiding, and their mission had been to fight partisans and Jews. With sardonic understatement, Kosinski had commented, "Had we met then, I might not have had the opportunity to meet you in Munich today."

Kosinski acknowledged that, aside from this reponse, he was confounded in trying to react. Again, the questions tumbled out: "Was I deadened to what had happened? So I live too much in the present? Should I summon the feeling that he is my enemy? (He was not, not in Munich.) Should I write about it?"

But however he, the writer-survivor, responds to his past, Kosinski observed, he does so only as an individual. After referring to those who had been crippled or otherwise maimed for life by the Holocaust, he commented that, "I am uneasy about having survived without visible scars. I have no right to be a spokesman for the children who emerged from what was the worst time ever to be a child."

In this case, of course, the writer is also a Jew. Kosinski recalled that his father felt that for a Jew to be happy, he has to be invisible. Yet, observed the son, there came a time when the members of his entire immediate and extended family—mild-mannered scholars, unobtrusive doctors and lawyers, and others—were all too noticed. And he, as a young boy in hiding, had the potentially mortal visibility of circumcision. "To be a Jew is probably not to be transparent," Kosinski concluded.

If there is a lesson to be drawn from all this, he ventured, it is not in one's external appearance but in appreciating that "the ultimate reality is that of my own being." By this, noted Kosinski, he did not mean physical being, for there is something "dead" in the mere organic functioning of an animal or plant. Rather, he referred to the distinctly human—and particularly Jewish—awareness of the "sanctity of life," a life which "imposes great obligations and a sense of privilege." In light of this feeling, for one not to speak fully about oneself and one's past constitutes "an act of betrayal."

And yet—for Kosinski, there is almost always an 'and yet'—this personal, full confrontation with one's past must be "controlled," or more than merely subjective. The writer-survivor-Jew should appreciate that there are historical reasons and a societal context for what happened to him, and that these reflect the rift in contemporary western, Christian civilization. As such, his condition takes on an emblematic quality: "This is the twentieth century at its best because I am here—and at its worse because so much of my family is not."

# *Penthouse* Interview

## Barbara Leaming/1982

Published in *Penthouse* July 1982:128–30, 167–71. Reprinted by
permission of the Wallace Literary Agency, Inc. Copyright © 1982
by Barbara Leaming.

Jerzy Kosinski is one of America's most controversial novelists. He first
shocked the literary world in 1965 with *The Painted Bird,* a graphic
account of a mute child's odyssey through violent, war-torn Poland.
Readers suspected immediately that this, like many first novels, was
autobiographical—and that the young Kosinski had himself been a mute
witness to the unthinkable. In each of his subsequent novels, Kosinski
continued to mingle art and life as he created a bizarre mystique for
himself. Although his books were labeled "fiction," they hinted at
Kosinski's real-life experiences of the perverse. The protagonists of
*Steps* (1968), *Cockpit* (1975), and *Blind Date* (1977) are aficionados of
violence whose roguish and random adventures around the world may
have paralleled Kosinski's own—or so he suggested in frequent talk-
show appearances.

It comes as no surprise that this popular TV raconteur has registered
his fascination with the mass media in one of his most popular novels,
*Being There* (1971). His forays into the inner sanctums of the American
superrich are amply recorded in *The Devil Tree* (1973, revised and
expanded in 1981), and his well-known fascination with high-risk sports
is reflected in *Passion Play* (1979). Most recently, in *Pinball* (1982),
Kosinski meditated on the conflict between privacy and publicity that
has haunted his career. For as much as he has revealed about himself
and his obsessions, Kosinski has also conducted a profoundly secret
life—which he talks about now in this month's *Penthouse* interview.

In 1957 penniless Kosinski arrived in the United States from Poland.
He worked at various odd jobs until he fulfilled the dream of many
immigrants: to marry a fabulously wealthy American woman. Mary
Hayward Weir was eighteen years his senior, and the widow of a steel
magnate. She died six years later and left Kosinski without inheritance.

During their marriage, however, he had managed to produce *The Painted Bird*, launching his international literary career. His second novel, *Steps*, won the coveted National Book Award. Then tragedy struck Kosinski's life again with the brutal slayings of Sharon Tate, Jay Sebring, Wojtek Frykowski, and Abby Folger at the California home of his old friend, filmmaker Roman Polanski. Kosinski said he was on his way to the Polanski household that horrific night but was delayed by a baggage mix-up, which saved his life. Later, he detailed his vision of the Charles Manson murders in the novel *Blind Date*.

*Penthouse* interviewer Barbara Leaming met Jerzy Kosinski while researching her new book, *Polanski: The Filmmaker as Voyeur*. Shortly before the publication of Kosinski's new novel, *Pinball*, she met with him again in his midtown Manhattan apartment to discuss a vast array of topics.

In this month's *Penthouse* interview, Kosinski makes clear how much of the bizarre material in his novels is based on his real-life obsessions. He talks at length about his lifelong interest in nude photography—a subject that comes up in *The Devil Tree, Steps, Cockpit,* and *Blind Date*. He explains his fascination with transsexuals—shared by the protagonists of *Passion Play* and *Blind Date*—and with the disguises and sex clubs that figure so prominently in *Pinball*—and Kosinski here recounts his volatile correspondence and meeting with the brilliant writer-killer, to whose violent youth he compares his own. Finally, Kosinski speaks revealingly about Peter Sellers's appearance in the film version of *Being There,* and about his own off-screen encounters with Warren Beatty when the novelist-turned-actor starred in *Reds*.

**Penthouse:** Is some of your writing pornographic?

**Kosinski:** Some might think it is. Others think it is spiritual.

**Penthouse:** What is the difference between your novels and pornography?

**Kosinski:** Pornography views sex as physical, not spiritual. It does to sex what totalitarianism does to politics: it reduces it to a single dimension. But for me, as for all my fictional characters, sex is a spiritual force, a core of their being, indeed, the procreative basis for self-definition.

**Penthouse:** Are you at all interested in literary pornography? Do you see any difference between literary pornography—something like *The*

*Story of O* or the work of the Marquis de Sade—and commonplace
pornography?

**Kosinski:** I see an enormous difference. If writing about sex
enhances our view of life, then it is art. If it doesn't, if it counteracts the
wholesomeness of sex and degrades it, then it belongs in the Yellow
Pages, under a more commercial listing.

**Penthouse:** Have you, like countless other writers, ever tried to write
undiluted pornography?

**Kosinski:** No. Why should I? I abhor pornography. I express my
interest in the more obvious physical aspects of sex in the photographs
I've taken. Since the age of fifteen I have done a great deal of nude
photography. For me, by nature, the visual is one-dimensional, with
limited complexity or ambiguity. As art, photography interests me
because it portrays surfaces and only surfaces. I like to think that, in
my novels, I give these surfaces depth.

**Penthouse:** What is your relationship with the people you photograph?

**Kosinski:** A limited relationship. By shortening the social distance
between us, the camera mediates between me and the person I am
interested in. The camera makes no phony claims. Its presence states
clearly that as a photographer I am after a visual being. Since I photograph only the face and the body, social complexities between the
photographer and his model are out of place. The idea is to get the
person, or persons, in front of the camera as quickly as possible. There
is no need to go through a great deal of anything else. I have access to
photo studios, each with a darkroom, which I can use at any time. No
matter where I am in New York, it is no more than a ten-minute taxi
ride to a place where I can be alone in a darkroom or where I can
photograph those who went there with me.

**Penthouse:** Do you ever photograph people without their knowledge?

**Kosinski:** No, but often without their clothes. In intimate circumstances, I did not and never would take pictures without people's knowledge. I have often photographed some of my friends—consenting
adults, I might add—in various circumstances of a sexual nature.
Occasionally, I might take pictures without their knowing precisely
when I'm about to depress the camera's shutter.

**Penthouse:** Why would you do that?

**Kosinski:** To get their authentic, unpremeditated expressions. To avoid physical clichés.

**Penthouse:** For what purpose?

**Kosinski:** Because I'm interested in the human body. It excites me sexually and aesthetically. During the war I came to view the human body as a target of destruction, the enemy of mankind beaten, raped, mutilated, gassed. After the war I came to know it as a source of life and love. There was no stronger bond than the embrace of lovers, and none more beautiful. I still see it that way.

**Penthouse:** Who are some of the people you photograph?

**Kosinski:** Usually women, alone or with their intimate friends of the moment. Some of them are, or used to be, performers in nightclubs and burlesques. Some of them I have known only fleetingly, others are friends and acquaintances whom, over the years, I have photographed every few months. Many have allowed themselves to be photographed in exchange for the photographs or photographic portfolios they need in their professional work; many have done it as a favor; many out of vanity. I enlarge their photographs myself and I mount them in several albums, a progression of faces and bodies, through all the stages of undress—and time. Ever since I began doing all this, at the age of sixteen, I've also been developing an elaborate system of filing slides, proofs, and enlargements—and of their quick retrieval, should I suddenly run into one of my photographic subjects.

**Penthouse:** How many women have you photographed in the nude?

**Kosinski:** As a serious, creative project? Several hundred, over more than thirty years, I guess. But then I do take photographs of other women subjects in less creative circumstances.

**Penthouse:** What do the photographs of these women reveal?

**Kosinski:** They obviously reveal many things—how, through their poses, they view themselves as physical beings, and about the flesh and what time does to it. Also, these photographs reveal a great deal about me. It seems that as a visual being I am very idiosyncratic, almost fetishistic, in my pursuits. Looking at the contact sheets and albums, I noticed that, over the years, I used certain angles, distances, and close-ups far more often than I did others. Suddenly, the photographs began to facilitate a revealing analysis of my sexual drive and of its aesthetics. They show how, whether for cultural or personal reasons, I respond to—or prefer—certain parts of the body and certain poses of dress and undress. Why did I press the shutter then, and not three seconds before or after? And why would I use the same angle, the same close-up, with several hundred women I photographed over the years? Before this self-discovery, had someone confronted me with the suggestion of my preferences, I would have quite likely denied them. But the photographs proved otherwise. I was pleased by this newly found source of self-knowledge. But, in some instances, I also told myself that enough is enough and attempted to alter my sexual self.

**Penthouse:** You have both photographed transsexuals and written about them. Why?

**Kosinski:** All my fictional characters are seekers and questers, preoccupied with self-definition. A transsexual's need for a new self-definition is far greater than most of us have. And the price a trans-sexual pays for redefinition is obviously very dramatic—and often irreversible. That's why, at least twice, transsexuals have appeared among the protagonists of my fiction, and that's why I've photographed some eighty of them at various stages of their metamorphosis.

**Penthouse:** In your treatment of sex, do you consider your novels unusually explicit?

**Kosinski:** Not at all unusual, given the role of sexual behavior in contemporary life. Comparatively, the treatment of sex and violence by many of the nineteenth- and early-twentieth-century writers is far more advanced than mine. Look at the fiction of Stendhal, Balzac, Kuprin, Twain, Poe, Zola, or Dreiser. Taking into account their time and literary mores, isn't their portrayal of sex and violence also more graphic than mine? Also, in matters of sex I trail way behind television and contemporary magazines, including the one in which this interview is to appear. As a novelist, I haven't been part of our sexual avant-garde.

**Penthouse:** Why do you think sadomasochism is such a prevalent theme in current popular culture?

**Kosinski:** Popular culture uses these images as shock treatment in a desperate attempt to wake up its audience, which has been made sexually neutralized—or should I say neuterized?—by overexposure to a bland diet of television. The preoccupation with S&M is nothing but a short-lived scream for attention.

**Penthouse:** Some authors, like J. D. Salinger and Thomas Pynchon, seek to conceal themselves. Why do you choose visibility?

**Kosinski:** Since the end of World War II, when I was twelve, I have structured my life to be both private and public. I like to openly participate in the life of the community. I am committed to certain ideas and I want to be able to fight for them. Nothing interests me more than people. In the States, I felt safe enough to go public both as a writer and as a social activist in the field of human rights. For an artist there is no better safety than to go public. Once you are public, the public looks for what it has already seen. At one time, everyone tried to trace Salinger, to find Pynchon. No one tries to find Kosinski. In a sense, my visibility is my ultimate camouflage: nothing hides one better from the public than appearing on the Johnny Carson show, because everyone thinks they know what one is doing and what one is all about—and yet there are 364 other days in the year, when they don't.

**Penthouse:** Is it true that you often go about in disguise?

**Kosinski:** I do, but not too often and only for the sake of privacy. Once in a while, though, I don't mind a little prank. Last night, for instance, I went out, in disguise, with two friends. At one of the places we visited, we met a Yale graduate they knew—and who, when I taught there, was once my student. Testing my disguise, my friends began discussing Kosinski with him, and for part of the evening, the conversation was about Kosinski—my teaching method—and what he, and others like him, thought about me.

**Penthouse:** Did you participate in the discussion?

**Kosinski:** No, I sat next to him, drank my drink, and, pretending to be tired, just listened. The disguise worked.

**Penthouse:** Did you enjoy this?

**Kosinski:** I loved it. I acquired yet another insight into my own past. I had an enormous charge out of it.

**Penthouse:** Do you mind being recognized by your readers when you go to the various sex clubs?

**Kosinski:** No more, no less than when I go any other place. Sex clubs are open to the public and profiled in *Time* and *Newsweek* and on prime-time television, and are aspects of our life. And as a writer I'm just as curious about them as I am about industrial exhibits or sports events. Most people at the sex clubs aren't into recognizing others. Usually, they are there to seek inner recognition.

**Penthouse:** Do you ever visit the sex clubs in disguise?

**Kosinski:** Once in a while. But when I want to remain anonymous,

I also wear disguises to museums, industrial exhibits, or cinemas. In disguise, whether alone or accompanying someone in particular, I am more abandoned, as if an outer censorship has been lifted. After all, I don't go to these places to discuss my novels, or my politics. I am there to be myself, to watch or even to do what interests me.

**Penthouse:** There are many public figures who complain about the press's violation of their privacy. Do you feel that there is an area of your life which the press should leave alone?

**Kosinski:** Ours is an open society. If by virtue of my writing and my other social activities I become a public figure, the press has a right to go after me. Still, there are many areas of my life which are private and anonymous. That's why I conduct myself the way I do. If I am big enough to make myself a public figure, I should also be small enough to hide well.

**Penthouse:** Have you encountered dangerous situations in your nighttime wanderings? Do you carry a weapon?

**Kosinski:** I encounter the same dangers most people do. As for weapons, I have my own ways of dealing with these things.

**Penthouse:** A gun?

**Kosinski:** Never a gun. Still, I have my own ways.

**Penthouse:** Will you talk about them?

**Kosinski:** No.

**Penthouse:** You used to race GT cars and motorbikes. You are also a relentless polo player and jumper, as well as an aggressive downhill skier. Do you enjoy high-risk sports and danger?

**Kosinski:** I don't. I'm extremely careful. I take more precautions against danger than any sportsman I know. I want to stay alive and unharmed for as long as chance will let me—I love life too much to risk it in a silly way.

**Penthouse:** Are you afraid of dying?

**Kosinski:** Not at all. Not even remotely. The notion of death—and its imminence—enhances life.

**Penthouse:** In *Pinball*, Andrea Gwynplaine, the beautiful and talented Julliard student, seeks revenge. Revenge is a frequent obsession of your characters. Why?

**Kosinski:** Defense, rather than obsession. My characters often defend themselves against entrapments by oppressive societies. I see revenge as the last vestige of the eminently threatened self. When I was a student at the Stalinist university and the party threatened me with prison unless I would reform or openly perform an act of self-criticism and repent, I warned them, "Don't forget, if I go down, some of you will go with me." Revenge can be a positive force—the victim's final dignity.

**Penthouse:** Norman Mailer said that, for the sake of culture, he would be willing to take the risk with Jack Henry Abbott again. Would you?

**Kosinski:** Culture is a risk already. Society doesn't really need it. A lot of societies go without much of it; others kill it easily.

**Penthouse:** Was culture worth the risk Mailer and others took with Abbott?

**Kosinski:** Absolutely. Yes.

**Penthouse:** Jack Abbott was released from prison, with Mailer's help, and then Abbott killed again. Could someone like Abbott ever function in society as a "normal" person?

**Kosinski:** Yes, but after the proper transition. With Abbott, there was no provision made for a meaningful transition from the traumatic reality of prison to the traumatic reality of Manhattan. We all assumed that a violent man, coming from a violent environment, would become peaceful, simply because he happened to be an intellectual. Abbott also might have assumed that simply because he was a writer, he could now deal with his own emotional terror.

**Penthouse:** Why would Jack Henry Abbott write to you? What were his letters to you like?

**Kosinski:** I'd just been elected president of P.E.N., the association of writers and editors, and I had advocated the reenforcement of the P.E.N. prisoners' program, whereby books were sent to prisoners, who were encouraged to enter writing contests in poetry, fiction, and nonfiction.

As far as I know, Abbott entered one of these contests, in fiction. He wrote his first letter to me in 1973 because he had read *The Painted Bird*; and because in the novel the boy is saved by the Red Army, Abbott assumed that as a result of my own childhood I was, like him, a Soviet sympathizer. Needing help from P.E.N. and wanting to get out of prison, Abbott seized the opportunity to consider Kosinski his ally. The letter began in a friendly tone. But midway into it he had read other works by me, including my two studies of the social psychology of the Soviet system, which were obviously critical of it. The letter's tone became hostile. He called me a Rockefeller coupon-clipper, an enemy of mankind, who corrupted himself by escaping the possibility of becoming a member of the Communist party and living in the East.

When, after having read *The Devil Tree,* he learned that, like *The Painted Bird,* it too was strongly autobiographical and that I was once married to an industrialist's widow, his negative picture of me was complete. The assault continued for two years and many letters. Abbott embarked on the most sustained, vile barrage of personal, sexual, political, and aesthetic abuse, dissecting my novels and filtering them through his notion of my betrayal of mankind, and of my attachment to what to him was the worst of it—the contemporary theological Judaic concept of radical self-understanding and the Protestant message of the human boundary situation, both of which he easily detected in my fiction. To him, my preoccupation with the individual's freedom to define himself was nothing but an attempt to create a capitalist-market ideal consumer.

I wrote to Abbott once, then twice more, after which I stopped. When, after my second term as president of P.E.N., I became active in the International League for Human Rights and in the American Civil Liberties Union, Abbott decided his enmity wouldn't take him any-where. He then sent me several conciliatory letters, saying he'd been wrong in his initial assumption, and that after a second reading of my fiction he'd come to the conclusion that I had a right to my—however individualistic—philosophy. But I didn't reply, and he abandoned me as a potential rescue system. Abbott waited, until he came across Norman Mailer, who was writing *The Executioner's Song* and who, having had brushes with violence in his own life, would be—Abbott must have assumed—a more receptive ally than Jerzy Kosinski.

**Penthouse:** When you finally met him, after his release, what was the encounter like?

**Kosinski:** The meeting was very friendly. I was invited by him to come to dinner, and ever since I blame myself, for I shouldn't have gone. After all, the dinner was to pay tribute to Jack Abbott and to his book. The book restated the philosophy which in my life I had so often rejected—and yet I went to pay tribute to Jack Abbott.

**Penthouse:** Why?

**Kosinski** Because I became corrupted, that's why. Because I was corrupted by my exaggerated responsibility to society, and by the superficial requirements of my own social visibility. And because of

my temporary—I like to think—inability to sort out what was moral
and immoral about the whole affair. Come to think of it, some of the
greatest corruptions in history might have started with such an innocent
invitation to a dinner. Photographs taken during the dinner by a friend
of mine show Abbott passionately embracing me, and—I am sorry to
say—my responding in kind by toasting him and so forth.

During the dinner, with reference to our correspondence, I asked him
whether, if he were to join the Communist party and it took power in
the United States, he would go after me and put me in prison. He said
that it would depend on historical circumstances as defined by the party,
not by him personally. I asked him then whether as a free man he intended to continue to apply his philosophy of pragmatic violence of
the "school of gladiators" he wrote about in his book, and he said that
this, too, depended on circumstances—personal ones. I said that as a
child of World War II, I, too, had come from a gladiator school, but
that I had advice for him: in our world, if one is accosted by a violent
man, one must move aside. To confront such a man with violence
would mean to subscribe to his code, and I loved life too much to risk
it on somebody else's terms. "Well, I would never let anyone push me
around," Abbott said. "Then," I said, "you might die in the hands of
another gladiator. I have been out in this city, and in Chicago, and in
Los Angeles, and in Denver, and in New Orleans; in big towns and in
small towns; I have been to the gambling resorts, the whorehouses, as
well as in universities and the churches. It happens to be a very violent
country, so when they hit you, and you don't move away, they'll hit
you again." "Well," he said, "that is not what I would do, Jerzy."

Meanwhile, I advised him to look for an apartment on Staten Island,
outside New York. I felt Staten Island would expose him to the sea,
which he didn't know at all. I thought the sea might give him an idea of
the world as an open space rather than just as Manhattan—an urban
prison cell. But then, all of his talk dissolved into chatter. It was my last
and only meeting with Jack Henry Abbott. You know the rest.

**Penthouse:** After World War II, Jerzy Kosinski also had to emerge
from a violent milieu.

**Kosinski:** And initially at least, I didn't necessarily deal with it any
better than Abbott. When the war ended, I was placed by the authorities
with hundreds of other parentless kids in an orphanage, where we
fought each other with the skills acquired in our survival and with the

venom learned from our Nazi and Soviet oppressors. As a mute (I lost my speech at the age of nine), I ran an additional risk of being considered retarded—and treated accordingly, particularly by other boys: In the orphanage violence reigned: once again, though this time not from the peasants, I learned firsthand (though it wasn't just a hand) what rape meant—both sides of it.

After my parents traced me to the orphanage and took me out of it, I lived with them and with their newly adopted baby boy, who, I felt, had usurped my place in the love of my parents and whom I hated more than the memory of war. And so I began to go out at night and seek the attention, respect, and love of strangers, even though the authorities warned my parents I was a potential runaway. Imagine! I survived the war by running away from one village to the next in the rather harsh region of Eastern Europe, and when the war ended, the authorities warned my parents I might run away! On several occasions, I was picked up by the police as a runaway vagrant.

**Penthouse:** As a runaway vagrant?

**Kosinski:** Yes. But I wasn't really running away. I was merely running. Had I wanted to disappear, I was equipped to do it without ever being caught. I just wanted to go out at night, where I could test my freedom to hide, and when fewer people seemed to mind a mute kid. But I always wanted to come home. And in the morning the police would deliver me to my poor parents, as a runaway child. As a result of these escapades, and my brushes with the law five months after my parents found me, we had to leave the big town we lived in and moved to a small town in the mountains. There I was placed in the care of a deaf-mute ski instructor. It was thought that, since there is no nightlife in the mountains, I could not enter into conflict with the law.

**Penthouse:** Many of your novels offer a catalog of the cruelties you yourself witnessed. What is the cruelest thing you saw in postwar Eastern Europe?

**Kosinski:** The cruelest thing I witnessed was the steady, relentless manipulation of individuals by the party. The constant interference in the lives of innocent, decent people; the constant censoring of every act; the steady presence of the totalitarian philosophy. And the oppressive fear it introduced to our daily existence. In Communist Poland, an interview with a critic like you would have been a source of unbearable terror to me and my family. The terror would start long before your arrival and continue long after your departure—not to mention the unpredictable outcome of its publication. The consequences of an interview could have been terrible. If I said only what I was supposed to, you or your editors could accuse me of not telling the truth, of just trying to please the party. If I became openly hostile and spoke the truth—we know the consequences of that.

And so, the constant, unresolved predicament of being at the mercy of the most sinister political apparatus ever developed, in whose hands your life and the life of your family is vested at every moment. At any time, when I took nude pictures, it was considered, by the party, as an act of bourgeois preoccupation—for which I could be expelled from the university and punitively drafted into the army. When, for instance, I spent hours in the library, I had to keep in mind that someone would make a tally of how many hours I spent there reading what books. Then, at a student meeting a party member might get up and start a general discussion of the reading habits of certain people. "For example," he would say, pointing an accusing finger at me, "in the last few weeks, betraying his contempt for our socialist tasks, Comrade Kosinski has escaped into the capitalist niche of Romantic poetry."

**Penthouse:** You were never a party member?

**Kosinski:** No. I refused even to join the student union—an obligatory membership for anyone studying. In Lodz, the nation's second largest city, I was the only one who didn't belong, and because of such open defiance I was twice thrown out of the university by the student union. Threatening to resign, the rector and the dean had me reinstated, because they claimed that if the students could so arbitrarily remove a perfectly good student like me, they could also, if they wanted to, remove a rector or a dean.

Ironically, soon after, the party decided to utilize for its own good even my anti-Communist stance. Twice, in 1955 and in 1957, I was appointed to be in charge of the Western honorary dignitaries—scientists, writers, theologians—at both the Warsaw and Moscow Youth Festivals—precisely because I was a known anti-Communist, and so were many of the Westerners. Officially, I was assigned to this task simply because I spoke some foreign languages, but in fact this was done to convince the West that in a Communist state dissent was allowed. When the foreign dignitaries arrived, they were told that in charge of them was

Jerzy Kosinski, the young, multilingual social scientist—and well-known dissident. That's how perverse the system is.

**Penthouse:** You are a survivor. Is there any act which is not justified by the need to survive?

**Kosinski:** A great number of things would not justify my surviving. There was a time when, planning my escape to the West, I pondered suicide, simply because if caught, I would be given a long prison sentence and I didn't think that going to Communist prison for seven or twelve years was worth living for. I carried cyanide, and if they came to arrest me, I was perfectly ready to lick it. Also, I would have committed suicide had I been used against anyone else. The time they threatened to draft me—once into the army intelligence and once into the Polish secret police—I told them point-blank: "It's a useless act: the minute you do it, I will kill myself." To show that I was perfectly capable of it and that they couldn't stop me, I described three or four very pragmatic ways I might use to kill myself. After this, the party took a second look at me and more or less they left me alone. I would never let myself be used against anyone else—even if my life depended on it. Since I view life as a process that can end at any time, and arbitrarily at that, I see nothing wrong in using suicide as a safety device—one more guarantor of the decency of my life as it goes on.

**Penthouse:** Why did they want you for the army or police?

**Kosinski:** Because I was a survivor, with a history of violence, yet intelligent enough and—they probably assumed—Byzantine enough to serve them. That's where they misjudged me: precisely because I was Byzantine, they could never get me alive.

**Penthouse:** Because of your brutal childhood experience, do you perceive yourself as a victim?

**Kosinski:** I saw myself as a victim only from the age of six, when, at the war's outset, I was separated from my parents, until three years later, when I lost my speech. Ironically, as a mute, I accepted myself as being apart from others—and thus no longer a victim. Since I couldn't communicate with their world, the conflict ended. If I could no longer answer questions asked of me by their world, I didn't have to worry about those who would ask them either. I ceased being afraid. I looked at myself from within. I listened to my own inner voice. I knew my answers. Nobody else did.

**Penthouse:** What was it like for you before you achieved this inner peace?

**Kosinski:** I hated life. I was afraid of pain. Of being molested, raped, drowned, starved, killed by a German bullet, or taken to a gas chamber. Between the ages of six and nine, I made several suicide attempts. Once, I threw myself from a tree; another time, from a fence. I wanted to die because I had been badly abused and beaten up, and I didn't want to go through all this again. Once, to kill myself, I pondered swallowing nails.

Between the ages of nine, when I became mute, and fifteen and a half, when I got my speech back, I developed inner peace. Though I was beaten and maltreated a lot when I was mute, I led an extremely rich inner life. I had no quarrel with myself. But then, once I regained my speech after the war, the trauma began. The Stalinist society went after me, asking questions I didn't want to hear, demanding answers I would not give.

**Penthouse:** How did you lose your speech?

**Kosinski:** In a church, on Corpus Cristi in June 1942, while serving in a Mass as one of the altar boys, I was supposed to transfer the Bible from one side of the altar to another but fell with it. Since moments before it happened I knew I was going to fall—both physically and, I thought, forever in the eyes of the church—I am convinced I lost my speech from the tension *before* the actual fall.

**Penthouse:** How did you finally regain your speech?

**Kosinski:** A skiing accident eventually brought it back. I was skiing downhill toward my ski instructor, himself a deaf-mute, a warm, older man who had lived in the mountains all his life. There was a precipice on the way, and sliding toward it I was gripped by the fear that something unavoidable and horrible was about to take place—the same fear I once felt during that Mass. This fear, I think, snapped my muteness, moments before I actually fell into the precipice and fractured my skull. My speech reemerged a few weeks later.

**Penthouse:** Could something like this happen to you again?

**Kosinski:** It could, though I don't think there is anything right now that could generate such terror in me. I'm not so fearful anymore. Maybe I'm too old to experience fears of such intensity.

**Penthouse:** You are now working on a screenplay based on your novel *Passion Play*. Would you ever consider directing a film?

**Kosinski:** Directing doesn't interest me. It's collective and highly restricted by the never-ending responsibility vis-à-vis screenplay, actors, investors, studios, etc. Writing fiction leaves me uncensored and free to

do what I want to do most. Now that I've acted—in *Reds*—I realize
even more fully that no artist is as free as a novelist.

**Penthouse:** Can you tell me why, in *Reds,* Warren Beatty cast you in
the role of Grigori Zinoviev? And were you strongly directed by him?

**Kosinski:** Profoundly directed. My performance owes far more to the
director than, as an actor, I would like to admit. Initially, I turned down
the role. But it was pointed out to me that while, as an actor, I could
afford not to play in *Reds,* as a novelist I couldn't afford to miss the
opportunity of such an experience. Then, I realized that I probably
wouldn't have another chance to play in a Hollywood epic—and *Reds*
might be the biggest epic ever made.

But the prime motivation Warren provided was moral and political.
He said that, after my having been imprisoned for twenty-four years by
totalitarian philosophy, I now had a chance as Grigori Zinoviev to show
millions of Americans what a committed Communist is really like—
both ideologically motivated, bureaucratic, and detached from concrete
human existence at the same time. Warren said I could show such a
bureaucrat in confrontation with John Reed, who was a writer very
much like I am today, a man defending his moral right to write what *he*,
not the party, perceives to be truth. Regarding one of the film's final
scenes, when Reed screams at Zinoviev, "You don't rewrite what I
write!", Warren said, "Isn't this what Kosinski had been doing for the
last twenty years? Defending himself and, as past president of P.E.N.,
other writers and intellectuals like him against censorship?" Thus, said
Warren, in the confrontation of Zinoviev and Reed, I would speak for
the philosophy that once oppressed me in the first half of my life, and
Warren would defend the very principle that has rendered me free as a
writer in the second half of my life. To make certain that I was free to
convey the essence of Communist doctrine as proposed by Zinoviev,
I would write my own lines.

**Penthouse:** You contributed dialogue to the screenplay?

**Kosinski:** Yes, I wrote all Zinoviev's dialogue, with Warren going
over it. Then, to match Zinoviev's, Warren would write the lines of
John Reed.

**Penthouse:** How did Warren Beatty deal with you on the set of *Reds*?

**Kosinski:** To throw me back into my past, Warren did something
very clever. The extras he selected to surround Zinoviev in his committee were actually Soviet bureaucrats who had left the Soviet Union very
recently and lived in Spain and France. Because they spoke only

Russian, I was forced to speak Russian to them. Once they learned who I was, they did not hide their dislike for me, both as a writer who abandoned his native idiom to write in English and as an actor portraying Zinoviev, a Jew and a character they did not think much of. Soon they made me profoundly uncomfortable. I was in a state of emotional siege and, willy-nilly, in the process, emotionally I *became* Zinoviev.

Equally soon, as Kosinski/Zinoviev I began to dislike Beatty/John Reed, who in his American naiveté knew nothing of what I had to go through with these Russian hard-hats. I guess that my hostility, however, minimal, permeated my performance and possibly made it more authentic.

Very early in my acting, Warren also noticed how in the midst of a take of one of my passionate tirades I became discouraged when I suddenly saw four crew members deeply asleep behind the cameras. After that, in all other takes, he banned everyone from my field of vision, so I couldn't assess the impact of my acting on others.

**Penthouse:** Did he ask you to watch the rushes?

**Kosinski:** He said I could see the rushes, but he said it in such a way that I sensed he didn't think I should. So I decided against looking at the rushes. I did not see myself in *Reds* until two days before the movie opened.

**Penthouse:** Were you happy with your performance?

**Kosinski:** No, I was not. I would rather have played John Reed, and be handsome and glamorous, and kiss Diane Keaton.

**Penthouse:** Tell me about that other famous actor in your life—Peter Sellers in *Being There*.

**Kosinski:** For a long time, I thought the role of Chauncey Gardiner should be filled by an unknown actor, not by Peter Sellers. I even conducted a video test with some fifteen nonprofessionals. Every one of them proved that, even if given the role, he would *remain* unknown. Then, after bombarding me for nine years with calling cards and letters—in which he called himself Chauncey Gardiner—one day, in a small garden, adjoining a beach house in Santa Monica, Peter Sellers demonstrated to me how he'd play the role. I was staggered by what I saw. But it wasn't easy to sell Peter Sellers as Chauncey Gardiner. Everyone thought he was overly identified with *The Pink Panther*. Finally, I managed to convince them. As the role called for no visible signs of aging, without much fanfare Peter Sellers underwent plastic surgery, knowing that immediately after plastic surgery, his face would become a bit blank, its facial muscles slightly rigid. You might have noticed the difference between his face in the last *Pink Panther* and in *Being There*—his last serious film.

**Penthouse:** Will you say something about your next novel? Is there one already in the works?

**Kosinski:** My next novel will be about intimacy, and I have already begun it. It will focus on the spiritual background of intimacy, and on its taboos and rages. How is society present in the lover's embrace? Is some of love pornographic? Is some of the body pornographic?

**Penthouse:** George Steiner has argued against writers making erotic life too public in their works. What do you think?

**Kosinski:** I think that since a novel is itself an intimate act, it is eminently suited to examine intimacy. A novel is the most intimate thing I can make. Right now, until my next novel is out, nothing I do or say or show is more intimate than *Pinball*. No relationship with me could be more intimate than reading it.

# Jerzy Kosinski Leaves 'em Amused, Bemused and Confused

Garry Abrams/1984

Published in the *Los Angeles Times*. 14 November, 1984:Sec.5:1,12.
Reprinted by permission of the Los Angeles Times Syndicate.

Novelist Jerzy Kosinski knows how to leave them amused. He also knows how to leave them bemused.

Both conditions apparently were his aim last week when he made a rare public appearance to deliver a lecture sponsored by UCLA and the Streisand Center for Jewish Cultural Arts. The crowd of about 1,000 that turned out for his talk, spent much of the evening laughing at Kosinski's jokes about circumcision, sex, self-help books, his readers, himself and the nature of fame. But in the question-and-answer period that followed it was clear that many were trying to discover a unifying thread and thrash some overall meaning from Kosinski's discursive, disgressive talk.

Some probably felt frustrated in their efforts. Kosinski gave a series of elusive replies, including this one to a question about how much of his fiction is autobiography: "I am a storyteller, my man. There's no way to tell." A little later, however, he conceded, "There's nothing in my novels that isn't derivative (of my life) in some way."

For those thirsting for a key to his artistic methods Kosinski did, however, offer clues. "I have a fear of plot, plot is an excuse," he said, explaining that the fictional device imposes order where none may exist. At a reception after his talk, Kosinski repeatedly told admirers, "I am not didactic," adding that each listener should find his own meaning in his lecture.

For those who have followed his career, the performance was vintage Kosinski. Since the publication of *The Painted Bird* made him famous in 1966, the native of Poland, now 52, seems to have relished cultivating an enigmatic image—a secretive man who is also a polo player, friend of the rich and famous, even a movie actor with a role in "Reds."

Kosinski, who is currently finishing a book, now divides his time between New York and Switzerland. Whether he intended to or not, the line between Kosinski's life and those of his characters has become blurred, at least for some readers. For instance, *The Painted Bird* is based in part on his boyhood in World War II Poland, the writer has said many times while insisting that the book is entirely fiction. And it seems likely that the blurring will continue with his next book, *The Hermit,* which Kosinski said is about a writer.

In his lecture, titled "Facing the World: Confrontation and Conviction," Kosinski admitted that his real identity is a problem, even to himself. One major element of that problem, he said, is others' perception of him. He is just famous enough to be inaccurately identified, he said, citing an incident in a restaurant when four Japanese businessmen mistook him for mime Marcel Marceau. The businessmen didn't realize their mistake until they saw the autographs he had given them, he said. They all then politely returned the handwriting samples, obviously never having heard of him. The experience was unsatisfactory, he added, even though "for all practical purposes the act of fame was accomplished."

A more common occurrence, he said, is the reader who writes to vent rage over what happens to a character in a novel. Kosinski produced a letter from a reader named "Fat Pat" who objected to the way a female character was treated by a male character on page 158 of *Passion Play.*

After telling Kosinski that "you treat people like trash," Pat went on to object to Kosinski's treatment of women, especially the overweight, and noted that Kosinski himself could be considered unattractive. "You could go sucking up ants with that nose," she wrote.

After ruminating aloud on courses of action, Kosinski concluded that Pat was "writing to my fictional character" and that it was not necessary to get in touch with her. "Why should I do what my character would not do?" he asked.

During his talk, Kosinski referred constantly to a fistful of large index cards that contained notes or were stapled with newspaper and advertising clippings. From these cards Kosinski produced offbeat facts and quotations about what he perceives as dilemmas in determining identity and truth.

Two were obvious favorites of his—an ad for a voice stress analyzer and a Swinging Singles passport he had received in the mail.

After assuring the reader that the analyzer is "ethical" the ad claimed that the machine, used in place of a lie detector, was developed during the Vietnam War. Kosinski looked up and said, "Now we know we have an ethical basis for this," drawing a big laugh. The ad went on to claim that the machine could be used for entertainment—testing the veracity of a newscaster—as well as practical reasons—finding out if the check really is in the mail.

"We don't want something that's gruesome or awful or boring, we want to have fun with it," Kosinski commented.

Despite the claims made for "truth machines," Kosinski said his research found that a small but significant (80 out of 1,000) number of people tested on these machines are found to be lying when they're actually telling the truth. "Would you trust your life to these sorts of statistics?" he asked.

As for the passport, Kosinski seemed most amused by the fact that it contained translations of the phrase, "Take me home, I'll show you a good time," in several languages, including Chinese and Hebrew. "In Eastern Europe there would be no way to travel on this passport," he said. "It would be the fastest way to disappear."

The point, Kosinski said, is that it's difficult to get at the truth of who someone really is—expecially given the many ways people today can identify themselves, including with a Swinging Single passport.

Kosinski also addressed in an oblique way allegations raised in the *Village Voice* two years ago that he has received substantial help in writing his books. The issue was a cause celebre in 1982, sparking numerous articles in the nation's press, including many in Kosinski's defense.

Early American novelist James Fenimore Cooper sued newspapers with which he disagreed, Kosinski noted. But he is prevented from taking such action because he believes in the absolute freedom to publish, he said, even if what is printed is inaccurate, "That article must be published. (Other writers) must be as free as I am," he said, receiving a warm round of applause. "Freedom is the only commodity that is truly unique in this country." He chose his career, Kosinski said, because "to be a writer is to be removed from the world of violence" and because "more than anything I would not be responsible for anyone but myself."

# Encounter—Jerzy Kosinski

Mike Leiderman/1987

Television interview, November 1987, *WJUF-TV*, Jewish Federation of Metropolitan Chicago. Reproduced by permission.

Hello, welcome to the program. I'm Mike Leiderman. With us is author, teacher, actor, activist—and many more things can describe Jerzy Kosinski. But we all know him as one of the foremost writers in the world. He was born of Polish Jewish parents in Poland, survived the Holocaust, later came to the United States where he became one of the top writers, not only in this country but internationally. *The Painted Bird, Steps, The Devil Tree, Being There,* are some of the books that he's written. *Being There,* of course, was made into a movie with screenplay by Jerzy Kosinski and starring Peter Sellers and Shirley MacLaine. Good to have you with us. You are working on a new book?

**JK:** I just finished it; delivered the last galley page to the publishers on the way to Chicago.

**ML:** You don't work real quickly, do you? It takes you a long time to put a book together I heard?

**JK:** Given the size of the book, real quickly.

**ML:** How big?

**JK:** Oh, about 600 and some pages.

**ML:** *The Hermit of 69th Street.* Tell me a little bit about it, since we haven't seen it or heard about it yet.

**JK:** Well it's an attempt at portraying the thinking process that goes into writing of a novel. It's a novel about the state of mind in which a novelist lives—state with a capital 'S'. When one conceives of a novel, I don't think I can describe it in any better way. It's the state of mind as the environment of action—what happens in one's head, when one tries to envisage someone other than oneself, circumstances other than the ones one knows. In other words, what is this reactor? It's a novel about the spiritual reactor, the head, the mind.

**ML:** And the mind and the process. . . .

**JK:** Yes. Fiction and non-fiction fused together, as it is in our conversation right now. We talk about things which are speculative, "being there," hypothetical fictional devices, yet an artifact, a footnote therefore—Peter Sellers, Shirley MacLaine,—these are real things. The movie is not real. It's a figment; it was at least, once, a figment of my imagination as a novel, not as a movie. Movie, that's the second footnote, which means *Hermit of 69th Street* is a mixture of spiritual and actual. Action and reaction, fiction and non-fiction, and since the character is a foot fetishist, a lot of footnotes. And the footnotes very often tell the story.

**ML:** Are you into one of those kinky sex novels again? Remember the kind of program this is.

**JK:** The idea was that I felt that the traditional novel, the kind of a traditional novel I wrote until then—with plot, whether broken or not, nevertheless truly fictional—ran out on me. I had nothing more to say in that. Eight novels, enough!

**ML:** But you have an awful lot of sex in the books that you write.

**JK:** Not enough.

**ML:** Not enough. Why not?

**JK:** Because it's a force of life. I don't know of any other. You wouldn't be here without it. I wouldn't. Sex for me, it's an instinct of life. It's pro-creation.

**ML:** Some of the action could be actually described to be anything but pro-creation, however.

**JK:** Well, it's a matter of opinion.

**ML:** Let's go on to another topic. In some of the information that we received about you, it said that in part *The Hermit of 69th Street* is going to deal with the influence of Rabbi Heschel on you. Why is Abraham Heschel an important figure in the life and work of Jerzy Kosinski?

**JK:** Heschel was an extraordinarily important figure in my life, for many reasons. One, is that he was probably the first philosopher I encountered in translation in 1950 in Poland who confronted what happened in Eastern Europe as part of a long spiritual process without assigning too much importance, spiritually speaking, to the period 1939–1945. In a book he published in 1949 in the United States, *The Earth is the Lord's,* Heschel looked upon the 1,000 years that we, the Jews, have spent in Eastern Europe as the golden period in the development of our soul. This was the picture of the inward Jew. My father bought the book in 1950, I think, in the mimeograph translation. (It's going to be published in Poland I gather only now.) And he asked me to read it simply because, I imagine, after the war I tended to see myself as an ahistorical person. I felt that history had turned against me. I was on the margin of history; I survived but only in a marginal fashion.

**ML:** Let's back up just a little bit. Coming out of the war it's well known that you were wandering through that period, that you had lost your power to speak. Where were you in 1950?

**JK:** I was back in high school, I was functioning perfectly. But nevertheless, spiritually, I saw myself like many members of my generation—as those against whom all civilization had turned. I lost most members of my family; only my parents survived. There were some 16 members of my family in 1939. By 1945, there were just two, my parents. And then, of course, my life was in no way different than the life of thousands, if not hundreds of thousands, of other children, Jewish and Polish-Jewish. The idea was how one perceives oneself.

Does one see oneself as a part of a long historical process and therefore should one overlook what happened, including the loss of the family? People do die, even if they do die in the most tragic fashion possible. But if I were to define myself only by the years of the war, I would see myself permanently as a victim who was almost slaughtered. Heschel says not at all. You have been a part of an extraordinarily fascinating period in the history of the Jewish soul; so look for what else there is. The flesh dies anyhow, but the soul does not. The way you speak, the way you sit, the way you think, the way you imagine things—these things are old; they cannot be burned; they cannot be destroyed with relatives; they stay. And Heschel wrote that in 1949, only four years after that event without any precedent, in which Jews and non-Jews but particularly Jews, died in a fashion like no one else has ever fashioned.

It was very important, therefore, to say to oneself: here is a Polish-Jewish philosopher—he was born in Warsaw—who, only four years after that event, the event which I considered to be critical in the sense that it would define me, maybe forever, and all Jews in that we would always see ourselves as victims. Heschel said not at all, this was the golden period in the development of your soul. And I took another look at myself in the mirror: I said I am 800 years old, and Mr.

Goebbels lost the war. That's how Heschel began. The role of Heschel in my life.

Then about ten years ago Rabbi [name unintelligible], I'm the god-father of his child, came to New York and he mentioned Heschel. I said, "Heschel, what about Heschel?" He said, "I was a disciple of Heschel, I was his secretary." I said, "Abraham Joshua Heschel?" And that was my second encounter with Heschel. And, of course, Heschel was part of my books—there are echoes, here and there, and my whole attitude that life is to be made moment by moment, that one is a unique event, a unique occurrence. Unique and, yet, part of the development of the soul.

**ML:** Heschel's writings have such a reverence for man, really, that man is important, that God is in search of man. Is there any . . .

**JK:** *Who is man?* in particular. These are the two books I travel with. One is *The Earth is the Lord's*, and the other *Who is Man?* In fact, I have them right here. Assuming that I was in trouble with you, Heschel would help. Heschel would tell me I must disregard, if necessary, you or this program. Life is made moment by moment; you define yourself as you are. It's the ability to do that that makes you spiritually Jewish. But you need your tradition to select the spiritual elements which allow you to arm yourself from within. You may be an average person from without; you may be criticized from without and rejected from without; but from within, you are luminous and you know it. And if you know it, then life is a dream. And it's a blissful force and full of life, including the instinct of life. I don't think that Rabbi Heschel devoted that much of a role to sex. I think I did it for him.

**ML:** Yes. But how much of that Jewish spirituality do you see as being important to your literature, to your books? How much of that Jewishness runs through your books and how?

**JK:** It runs in the fashion in which they are written. You may have noticed that I don't stress plot. I don't believe there is such a thing. I stress the moment, the element of drama in every specific moment of life; hence my novels are devised, and designed, as encounters with each particular manifestation of life. There is no promise to the reader that at the end of the book there will be a resolution of some sort. No. You meet my characters and life within my books the way we meet each other. Confrontation.

**ML:** But you can read other people's books and know, well, this is a

book about a Jewish theme, a Jewish person, a Jewish situation. You
don't get that reading you.

**JK:** No. Life is not Jewish. Life is universal. We partake in it. And
what role we play in it, I don't have to stress it. In my first book, *The
Painted Bird,* the boy may have been a Jew or Gypsy, and *Steps,* my
second novel, like *The Painted Bird,* was totally ahistorical in a sense.
A novelist is about the development of character—the development of
the soul of the character. There is no need to give names to it.

In *Being There* I departed from it. But *Being There* is, ironically,
a very Heschelian novel. It's a novel about someone who leaves his
garden, the garden is no longer retrievable, it is gone; it is the garden of
my history. What is left is the industrial civilization which makes something else of Chauncey Gardiner. He's there by chance, he survived by
chance. His name was Chance. But when he steps out of the garden, the
garden is not there anymore. He cannot say, "I'm an innocent man.
Look at me. I'm this, and this, and this." Because everyone would say,
well, where are you from, buddy? And he would say, my wall has
vanished. and Heschel says it somewhere: the wall has vanished, but we
hold the key to it. Chauncey Gardiner is the key to that garden.

**ML:** But Chauncey Gardiner almost seems to be someone on a moving stair, someone who is being carried along by events.

**JK:** But he's luminous from within, isn't he?

**ML:** You wonder, though. It seems that everything that happens to
him, happens to him, no pun intended, by chance.

**JK:** It doesn't happen, anyhow? You think I'm here by design?

**ML:** Well, there is a feeling, of course, that you do control your own
destiny to some extent.

**JK:** A feeling—a very subjective feeling. I think if one is controlled
by a force, I would like to think it is the force of tradition, it is the
spiritual force that makes me sit like this and hold my hands that way to
contain myself more. I learned it in Poland. I learned practically
everything there. I was 24 when I came to the United States. It would
be awfully unfair for me to say that I came unformed. I came very
formed, but I came formed by a great number of forces. I'm almost 55
now. I have spent 30 years in the United States, and have not been back
to Poland or to Eastern Europe. Clearly the 30 American years have
contributed a great deal to me, particularly, freedom of expression,
ultimate American value, and one I value so much that I literally would
die for it. Since without that freedom of expression, my tradition would

be without meaning. And the reason I would not go back to Eastern Europe (though I might go next year) is that until now I felt there was no place for me to express the uniqueness of my being. There was no way for me to say that I considered my history in Eastern Europe to be extraordinarily rich and valid for me, for you, for civilization, for Poland, for Eastern Europe. That in many ways, I was a central figure there, a centrifugal mind that stimulated others, that contributed things to the culture around me throughout diaspora; that for every dying Jew, or for every Jew who died, there is a spiritual monument left somewhere, and it's not only the monument to the victims to the Holocaust. It's a monument to our accomplishment, that we are in fact extraordinarily spiritually accomplished. No one would deny that. And therefore one should look at the Second World War and what happened to us, crying, as I cry by not having my relatives right now. I would love my relatives to watch this program with you right now. I would love my grandparents or some relatives to say; "Hey, there is Jerzy Kosinski. Look at him, he turned out to be a nice kid." Well, they are not here. But their tradition is here, their accomplishment is here. It is in Eastern Europe, but it's here too.

**ML:** When you think about Eastern Europe today, the remnants of the Jewish community in Poland, what do you think of the 4,000 or 5,000 mostly elderly Jews? Is that tradition just disappearing? Is there anything there for you to go back to?

**JK:** One thousand years. A wealth like no other.

**ML:** What happens when the people are gone? When all the people, when all the Polish Jews are gone which may not be. . . .

**JK:** Well, we are here, we are Polish Jews. As long as I'm around not that much will be lost. Things have been preserved. There are crates upon crates of things which were packed in 1939 because no one expected what would happen. They have to be decoded. They have to be preserved. I think there is a greal deal of work done already. I work for the American Foundation for Polish Jewish Studies in New York, Chicago, Boston, Miami, Oxford, and we are trying to recreate the bridge between civilization and what we have left behind. We'll be able to do it, now, given the opening in Eastern Europe. I might go there next year for the 45th anniversary of the uprising in the Warsaw ghetto.

**ML:** One of the items on the agenda of the recent meeting between the Pope and Jewish leadership has been the tendency of the Polish government and the Catholic church to internationalize the Holocaust.

Jewish leaders feel that when you go to some of the death camps in
Poland, the plaques, the inscriptions, are more international—saying
millions of people died here but it doesn't single out that although other
people died the Holocaust was a war against the Jews.

**JK:** It was both. Civilization turned against the Jews, but it also
turned against itself. Jews were not the only ones who died, clearly.
Jews were not the only ones who were exterminated, there were others.
It's unique in a sense that we were singled out simply for being Jewish.
In this sense, it's ultimately unique. But the manner in which my family
perished, as much as I would love to see it as being unique, was not.
Gypsies perished; Soviet prisoners of war, 4 and ½ million of them,
perished in a very similar fashion. Mobile ovens. Great number of
Poles, two out of five Poles perished—the cream of Polish society.

**ML:** But not for the same reasons as the Jews.

**JK:** Perishing is perishing. Life extinguished is life extinguished.
Life is the greatest gift we have. We, the Jews, have no monopoly on it.
We have an understanding of it, which is perhaps unique and very
precious to us. But I would love to think that we once again in some
way have pioneered. The Holocaust is not our responsibility. It belongs
to those who unleashed it upon us. I don't blame my family for dying
the way they died. That's not my business really to think about it. I
mourn them, of course. But somewhere in the back of my mind I have
to say, look, they would have died anyhow. Not the way they died, no.
But we are all mortal. In this sense, eventually, they will be gone. The
essential thing is that civilization, and Heschel says it very wisely, is not
the issue here. We have to go beyond it, because if you sink to the level
of civilization, then we will have to assume that we will not be around
for too long. And I think we surpassed this. I certainly have surpassed
civilization; I don't use it as a yardstick for my being. I use Heschel.
And he says, Kosinski, surpass civilization. Learn a lesson from your
past, from your tradition. Don't define it as this and that, and I think I
do.

**ML:** How is that different from just accepting what happens to you?
The Germans want to exterminate Jews, well, they have the power to do
it, and we must learn from this.

**JK:** And we learn from it, yes.

**ML:** But as opposed to saying we have to rise up or we have to learn
from the fact that we were not able to rise up.

**JK:** Rise up in what sense?

**ML:** To try to countermand what was happening.

**JK:** How? We have. I'm here. You are here.

**ML:** Six million people are not. But the point I'm trying to make is that are you afraid that Jews are using the Holocaust as something uniquely personal as opposed to getting on with their lives? How should a Jew look back, let's go over this a little bit: How should a Jew look back on the Holocaust and say what can I learn from this? Or how dare this have happened? Or, if I had been there it wouldn't have happened.

**JK:** All this and more. I think we should look at it as part of history, and not only ours. Clearly it was unleashed against us. But not only against us. I think we should look upon it in terms of an extraordinary lesson that history has taught us, that we have to rely on elements other than historical developments. That we have to develop emotional and spiritual strength to deal with this, even with the memory of it. But that we have to transcend it, that we have to see it the way Heschel does, as part of our spiritual development. Therefore, I hate to say this, but I must. In some way, rejoice that in spite of all life goes on, and that I see myself redeemed, in a way, by what happened. That once again I have proven to be bigger than history, even though to many I might appear to be a speck of it. No, not at all. I'm able to transcend it, look at it and say it was terrible, but it happened, and I will incorporate it in my rejoicing of a life that goes on. I will become more creative as a result of this. And knowing how perishable life is and how quickly you and I and all this set up here can vanish, I can say to myself, my God, life is extraordinary. And thank you for it.

**ML:** But to those who say never again, what do you say to them?

**JK:** How do they know? Do they know something I don't? Why not, never again? What if the next time it's somebody else? We have pioneered, we have proven that you can make soap of human flesh and luggage. It doesn't always have to be Jewish luggage and Jewish soap. I'm part of history and I'm proud of that. In this sense, suffering is universal. It's mine, no doubt about it; it's mine because I lost my members of my family there, all of them practically and, of course, it's mine. But it's not only mine. It belongs also to those who have done that. It's theirs, too.

**ML:** But Jews have traditionally been sufferers and survivors.

**JK:** I don't believe that.

**ML:** You don't?

**JK:** No. Not at all. Not at all. When I pick up a book, a too much remembrance book which lists only the Jews who died, 1390, a pogrom in 'xyz'; 1667, 35 Jews crucified, I don't want to read that. It's not true. Of course they died. But I would like to look at history as the history of our accomplishments. We have been as important to history as anyone else I can think of, perhaps more. Why not remember that we have been the contributors; that we have been those who conquered; that we have been the ones who contributed extraordinary values and an extraordinary spiritual point of view to every aspect of life in every country on earth with Jews or without Jews including this blessed country of the United States? I repeat this again. For every Jew who died and who was martyred in whatever terrible fashion, we have left a spiritual monu- ment that will outlive us all, and it will outlive them as well.

**ML:** Aren't you concerned though about how much more would have been accomplished had there not been the Holocaust, pogroms and all these other things?

**JK:** It's not for me to speculate about that.

**ML:** There is a great deal of controversy now, a great deal of friction between Jews and Poles in the United States. It was precipitated by the release of the film *Shoah.* You, yourself are working on Jewish-Polish relations. How big an issue do you see this as being? [*Shoah* is a film about Nazi death camps in Treblinka and its survivors that uses contemporary footage and in parts shows continued signs of anti- Semitism in present-day Poland.]

**JK:** I don't see an issue in that. My name is Jerzy Kosinski, it's a Polish name. I have no trouble with that. I came to my spiritual fullness in Eastern Europe, in Poland.

**ML:** But, really, when we talk abut Jews and Poles we are talking about Jews who lived in Poland and non-Jews who lived in Poland, the friction between those.

**JK:** Both were Polish citizens.

**ML:** Right. But here in the United States the non-Jewish Poles are upset with Jews about the feelings expressed in *Shoah.*

**JK:** From one point of view, there is an authentic pain that Jews feel because of what happened in the Second World War. We were burned in a house that practically perished. There is the tendency I notice in us Jews, East European Jews, to blame not only the fire and those who started the fire, the Nazis and the Germans, but somehow we feel that because the house was where it was, we should also blame the owner of the house and maybe the insurance company. A great number of them died with us in the house. We were not the only ones. Two, I think, one has to remember that Poland was the most traumatized country of the Second World War. That of all the countries occupied by the Nazis, including the countries which were incorporated into the Third Reich, Poland was the only country in which practically on every street corner, and on every tree, there was a poster announcing in pure Polish that anyone helping to save a Jew would face the death penalty; and anyone not denouncing one who helped a Jew would be sent to concentration camp. We tend to forget that. *Shoah,* from this point of view, is the biggest lie in the whole world. I gather it's a great film visually, but as a Jew the visual medium is not mine. I read the screenplay of director Claude Lunzman, and I'm absolutely convinced that one could make, using the principle—a movie about Switzerland, portraying the Swiss as a people who hate the mountains; who, in fact, don't have mountains. You could actually use this method to interview the Swiss saying, "You are a people of the lakes, don't you love water?" "Why, yes, we have some lakes here." Mountains would never be mentioned.

**ML:** You're saying that *Shoah* is a distortion of the actual attitudes between . . .

**JK:** A distortion? I'm saying it's a fantasy trick. Maybe, visually, a great one. Historically, I know of nothing, nothing, that is more distorted than that. Because to use Poland and to revert to the most banal, dried out, stereotypical attitudes and use them as the yardstick of what happened in Poland, the most traumatized,—I repeat that,—the most traumatized country of the Second World War, the country that suffered more than any other country in history in fact, is as unfair as anything I can possibly think of. Maybe the great artistry of the film redeems the lie that it contains. If it does, hats off to the visual aspect of *Shoah.* Other than that, I don't want to see the film.

**ML:** And you feel the friction between Poles and Jews shouldn't be there . . .

**JK:** The friction between Poles and Jews was a friction stemming from the proximity. We sat on top of each other. The church faced the synagogue and the synagogue faced the church, nonstop. We were part of the same historical process of the partitions, freedoms which existed for both the Poles who were non-Jews and the Poles who were Jews, the partitions by other countries, the partition by the Protestants, by Bismarck, by the Greek Orthodox Church. It's a very complex history. It's a history as complex as any history of a tightly-knit family. We have to leave it to the historians, and the Foundation for Polish Jewish Studies will gladly assist anyone who has any difficulty with *Shoah*. We produced the film.

**ML:** You have said some very interesting and controversial things, and now we have got to go, but thank you very much for your time. We look forward to *The Hermit of 69th Street* from Jerzy Kosinski with an assist from Rabbi Abraham Joshua Heschel.

Our guest has been Jerzy Kosinski. Thank you for joining us. We'll see you next time. Shalom.

# Jerzy Kosinski, the Last Interview

## Pearl Sheffy Gefen/1991

Published in *Lifestyles* Magazine. Winter 1991:18–24. Reprinted by permission of Pearl Sheffy Gefen.

A. M. Rosenthal tells a story about Jerzy Kosinski which sums up a basic trait of that extraordinary man. *Lifestyles* interviewed Rosenthal just a few days after Kosinski tragically took his own life. They had been close friends for years, and Rosenthal was visibly upset.

"I remember once," recalls the former *New York Times* executive editor, "when I hardly knew him, I had gone to the Dominican Republic and happened to stay at the same resort. I had had a knee operation, and I was walking through the water to exercise it. I happened to look back, and I saw Kosinski was walking behind me, watching to make sure I didn't fall."

I met with Jerzy Kosinski less than three days before he died. He admired *Lifestyles* and knew that his words would be accurately reported. His wife recently told me that he had known it would be his last interview, but I did not.

It was an exciting conversation, full of wit and philosophy, deep thoughts expressed in the inimitable, always original way of this brilliant man, whose knowledge was vast and whose intellect was sharp, penetrating and uniquely individual.

After Kosinski's death I was left with a feeling of profound privilege, and a sense of responsibility to share his final words with a wide readership. They reveal at least part of the nature of what Rosenthal describes as "a very tender, funny and tortured man; a brilliant writer much of the time, who synthesized the madness of the Holocaust and man's inhumanity to man that he himself had experienced."

Both Rosenthal and Mrs. Kosinski have confirmed that Jerzy was terrified at the idea of having a stroke and becoming helpless, a burden on others and a negation of his philosophy of being in control of his life. His father and other members of his family had suffered strokes, and the probability he felt of sharing that fate devastated him. I didn't know that when we met, but the letter he left behind confirmed that fear.

227

A few facts: He was born in 1933 in Lodz, Poland, to a family which, he said, worshiped writing and reading. Most of his relatives were killed by the Nazis. After he was separated from his parents at the age of six, and until the war's end, he was forced to wander the Polish countryside alone. He graduated from university in Warsaw and in 1957 immigrated to the United States and received a degree from Columbia University. He became an American citizen in 1965. He was the winner of the National Book Award for *Steps,* his second novel. He also won the American Academy of Arts and Letters Award in Literature, two Best Screenplay of the Year awards for *Being There,* the B'rith Shalom Humanitarian Freedom Award and the American Civil Liberties Union First Amendment Award.

For the rest, judge for yourself as I recount our conversation.

With hindsight, the thoughts and feelings that led to his tragic suicide, six weeks short of his 58th birthday, are easy to detect. But in a wide-ranging, two-hour interview, the last he ever gave, he talked of his plans for the future, of the gift and the joy of life.

He also spoke of aging, of death, of his angry resentment for his fickle, failing heart, which made it difficult to write and difficult to play polo, a sport that was far more than a game to him.

Writing was his life. "I don't want to do anything else," he said. "I cherish the idea that my life has lasted so long and allowed me to write freely." Polo, the subject of his novel, *Passion Play,* was something "I love, an extraordinary release, a reinforcement of masculinity. On horseback, I see myself as a potentially far more dramatic figure than I actually am. It's the only activity that fills me with such physical joy and mental relaxation to the point where I can contemplate. I could do it forever." He paused and added softly, "But I can't now because I'm physically impaired."

Dressed in a brown turtleneck and trim gray trousers, his lithe body was like a coiled spring; his darkly handsome face that of a complex man. During the course of the afternoon, he was by turn animated, forceful, meditative and sad, but always courteous, always original, a man his friends describe as immensely kind and caring, an active worker for the rights of the individual.

He lived in a two-room rented apartment on West 57th in New York, with his wife Katherina. He called her Kiki and dedicated most of his books to her. They had lived together for over 20 years before marrying four years ago because, Kosinski revealed, "a sense of great mortality suddenly descended on me at that time. Given the nature of society, Kiki, who has been an extraordinary presence in my life, would otherwise have been left with no proof of or access to our past."

Drawings of naked women hung in their small living room, made "by friends who haven't read my books but believed that was what they were about." In one corner, an old bear trap—"a metaphor for the literary critic," he laughed—hung beside some primitive farm tools "to remind me how much and how quickly life changes."

The other room was a combined study and office—complete with copy machine—and bedroom. "It would be nice to have another room," he sighed. "I have to sleep on this cot, and I cannot quite stretch, and I hate the copy machine." The shelves behind his desk were so crowded with books that the overflow "sometimes falls on my head." On the desk, a shiny artificial hip bone served as a paperweight and "a reminder that life isn't perfect." Above the covered bed were caricatures of himself by various painters.

"I try to write every day," Kosinski said. "I don't want to write novels anymore. It takes too long to write and too long to publish. I'm writing short fiction, perhaps a collection of stories, perhaps a novella. You see them here on this desk." There are many corrections, in ink, "because writing is rewriting. Walt Whitman was rewriting *Leaves of Grass* until he died.

"I'm bored with myself. I don't want to write the way I used to. I don't want to repeat myself. I want to open up much more if I can and if there's something to come up with. There may not be enough inspiration. I will judge.

"I don't think in terms of the future. I rent everything, other than the gift of life itself, which was given to me without any predictable lease, a gift that can be withdrawn at any time. I'm not afraid of death, not at all. It's something I take for granted."

Kosinski learned about death at an early age. Other than his parents, his entire family was wiped out in the Holocaust. "Now that my parents are dead, I have no blood relatives. I have an adopted brother in Poland whom I will see next week when I go there for the opening of the first American bank in Poland, on May 17. I will stay there for 10 days."

Kosinski was instrumental in founding the Polish-American bank,

which he said is 80 per cent American-owned—and with which Kiki
Kosinski remains actively associated.

In the past, the Polish government bitterly attacked Kosinski because
of *The Painted Bird,* his first and best-known novel. He recently became involved again in his native country because, he told me, "Poland
was the crib of a substantial chunk of Jewish civilization. Jews lived
there for 800 years."

For that reason, he was deeply committed to creating "a center of
Jewish presence in Kazimierz, formerly the center of Jewish life in
Krakow, only 40 kilometres from Auschwitz," through The Jewish
Presence Foundation, which he founded two years before his death.
"Our basic aim is to resurrect the Jewish spirit, to return to the notion
that Jews are lifebound. The Holocaust was a German-Austrian-Nazi
invention, not ours. I am a victim of it, my memory registers it, but my
emotion is not devoted to it. Jews are life, not death. Jewish presence is
not quantitative, it's qualitative. We reside in every head. Every anti-
Semite lives on Jewish juices, Jewish creativity, Jewish humor and
Jewish songs without knowing it."

His last book, *The Hermit of 69th Street,* is a vast work riddled with
literary quotes and footnotes. Kosinski called it auto-fiction, rather than
autobiography, though the main character, Kosky, is clearly himself ("If
you take the 'sin' out of Kosinski, you get Kosky," he chuckled.)

"Anything written is auto-fiction, because in everything we write and
almost anything we say, imagination interferes. I would like to see most
writing, including journalism, defined as auto-fiction. What you will do
with this interview—extracting, editing, the way it will be set in print—
will turn it into yet another form of narrative. It will not be my voice,
even though my voice is already auto-fiction.

"I invent and reinvent myself. There are days when I see myself as
a profoundly heroic figure, and there are days when I see myself as a
decrepit figure about to die. I'm not willing to readily accept aging.
I inherited my heart trouble, and I resent it.

"But," he maintained, "it is not me who is depressed, it is a depression caused by the drugs I have to take for my heart. It's the medically
created self versus the spiritual self.

"I cultivate my vanity, my image of myself, not because I want
everyone to admire me, but because I want one person to admire me,
and that is *me,* Kosinski. I have to admire myself because I must admire

the life that runs in me. The minute I stop admiring that gift of life, I will lose contact with who I am.

"I love social life and yet, yes, I am also a loner. There's no contradiction. I like to watch, to observe. Here I have a great deal in common with the character of Chance in *Being There*."

Kosinski won awards for his screenplay of the film, which starred Peter Sellers as Chance. He originally refused to let Sellers play the role because "he was too well-known and the audience had an image of him and wouldn't be able to suspend its belief in that image. I wanted an unknown actor. But Sellers convinced me, and he was right.

"The screenplay took a great deal of time, and frankly I thought it could have been better spent. I realized I could have written the novel differently, and that's a wrong thought for a writer to have.

"I rewrote *The Devil Tree* completely because I wasn't pleased with the first edition, and *The Hermit of 69th Street* is very different in the paperback edition. But I cannot do that all the time. That's why I try not to reread my books now."

Because *The Hermit of 69th Street* is a difficult book, requiring more than casual concentration, it did not sell as well as his other eight novels. But, he was quick to point out, "none of them could qualify as best-sellers."

Novels, no matter how autobiographical, are fiction, and Kosinski always refused to specify what is literally true and what is not. Referring to *The Painted Bird,* he noted: "Writing about the child is always easier, because it's non-verifiable. We have no way of verifying the state of mind of a child. To assign images of childhood as strictly autobiographical, as any psychologist would know, is profoundly naive.

"In a way, *The Painted Bird* was the easiest of my novels, and perhaps the one, under other circumstances, I would not have written, but I've grown up in a tradition that claimed you must start with a novel about childhood. So people assume this is my most autobiographical book."

And so, to the question everyone asks. Did the terrible things he recounts in *The Painted Bird* actually happen to him, or were some of them purely allegorical, or perhaps events that happened to other children?

Most of them are clearly based on his own experiences. At the age of six his parents sent him to the Polish countryside, hoping to save him from the Nazis. They entrusted his life to a woman who quickly abandoned him to the cruelties of a succession of peasants.

He spent the next five years surviving unspeakable conditions. He was regarded as a Jew or a Gypsy by the blond-haired, superstitious peasants, and lost his speech when he was thrown into a manure pit. He remained mute until after the war when a skiing accident somehow restored his speech.

The child in the novel viewed fair-haired people—including Germans—as blessed, because they did not have the "evil eye" they were convinced he possessed, since he was not a blue-eyed blond. (But then, neither was Hitler.)

Kosinski would not tell me, or anyone else, which stories in *The Painted Bird* were true—for a simple reason.

"I don't want to say, even to myself. That ambiguity is what fiction is all about. What is not ambiguous is that the novel is about childhood traumatized by the war. My elementary reactions were formed by the war. Things I like to eat now are the same things I liked during the war: potatoes, radishes, cucumbers, onions. I also acquired a fear of authority, the desire to be independent and free to move if I have to."

Kosinski survived the Holocaust only to grow up under communism, which he hated. He eventually escaped and became an American who wrote all his books in English and even lectured on American and English literature at Princeton and Yale. "English is the language of sociology and I was studying American sociology in Poland," he noted. "But I still have difficulty, no less so today. You see, I have dictionaries all over the place.

"Language is a matter of dispute. I performed a test once. I showed pages of Steinbeck to some friends, claiming they were mine, and they criticized those pages, by a totally American writer, as having a very strong Slavic tone to them."

Kosinski delighted in dropping clues to his own identity throughout his novels. In his brilliant, penultimate novel, *Pinball*, for instance, he examines the world of music. Kosinski's mother was a concert pianist, and his love and knowledge of music is mirrored in every page, along with parallels to his own life.

The novel's central character is Domostroy, who once played the role of a Russian composer in an epic Hollywood film shot, in part, in

Spain. Kosinski himself played a Russian revolutionary in *Reds,* a film
made by his old friend Warren Beatty and also shot partially in Spain.

Kosinski's work is often described as "bleak." Domostroy refers to
a music critic who wrote that he was composing himself into "radical
isolation." The composer wonders: "Was his music really so bleak and
naked that it would one day tempt its creator, as another critic had once
suggested, to cut his own throat?"

Kosinski told me: "I'm not possessed with greed. Take all this away
and I won't miss anything." Domostroy, who had been a famous composer but had stopped writing and withdrawn from that world, echoes
Kosinski's own philosophy: "Freed as he was from the deceptive
security of accumulated wealth and the chimera of success . . . he
rejoiced at being able to live his life as he pleased . . . and at being able
to follow his own ethical code of moral responsibility, harming no one,
not even himself—a code in which free choice was always the indis-
putable axiom."

"My books stress individuality," Kosinski told me. The theme of
living one's own life as an individual and controlling it totally is echoed
throughout *Passion Play,* It's hero, Fabian, a polo player, is perhaps the
closest thing to a mirror image of Kosinski himself.

And in *The Devil Tree,* the protagonist, remembering his life,
becomes dismayed: "If that is all I have," he says, "I would rather
invent my past than recall it."

Kosinski read reviews of his work, and was sometimes influenced by
them. "If someone points out an obvious lack of logic, I would clearly
rethink it. A critic is also a writer, and it would be creatively obscene
and unwise not to pay attention to what they say."

Was *The Hermit* written, as some believe, in answer to an article that
appeared in *The Village Voice* in 1982, claiming that Kosinski did not
write his own books? Not so, he replied. *"The Hermit* is meant to
illustrate the point of creation, the creative process. It was the greatest
fun writing it. For once I allowed myself a great deal of time, almost
five years. I didn't go out, I stayed in and delved into myself and my
own history, the nature of fiction and non-fiction and the nature of
history and oral tradition."

He refused to condemn *The Village Voice* story. "It was a perfectly
valid expression of someone's judgment," he informed me. "Truth has

nothing to do with it. There's no way to prove or disprove it. Of course it bothered me, profoundly. Vanity is a very powerful force in someone who likes to ski and ride a horse.

"It still bothers me now when someone stops me at a red light in the street and says, 'Kosinski, I love your books and I don't care who wrote them.'" He laughed. "It's like proving you're alive." Isn't that easier to prove? "Not necessarily. There are many people who are walking dead."

Sex is a recurring theme in Kosinski's books. "It's important to my characters and in my own life. Sex is a life force, a procreative force and a creative force. It is not yet entirely dominated by the apparatus of society. I forgot who said that in the embrace of lovers the universe is crushed. Sexuality, as an expression not only of free will but of natural instinct towards life, has, however, been one of the subjects of my fiction."

Because he is known to have spent many nights in such notorious sex centers as Plato's Retreat, and because his novels are full of explicit sex scenes, he is often asked if he actually participated in sexual orgies in public places. He laughed. "If I had been in a monastery, would you have asked me if I had any relationship with the monks? Possibly yes, possibly no. You'll get an answer from a novelist, and that is, read my novels.

"A novelist would say that whatever life is, it finds its remote, fictional representation in the work of art. I go to any institution of public learning. A sex club is probably the most public of places, so it's the least intimate place. There was no intimacy because there were so many people around. They were peculiar institutions with, literally, far less sex than met the eye. They were places I would meet with Goya, Cervantes, Balzac, Whitman, Twain: all of us were there in some way.

"They no longer exist, unfortunately: because for a voyeur they were extraordinary. They are gone now because society changed and we have TV and videos to watch."

There have been complaints that Kosinski's characters always seek to dominate their women. "It depends on how you define the division of roles," he encountered. "I perceive women as being much stronger than men. Men could never put up with menstruation. We are weak. We couldn't survive nine months of pregnancy.

"Hence, we need a uniform to compensate, to indicate that feasibly we protect life and so forth. There's no doubt that when I get on horseback, I feel superior to myself, and when I put on ski clothes, which are a uniform, I adopt another persona, that of a chevalier, a knight, someone stronger than even the mountain he slides down.

"My father once said," he interjected wryly, "that the only person who made sense on a horse was Don Quixote, and that nothing was ever produced while sliding down a mountain or riding a horse. My father was a very wise man." Kosinski's father died in 1962, his mother in 1972.

Kosinski had no children. "I wanted to at one time or another, but by then it was too late. A child is an enormous responsibility and an investment in time. I don't think in terms of the future. If a child would grow in 24 hours to be 18, I would have a great number of children. At one point, a woman I was close to wanted to have a child with me. She said she would take care of it; but luckily it did not happen, because it would have been an egoistic error on my part."

Instead, both he and his wife, Kiki, an immensely charming and intelligent woman, an American of aristocratic, Catholic, German-Austrian origin, totally devoted to her husband, were "adopted" by the children of many of their friends.

"Since I have no family," Kosinski explained, "my friends are my family, many of them people I've known for 30 years. To some, I'm considered a cousin, to others a brother, or an adopted son or a father figure.

"But I must tell you," he added, his eyes twinkling, "some of my dinner companions don't want to sit with me because they're afraid of what I might say or do. They believe my books and what is written about me. There are a great number of people I wouldn't want to sit next to either, so I'm not complaining. Either they're boring or they might detract from my vanity. I cultivate my vanity, no doubt about it. I play polo in white britches because they look better than jeans.

"I have to say to myself, 'Kosinski, thanks for being alive.' It's a form of prayer, rejoicing at being alive, over an accomplishment which nobody else can see. There are times when Kosinski is not happy, and then Kosinski says to himself, 'Let's look at your vanities, where you're deficient. Maybe you should start reading a book about another writer who comes from the same spiritual background: Maupassant, Stendhal and Whitman.'"

Kosinski tried to write every day, although he found it increasingly difficult because of his painful heart. "Whatever else I do is a hobby. I don't lecture any more, because I have no energy for it and I've done it. It's enough. I have to conserve energy now."

Until his death, Kosinski was a fellow at Yale's Timothy Dwight College, situated near the Kosinski's rented apartment in New Haven, Connecticut. "It's our vacation land, a place I love," he said. "It's so close to New York, yet entirely different.

"New Haven is hot and humid in the summer; but it has bookshops—so I have a sense of continuity, which is very important for me when I'm trying to be really creative. It has Yale, it has polo horses which we have access to because they're part of the university and I'm on the board. I've written the only full-length novel in the English language with a polo player as its main protagonist (*Passion Play*), so I can always get access to a polo pony." A shadow crossed his face as he remembered that his heart limited him in that pursuit.

Kosinski was the president of the American Center of PEN, the international association of writers and editors, for two terms. Civil liberties, particularly for writers imprisoned for political reasons, always concerned him deeply. He had a quintessential belief that "unless the liberties of the individual are to be preserved, one way or another we will not be able to maintain a free society. Jefferson would become a figment of the imagination, along with the whole Declaration of Independence and the Bill of Rights."

Kosinski said this belief in liberty is the basis of his Jewishness: "Judaism means the freedom to express a certain insight into the joy of life, life perceived as the tree of life with the roots and branches of equal importance, creativity for oneself and for others, a universal sharing. It means family, education, self-enlightenment.

"I see Israel as a great hope for the Middle East, a very colorful place, a cultural and technological force. I see Israel as a force for turning the Middle East into a greenhouse, as a state living eventually in totally symbiotic conditions with the Arab states.

"I feel it will happen, absolutely. I see no spiritual division between us. Islam is an extraordinary creative force. The *Koran* is one of the greatest works of art. Every Arab carries in his or her head a universal imagination from which we have all drawn.

"But history takes time. Israel did not exist before, now it does, and

I see things progressing very nicely. I see Israel as being quite different from what it's perceived to be. I see the Israeli presence as being misrepresented by those who look at Israel as a fortress. It is, in fact, an oasis.

"I've visited Israel three times," he told me. "If I go again, I would like to stay longer, in Jerusalem, and try to write there."

It was late. He had preparations to make for his trip to Poland. When he walked to the elevator, Kosinski said, "Call me anytime." When would he be back from Poland? May 20, he replied. Then he shrugged and added, "But first, let's see if I go." His eyes, intense, riveting, looked sad and troubled.

That was late Tuesday afternoon. In the early hours of Friday morning, May 3, 1991, Jerzy Kosinski put a plastic bag over his head and died quietly, cleanly. The gift of life was gone. He had chosen to return it, on his own terms.

When I arrived home after the interview, I read the slip of paper he had given me to paste in one of his books. It read, "With hope of future encounters." There would be none, and I, and all those who knew him, are the poorer for it.

# Index